The Politicization of Trans Identity

The Politicization of Trans Identity

An Analysis of Backlash, Scapegoating, and Dog-Whistling from Obergefell to Bostock

Loren Cannon

LEXINGTON BOOKS
Lanham • Boulder • New York • London

Published by Lexington Books
An imprint of The Rowman & Littlefield Publishing Group, Inc.
4501 Forbes Boulevard, Suite 200, Lanham, Maryland 20706
www.rowman.com

86-90 Paul Street, London EC2A 4NE

Copyright © 2022 by The Rowman & Littlefield Publishing Group, Inc.
Preface to paperback edition copyright © 2024 by The Rowman & Littlefield Publishing Group, Inc.

All rights reserved. No part of this book may be reproduced in any form or by any electronic or mechanical means, including information storage and retrieval systems, without written permission from the publisher, except by a reviewer who may quote passages in a review.

British Library Cataloguing in Publication Information Available

Library of Congress Cataloging-in-Publication Data

Names: Cannon, Loren, author.
Title: The politicization of trans identity : an analysis of backlash, scapegoating, and dog-whistling from Obergefell to Bostock / Loren Cannon.
Description: Lanham : Lexington Books, [2022] | Includes bibliographical references and index.
Identifiers: LCCN 2021053792 (print) | LCCN 2021053793 (ebook) | ISBN 9781793623812 (cloth) | ISBN 9781793623836 (pbk.) | ISBN 9781793623829 (ebook)
Subjects: LCSH: Gender identity—Law and legislation—United States. | Transgender people—Legal status, laws, etc.—United States. | Gender identity—Political aspects—United States.
Classification: LCC KF4754.5 .C36 2022 (print) | LCC KF4754.5 (ebook) | DDC 342.73/087—dc23/eng/20211202
LC record available at https://lccn.loc.gov/2021053792
LC ebook record available at https://lccn.loc.gov/2021053793

To the memory of my mother, Lynn Cannon

Contents

Preface: Late December 2023	ix
Acknowledgments	xiii
Introduction	1
Chapter 1: The Obergefell Decision	7
Chapter 2: The Anti-Trans Offensive	35
Chapter 3: The Case against Anti-Transgender Bathroom Bills	61
Chapter 4: Backlash	81
Chapter 5: Scapegoating: The Over-Blaming Account	107
Chapter 6: Scapegoating: The Girardian Account	131
Chapter 7: Dog Whistles and Virtue Signaling	151
Chapter 8: "But for" and the Bostock Decision	169
Epilogue	201
Bibliography	205
Index	215
About the Author	223

Preface

Late December 2023

Some years ago, I was asked to give a keynote speech about my ongoing political and moral analysis of recently proposed anti-trans legislation across the country. It was March 2020, right before the COVID pandemic would change our lives so drastically. I didn't know what was coming regarding the COVID plague but was focused on a different sort of national crisis that would impact our health, well-being, politics, and social climate. The harms of COVID were then unknown, but the harms resulting from the backlash against gains in LGBTQ+ rights and respect were already being felt by many.

This speech was to a large and friendly audience. I introduced the topic of my research, which later became this book in your hands. I reviewed events such as the SCOTUS ruling in favor of same sex marriage (*Obergefell v. Hodges*) and greater trans visibility and respect (here thinking of folks like Laverne Cox, Janet Mock) but also spoke about how, within that backdrop of good news for the LGBTQ+ community, there was an exponential increase of specifically anti-transgender legislation proposed across the country. On the horizon were concerns that expansions of the notion of religious freedom would be used to dismantle or limit full social participation and civil rights and that, while trans and gender non-conforming and non-binary individuals in our nation's history have always faced significant barriers, the new efforts to scapegoat this community were reaching a heightened level. As it turns out, it was just the beginning of an intensified level of antisocial and even violent rhetoric directed at one relatively small and intersectionally diverse and marginalized group: a potentially dangerous and historically relevant turn of events.

At the beginning of the speech, I began to recite the first few lines of Dickens's *A Tale of Two Cities*. Whether or not one has read this work (it took me five attempts), the first few lines are well known:

> It was the best of times, it was the worst of times, it was the age of wisdom, it was the age of foolishness, it was the epoch of belief, it was the epoch of incredulity, it was the season of light, it was the season of darkness, it was the spring of hope, it was the winter of despair.

To my surprise, the audience joined me in the recitation. Perhaps my fellow advocates of LGBTQ+ rights and respect were feeling as I did, a mix of optimism and pessimism. Many felt some optimism that after the ruling in Obergefell, backlash was predictable, but it would subside as the cisheterosexual majority learned to coexist with a new and more inclusive society—one more queer, not to mention decidedly less white. Yet even in the midst of cautious optimism was a growing feeling of dread. It seems, historically speaking, that once a scapegoat is created and supported socially by the powerful, it is difficult to undo. If the right conditions exist and enough power is on the line, bluster, irrational and dehumanizing rhetoric, and dog-whistling and its companion of virtue signaling can create a new scapegoat of contemporary focus. This is especially true in the present context of (anti)social media. In such a context it is difficult to permanently dismantle these scapegoating narratives so that they become less profitable for those looking to amass power and less enticing for those isolated and well-armed individuals whose insecurities have been transmuted into personal vendettas against imagined enemies. Conjured nemeses are made to seem that much more menacing due to the content of whatever series of internet links one has most recently clicked.

It has only been two years since this book was released in hardback in February 2022, and I am so appreciative that this new paperback version is now available. Though two years is not a very long time, the political and social climate now, at the end of 2023, has changed. I can't imagine a group of people in a chorus of Dickens's famous opening lines, especially those who are trans or gender non-binary, because these do not seem like the "best of times" or the "season of light." There are scores of individuals and families fervently looking to leave their home communities: internal refugees seeking contexts in which they can receive health care, live relatively free of violence, and lead dignified and respected lives. The worsening of the political climate certainly has created a "winter of despair" for many. Relocating, whether for oneself or one's family, requires not just the economic means to do so. For some, moving across the country is not an option due to ties to family, land, and regional culture. Those whose homes are found in the sublimely beautiful southern states, the expansiveness of the heartland, and the majesty of the Northern Rocky Mountain west should not, by those of us who live in more politically accommodating regions, be regarded as expendable. A 1980s-style queer flight to the coastal cities isn't the answer.

Living in a hyper-politicized age advantages only the few who benefit from pitting us against each other. It has long been the case that LBGTQ+ folks have lost friends and family members due to our commitment to craft unapologetically vibrant lives. What is different now is that the tearing of the cohesive fabric of connection is more due to the rhetoric of politicians, conservative religious leaders, and internet "influencers" than real conversations and shared human experience. The damage is done long before a family member blocks another on social media and commits to skipping the next reunion. Whether one supported the health guidelines of the pandemic and wore a face mask; is willing to assert that we have a problem of national gun violence; is concerned about the global climate; believes that critical race theory is unpatriotic instead of a desperately needed analysis of our shared racist history; or that policies that support the flourishing of trans and gender non-binary people are just or the result of a distortion of the natural order, all fall along party lines. Fear is passionately stoked through tunnels made by click sequences, bringing one to ever narrower echo chambers and more alarming content. Fear drives clicks. Clicks mean money. Subscriptions exist for those who want a constant reaffirmation of their worldview, however distorted. If not a subscription, then "Please Don't Forget to Click Here to Support Our Ongoing Efforts." It is within this kind of environment, a cacophony of faces, voices, innuendos, and fallacious reasoning, that the backlash against LGBTQ+ political gains has been made, demons conjured, real lives endangered, and worse.

Our ability to understand the breadth of this backlash has changed in the last couple of years. While my original research involved a decidedly inefficient and obsessive scanning of news for anti-trans legislation, we now have at least a bit more press coverage on these issues. Independent journalist Erin Reed, who reports specifically on anti-trans legislation and politics, just recently published her anti-LGBTQ legislation tracking for 2024. Before the new year has even been christened, there are 80 separate proposed bills and 195 others that can be rolled over from last year. Given that the new legislative sessions haven't even begun, we can expect these numbers to increase. These proposals, if passed, will further limit our ability to participate in society, education, and sports and enact serious barriers to health care. Included in the list are anti-trans bathroom bills, "Don't Say Gay," bills, gender-affirming health care bans, book bans, trans athlete bans, affirming pronoun bans, a mandated state control of the meaning of "gender" meant to erase the trans experience entirely, and more.

Still, even without following the rise in anti-trans legislation, the infiltration of anti-trans rhetoric in our politics is not difficult to notice. While watching a video of the Trump rally before the storming of the Capitol on January 6, 2021, I was shocked that Donald Trump Jr. explicitly demonized trans women in his speech. I thought to myself, "*Really*, demonizing trans people is so important to mention *now*?" Fast forward to the fourth Republican presidential primary debate, December 6, 2023, just one month shy of the third anniversary of the January 6 insurgency. Not five minutes into the debate, the conversation includes the "gender mutilation of minors." What started as an occasional nod to the far right has turned into serious presidential-nominee talking points. Evidence supporting trans health care in its age-appropriate varieties never makes it to the debate stage.

Some have said my research was "prophetic." Whether or not this is true, I am happy to lend these ideas to others in our attempt to make sense of these complicated times. The tools of directed backlash, scapegoating, and dog-whistling continue to be unimaginatively used by those who believe further marginalizing of others will add to their own coffers and their access to power. I believe it is worthwhile to recognize how these tactics are being presently used, especially against the intersectionally diverse LGBTQ+ community and all those who transgress societal assumptions of sex, sexuality, and gender. Important too is recognizing that a denial of reproductive rights; a refusal to acknowledge this nation's past and present structural racism; an increase in animus against "woke" policies (I'd rephrase "woke" as "compassionate"); and even the defunding of the study of the humanities in higher education are all related and mutually reinforcing. Professors are being targeted, programs discontinued, and academic freedom reduced. Even the publication of this book in 2022 resulted in me personally being included on the far-right "Professor Watchlist" of Turning Point USA. Given the caliber of scholars on this list, I might feel flattered, but the realities of living in a country unable to curb gun violence means that I, and others, can't take such targeting lightly. I firmly believe that going forward requires us to understand the mutually supporting forces of the present social and political climate and to recognize the threat to our collective and individual flourishing.

There are no coincidences.

Acknowledgments

There are many books that should be written, yet few have the privilege of time, health, and economic security to make those projects a reality. As important as the privileges just mentioned are, far too many of us receive implicit and explicit messages that we have nothing to add towards contributing to an understanding of our shared world. Regardless of the strength or weakness of this work, I am privileged to be supported in my efforts to share this analysis in hopes that it is a meaningful contribution.

This project is a product of years of thinking, writing, and presenting on this topic. The seeds of some of these chapters began as short essays in the *LGBT Issues in the Profession*, newsletter of the American Philosophical Association. I am appreciative of those who have worked on this newsletter throughout the years, especially Kory Schaff, who edited two volumes in which my work appeared. Such labors keep these kinds of philosophical inquiries alive and ensure that matters that involve LGBTQ+ lives remain topics of fruitful and respectful analysis and debate.

Some of the ideas expressed in this work have been presented at philosophical conferences including the Society for LGBTQ Philosophy (American Philosophical Conference, Central, 2017), the LGBTQ Advocacy Committee for the Society for Phenomenology and Existential Philosophy (Annual Conference 2017), Thinking Trans, Trans Thinking Conference (2018), the APA Committee Session: Roundtable on LGBTQ People in the Profession (Central Division 2019), and the Thinking Trans, Trans Thinking virtual conference in 2020. The labor involved in organizing these events results in this important work being showcased, sets the stage for personal and professional connections to be made, and helps ensure that emerging scholars realize that these topics are suitable for analysis and philosophical reflection. I am especially grateful to those who have been instrumental in the formation and ongoing work of the Trans Philosophy Project. This project is crucial in highlighting some exceptional philosophical work being done by scholars nationally and internationally. Through the Trans Philosophy Project, I have not only been able to present my work but have found a sense of community.

I received a sabbatical leave in the fall of 2019 from my lecturer position at Humboldt State University. Those individuals on the HSU Leave Committee spent their time and attention reviewing all sabbatical applications and were instrumental in supporting my goal of spending focused time on this project. As a lecturer, I realize that few others of my professional status (or, more accurately, lack of status) are even given the opportunity to apply for sabbatical leave. This opportunity, contractually negotiated, was only made possible by the advocacy and social justice work of the California Faculty Association, my union. I am deeply grateful, not just to benefit from the contract negotiated right, but also to work with my union siblings in making higher education in California more inclusive and socially just.

I have received other support from Humboldt State University. I am thankful for the funds I received from the Humboldt State University Emeritus and Retired Faculty and Staff Association (HSU ERFSA), who supplied a small grant to help fund some of the legislative research for this project. Thank you Marshelle Thobaben, for your support and the opportunity to discuss my work with ERFSA members. I have deep gratitude to the members of the HSU Department of Philosophy, who have so consistently supported my work over the last sixteen years. I am also appreciative of the advocacy of the HSU Department of Critical Race, Gender, and Sexuality Studies, which made a trans theory course a reality at our institution.

Receiving partial funding for research assistants or editors is only part of the story, of course. It is also the case that the work needs to get done—despite so many time commitments that pull elsewhere. Thank you, Kayla Santiago-Snyder and Roman Sotomajor for your assistance in helping me keep track of the legislative anti-transgender backlash in these last six years. You both were so helpful in making clear the scope of the backlash and its effects. Discussing the data, and this broader project, with you both was stimulating and meaningful. I also have great appreciation for Felix Boers, whose work was so crucial to finally getting this project ready for publication. Thank you, Felix, for your attention to detail, your insightful comments, and your patience for my habit of putting two spaces after a period. Lastly, I am appreciative of the indexing skills of Rose Ippolito, your timeliness and professionalism.

My own thoughts have been influenced by many philosophers, thinkers, activists, and students. Any list will be necessarily lacking. I studied philosophy as a second career and began my doctoral studies at age thirty-seven. Without the support of philosophers who were not just insightful but accessible and welcoming, I would not have had the confidence to attempt to change careers and devote myself to philosophical study. Thank you, Dr.

Shari Collins, Dr. Peter French, Dr. Margaret Walker, Dr. Michael White, and the late Dr. Jeffrie Murphy, all of Arizona State University. I have been also so fortunate to have been able to study and learn from the work of those in this and related fields. I appreciate the deep thinking and cogent analysis of John Corvino, Talia Mae Bettcher, and Jacob Hale; their work has been so influential on my own. All three have shown me both support and friendship, which is priceless. Thank you to Bob Fischer, whose invitation to contribute to his anthology, *Ethics, Left and Right: The Moral Issues that Divide Us*, was a catalyst for thinking how this work might come together. Thank you for reaching out to me, it was a pleasure working with you. My essay for this anthology, "Trans-Directed Injustice: The Case against Anti-Transgender Bathroom Bills," has been revised and is included here as chapter 3, copyright © Oxford University Press 2019, reproduced with the permission of the licensor through PLSclear. Thank you to those of Oxford University Press and PLSClear for providing this copyright permission. Other thinkers who have resolutely influenced my thinking are James Baldwin, Dean Spade, María Lugones, Jennifer Finney Boylan, Susan Stryker, Sandy Stone, C. Riley Snorton, Carlos Sanchez, George Fredrickson, Simone Weil, among others. Special thanks to the anonymous reviewer whose feedback on this work, I believe, made it stronger.

Lastly, I have appreciation for my family and friends who have supported me in completing this project. This includes my colleagues in the philosophy department; my friends who have listened to me discuss my ideas, especially Mary and Cat; my family members who have heard of this project for the last two years; my cycling buddies, Mike, Michael, and Leena; and my COVID pod members Mira and Jill. I am so grateful to my brother Steve, for his assistance on the cover of this book and his willingness to use his talent to produce images that are as beautiful and meaningful as is the depth and expanse of my indecision when choosing one. I am also indebted to Leo, Sky, and Magic, their (usually) easy company and canine loyalty. I trust all these thoughtful individuals will discourage me from trying to finish another book while in the midst of a global pandemic while also trying to learn to teach online. I will readily take their advice and I hope it never becomes again relevant.

I am especially fortunate to have the steadfast and constant support of my wife, Jess Pettitt. Thank you Jess for being tirelessly encouraging in all aspects of my professional life. Your commitment to help me reach my professional goals and to support my vision of the value and applicability of philosophy has been unwavering—even in the face of what seem intractable barriers and disappointment. Your level of commitment to these goals is matched by your willingness to review drafts and discuss my ideas with me. I cannot imagine facing the challenges of the last sixteen years without you . . . and of course, your life-enhancing fried potatoes.

Introduction

This book is about this politicization of transgender identity. The time frame of focus here is between 2015 and 2020, the years between the two most influential US Supreme Court (SCOTUS) rulings on LGBTQ issues in decades, Obergefell in 2015 that ceased prohibition of "same sex" marriage and Bostock in 2020, that made clear that discrimination on the basis of sexual orientation or gender identity is a form of sex discrimination and thus prohibited by Title VII. Yet, this is not a history book. I do present information in chapter 2 regarding the breadth of what I am calling the anti-transgender backlash, but the focus overall is more of a conceptual and legal analysis. Because I believe that the ideas of backlash, scapegoating, and dog-whistling can all be aptly used to describe what has occurred in the United States between 2015 to 2020 (and beyond), I spend considerable time on an analysis of these concepts and their application to the present context. As I make clear, this analysis of these ideas is not independent of morality. This backlash has caused a great deal of unnecessary harm and this harm has been perpetrated, in many ways, so that some amass more political power than they would otherwise. This analysis cannot help but bring up questions about the integrity of politicians, the value of truth and its distortion, and how to envision and then bring to fruition a just society that nurtures the flourishing of its individuals and groups rather than one that nurtures distrust and fear while using a dangerous fetishization of difference for political gain.

To be an advocate for trans equality and flourishing for all gender transgressive individuals, one must be also anti-racist. To be an advocate for this equality and flourishing, one must also be anti-sexist, anti-classist, anti-ableist. This is because this kind of animus, bias, discrimination, violence, and marginalization will always target those that are otherwise marginalized through perceived racial, ethnic, gender, and ability identities, expressions, and/or experiences. Discussions of backlash, scapegoating, and dog-whistling, herein, often include examples of racism, sexism, or other biases, as they occur together in their intersectional cohesion and interdependent simultaneous oppressions. I believe the term "cohesion" is relevant here in that racism attracts anti-trans animus, just as anti-trans animus attracts racism and other marginalizing forces. In the dictionary, cohesion is defined as "the sticking together of particles of the same substance." I am reminded of when, as a child, I played with the mercury from a broken thermometer. (I am pretty sure that this activity is generally not recommended.) I was fascinated how the little balls of mercury would be attracted to each other and then cohere as one glob when they got sufficiently close. Anti-trans animus and bias cohere with racism and other oppressive forces in similar ways. They attract each other, eventually becoming a larger glob in which the previously separate bits are no longer distinguishable. The separate aspects of racism, anti-trans animus, and other oppressive forces like sexism become indistinguishable, and thus, potential for harm is increased. Like so many theorists before me, here thinking of ecofeminist Karen Warren, oppressive strategies are "of the same substance." This is not to mean that racism, sexism, and anti-trans animus are the same, but that the strategies that the powerful and ignorant use to divide and marginalize tend to look similar. As racism, sexism, and anti-trans animus (or cissexism) cohere in a sticky self-similarity, their cohesion and their affects only reproduce, magnify, and exponentiate the degree of harm.

This book is composed of eight chapters, all that involve some aspect of the politicization of trans, gender non-conforming, and gender non-binary identities. The work is sequential, only in the sense that chapter 1 involves an analysis of the US Supreme Court ruling (*Obergefell v. Hodges* 2015) that allowed same-sex marriage (at least for those that qualify) and chapter 8 offers an explanation and critique of the "Bostock" ruling by the US Supreme Court (*Bostock v. Clayton County* 2020) that ruled that discrimination on the basis of gender identity and sexual orientation is a form of unjust sex discrimination. The chapters between these two are not sequential but involve a conceptual analysis of the concepts of backlash, scapegoating, and dog-whistling, and their application to what I call the "anti-trans offensive."

More specifically, chapter 1 is focused on the Obergefell ruling and an analysis of the legal reasoning involved, but also, more broadly discusses the politics and ethics behind the prioritization of the "marriage equality" movement itself. Chapter 1 serves to trouble this prioritization, even in light of its multiple benefits to many individuals and couples that has resulted from the ruling. There is a common argument that the prioritization of same-sex marriage by LGBTQ equality groups was a timely and prudent one. Indeed, it seemed that success in recognizing a more expansive understanding of marriage was at hand—and indeed it was. Social recognition of commitment as well as the material benefits of legal marriage have changed people's lives for the better. Indeed, there is no doubt that those of "same-sex" marriages should receive the same benefits of those of "opposite sex" marriages in the overly binary context of US law. Still, I offer the work of theorists of that time who would be more apt to consider who is left out by "marriage equality" as to celebrate who is included in this new privileged group. If marriage is important for is material benefits, why can't those benefits be available to all regardless of marital status? If the focus is on love and commitment, then what reason is there to believe that traditional marriage is the ideally organized relationship paradigm? It cannot be denied that this ruling, by which so many, including myself, benefit, is historic and in very many ways righteous, but it is important to question not only the substance but the trajectory of social justice issues and how much of the status quo we are willing to accept considering current social conditions.

Chapter 1 also includes an analysis of the SCOTUS ruling itself. I argue that the reasoning here is flawed, and it is flawed in a way that "marriage equality" critics would be apt to note. The supremacy of binary-conceived, assumed monogamous, two person commitments as the forever foundation of US or "civil" society is not justified. The reasoning of the court does not acknowledge even the existence of trans or gender non-binary persons, all of whom are affected not only by the ruling, but by its foundational reasoning. There was no mention of how transgender and non-binary persons have already demonstrated that a binary-conceived "opposite sex" state sponsored union was not just wrongheaded but was in active denial of our lives and our relational commitments. The Supreme Court ruled in favor of same-sex marriage, but the arguments offered do much to support the status quo. Perhaps this is not surprising. Without a doubt, Supreme Court decisions are at once legal documents and moral documents whose final rulings and reasoning will be influential into the future.

Chapter 2 is committed to an overview of the anti-trans offensive of proposed anti-transgender legislation between the years 2015 and 2020 and increased violence against trans and gender non-conforming persons in this time frame. This chapter is not meant to serve as an up-to-the-minute-guide to present anti-trans legislation in any given US state, but to focus on the wave of proposals that targeted transgender persons. If you are concerned about present laws or proposals in your own state, please research the current situation in your area, for they have been changing quite rapidly since 2015. In this chapter, I try to convey scope of the anti-trans offense while also attempting to humanize the data that so many of us are familiar with. When discussing anti-transgender violence, bias, and discrimination, the focus should be on how these forces reduce the flourishing of those targeted and those that, while perhaps not originally targeted, are harmed due to their resemblance. For instance, while transgender people are the stated target for much of this backlash, those who are cisgender but gender non-conforming may be affected due to their gender presentation. Additionally, this chapter includes a critique of these proposals and serves as a basis for further claims of backlash, scapegoating, and dog-whistling.

Chapter 3 focuses resolutely on anti-transgender bathroom bills. Portions of this chapter were originally published in *Ethics, Left and Right: The Moral Issues That Divide Us*, edited by Bob Fischer. I focus on bathroom bills since it is this issue that, I believe, is indicative of the first years of the wave of anti-transgender legislation and continues to be a flash point for those who are simply uninformed on this issue and whose ignorance supports their bias, or who have been misled by those who wish to capitalize on the demonization of the transgender community broadly understood. I argue that these proposals are morally inappropriate, are the result of severely flawed reasoning, and are the source of unjustifiable harm. These kinds of proposals actively seek to make social participation of transgender and gender non-conforming persons nearly impossible. Proposals like these that attempt to limit societal participation serve to target and marginalize trans persons, resulting in severely negative effects for those who are also persons of color. All anti-trans proposals are racist in terms of their impact. The trumped-up fear of trans and gender non-conforming folks using public facilities not only means that certain groups of persons are ostracized and put in harm's way, but that certain types of bodies and body types are demonized as wholly unacceptable, violent, or disgusting. Bathroom bills, like other forms of proposed anti-transgender legislation, are morally wrong.

Chapters 4 through 7 involve the conceptual and moral analysis of terms that are related to this present study of backlash, scapegoating, and dog-whistling. In each chapter I first present a conceptual analysis of the term, and then apply that understanding to the subject at hand. The conceptual analysis in each case is independent of its application and stands on its own as, I hope, a contribution to our thinking on these important ideas. Examples of backlash, scapegoating, and dog-whistling are provided to support the conceptual analysis as well as the application. Obviously, my central claim is that these terms, backlash, scapegoating, and dog-whistling, aptly characterize what has occurred in the politicization of trans identity since 2015. Both chapters 5 and 6 are devoted to the analysis and application of scapegoating. Scapegoating as over-blaming is the focus of chapter 5 whereas an analysis and application of René Girard's view of scapegoating is the topic of chapter 6. I believe that these two ideas, working together, complement each other and go a long way in understanding our present context. Ian Haney López's characterization of dog-whistling is the focus of chapter 7. To this now fairly well-known idea I couple the idea of virtue signaling. As I argue in that chapter, it is one thing to ignite the biases (conscious and unconscious) of individuals for one's own political benefit, but ignition, generally using fear mongering, is unhelpful unless there is someone who is seen as ready to alleviate those fears. Virtue signaling that one is the person to alleviate the fictionalized and trumped-up threat of harm is the other side of the coin of dog-whistling and is also relevant to the politicization of trans and other gender transgressing persons.

Chapter 8 is devoted to an explanation and critique of the Supreme Court ruling, announced in July of 2020, that discrimination on the basis of gender identity or sexual orientation is discrimination on the basis of sex. This 2020 ruling, of what I call the "Bostock case," is a landmark ruling for LGBTQ equality and, unlike the Obergefell ruling of 2015, does explicitly discuss gender identity and the rights of trans and gender non-binary persons. I present an explanation and analysis of the court's opinion in this case as well as the dissenting opinions offered. As I explain, the opinion of the court, written by Justice Gorsuch, seems to be a straightforward application of the law. The dissent, particularly the one penned by Justice Alito, demonstrates a worrisome level of anti-trans bias and ignorance. Just as the Obergefell ruling didn't "fix" all that was inequitable in this country with respect to marriage and the benefits thereof, neither will the Bostock ruling fix all that is inequitable with regard to discrimination against LGBTQ persons. Still, both of these cases will be highly influential in the lives of individual persons and in the influencing of future cases.

Lastly, I offer a short epilogue. A new wave of proposed anti-transgender legislation began in 2021, and thus falls outside the scope of this particular study. As is obvious, one of the great harms of the politicization of an identity or group of persons is that it is very difficult to have that identity or group become *de*-politicized. If politicians can win votes, demonization tactics will continue. If disinformation is transmitted in our highly polarized society in which political and religious affiliation is thought to require such high degrees of homogeneous thought, I fear that the politicization that has occurred to this/my community will continue to have negative ramifications into the future.

Chapter 1

The Obergefell Decision

The *Obergefell v. Hodges* ruling of the US Supreme Court, affirming the right to same-sex marriage nationwide, announced June 26, 2015, serves as the chronological beginning to this analysis and reflection.[1] The *Bostock v. Clayton* ruling, announced a full five years after that of Obergefell, which ruled that employment discrimination on the basis of sexual orientation or gender identity is a form of sex discrimination prohibited by Title VII, serves as the final bookend of this work. This organization is not simply conveniently parallel or an aesthetically pleasing chapter ordering, but these cases do rightfully serve as relevant legal markers spanning a time of unprecedented politicization of transgender persons. The Obergefell ruling, despite the efforts of those who criticized the ruling as misguided, still resulted in overwhelmingly exuberant celebrations across the country. There was, in many contexts, a sense of *accomplishment*, and that lesbian, gay, and queer (LGQ) relationships were finally being *seen* and *recognized* as valuable, meaningful, and legally on par with heterosexual relationships.[2] Obergefell represents a long overdue but righteous response to centuries of oppression of LGQ persons, a legal and moral rebuke of unjust tactics that have included the illegalization of sexual activities between partners considered the same-sex; social ostracism; violence; and psychological, spiritual, and cultural harm. Because the prioritization of heterosexual unions and denial of the legitimacy of LGBTQ lives and relationships is rooted in colonial ideologies, in recognizing same-sex couples, a very small but important step in the decolonization of the country's laws has taken place.

A LOOK BACK: MOMENTUM FOR SAME-SEX MARRIAGE

The change in national climate and levels of optimism regarding same-sex marriage from 2015 to 2020 is so dramatic as to be whiplash inducing. Even though President Barack Obama's campaign of hope had started to go stale by his second term in office, the fact that he was elected for a second term was seen as a reassertion of liberal values and evidence that the white supremacist state did not somehow *accidentally* elect a Black man into the nation's highest position in the first place. Obama's public "evolution" of opinion on the matter of same-sex marriage mirrored that of the dominant collective. The *Washington Post* reported that Obama's slow-motion support of same-sex marriage was intentionally timed to coincide with popular opinion in a way to insulate him from looking more progressive than would be politically prudent.[3] According the Pew report at the time, cited in the article, support of same-sex marriage turned a corner around 2012, when more Americans than not approved of the legalization of such unions. (Specifically, Pew reported a 48 percent approval rate in comparison to a 43 percent rate of disapproval.) Obama's own public avowal occurred first in 2012. Through national public debate as well as personal conversations over coffee, the telling and retelling of narratives that characterized the legalization of same-sex marriage as *the* civil rights issue of the era made inroads. These stories included that of then San Francisco mayor, Gavin Newsom, using his political authority to issue (illegal) marriage licenses to same-sex couples on February 12, 2004. Within twenty-nine days, four thousand couples enjoyed the fruits of some semblance of official recognition as well as the satisfaction that comes from participating in meaningful civil disobedience. Newsom's bold dismissal of California state law, as well as the legislative and legal attempts to legalize same-sex marriage in states such as Hawaii (1993–2013), Massachusetts (2004), Connecticut and California (2008), and elsewhere, meant that the scrambling for political power and moral authority for those both in favor of and against same-sex marriage grew to a dramatic tension by the time the Obergefell case was argued in 2014.

The now iconic picture of the White House glowing in the shades of the rainbow shortly after the Obergefell announcement explicitly illuminated the federal government's support of the ruling and of LGBTQ Americans. For the first time, marriage became accessible to many who had been previously denied this right throughout the history of the United States. The Supreme Court ruling that granted the civil right to state-sanctioned marriage and its myriad of benefits to couples regardless of assigned sex at birth was truly a turning point in our nation's history and its legal recognition of the value of LGQ identities and relationships. The United States, Finland, Ireland, and Greenland each found the collective will to legalize same-sex marriages in 2015, with seventeen nations doing so before 2015 and (so far) nine countries following suit between the years 2015 and 2020. According to Pew research, the thirty countries in which same-sex marriage has been legalized include the following: the Netherlands (2000), Belgium (2003), Canada (2005), Spain

(2005), South Africa (2006), Norway (2008), Sweden (2009), Iceland (2010), Portugal (2010), Argentina (2010), Denmark (2012), Uruguay (2013), New Zealand (2013), France (2013), Brazil (2013), England and Wales (2013), Scotland (2014), Luxembourg (2014), Finland (2015), Ireland (2015), Greenland (2015), the United States (2015), Germany (2017), Malta (2017), Australia (2017), Austria (2019), Taiwan (2019), Ecuador (2019), Northern Ireland (2019), and Costa Rica (2020).[4] Outgoing president Obama retweeted the iconic picture of the rainbowed White House on his last evening in the White House, January 19, 2016, before he handed over the house, and the executive branch, to the newly inaugurated President Trump. Obviously, Obama still looked favorably on the Obergefell decision and perhaps took pride in the fact that he found a place, whether it was personal or calculated, to take pride in his own support of LGBTQ marriage equality.[5]

It is vital to note, however, that whether one derives benefits or punishments as a result of becoming married depends on context. Disability activists have made clear that the Obergefell ruling does not mean that there is "marriage equality" for everyone. Many individuals with disabilities are financially punished for marrying since "tying the knot" can result in a reduction in social security and Medicaid benefits. Having liberty to engage in an action requires one not be punished for that engagement. One should not have to choose between marrying and being able to afford life enhancing services or being able to pay the rent. While celebrating "marriage equality" is understandable, it can also render invisible those who still cannot practically exercise this right.

The Obergefell ruling stands as the starting place for this study not because it was in any way a watershed moment for civil liberties for persons of trans and other marginalized genders.[6] While trans persons like myself and many others derived benefits from the Obergefell ruling either because we seek a same-sex marriage or because those who would refuse to recognize our gender identity might regard some of our unions as a same-sex relationship, the court's opinion failed to acknowledge even this. In fact, the decision, including the majority opinion and four dissents, does not even mention how the ruling is relevant to the experiences of lives of transgender persons or gender non-binary, or otherwise expansive, persons. The court did not argue, as I did in 2009 in "Trans Marriage and the Unacceptability of Same-Sex Marriage Restrictions," that a full recognition of trans persons and a rejection of the gender-sex binary was a sufficient reason to accept same-sex marriages.[7] The false set of beliefs that all individuals come in one of two sexes, that their gender identity is a function of sex assignment at birth, and that certain personal characteristics can be assumed from merely one's sex assignment at birth serves as the flawed starting position of any argument prohibiting "same-sex" marriage. In other words, accepting that not all individuals fit into one of two assigned sexes and one of two genders, or that personal character traits are independent of social roles involving marriage or parenting means that the "opposite sex only" provision of traditional marriage fails.

The rejection-of-the-binary argument against the prohibition of "same-sex" marriage is less common than others. This is not surprising, for it has long been the case that what came to be a mostly white, gay, and cisgender LGBTQ rights movement has failed to include the priorities and experiences of transgender, gender non-binary, and gender bending identities of white folks as well as members of the broader community that includes Black, Indigenous, and other people of color (BIPOC). If the focus of political action is on the needs of cisgender gay men and lesbians, the faults of the sex-binary system are generally not front and center. Additionally, in my own advocacy experience, those charged with updating policies and practices towards the inclusion of transgender and gender non-binary folks often wish to keep such changes relatively quiet, for fear of controversy and rebuke. The run-up to the establishment of federally recognized marriage equality meant that there was increasing pressure not to *muddy the waters* with discussion of transgender rights and the ever present, politicized, and weaponized cisgender fear of transgender and gender non-binary persons using public restrooms.

Even though transgender persons and our experiences were not seen as part of the Obergefell story, the ensuing years after the ruling ushered in a nationwide politicization of trans identity that birthed hundreds of explicitly anti-transgender legislative proposals and an increase in anti-transgender violence. To claim that the Obergefell decision was the sole cause of the anti-transgender political offensive in the years from 2015 to 2020 would surely be an example of an oversimplified causal analysis and the fallacy of *post hoc ergo propter hoc* (i.e., since the politicization of trans identity and the stoking of anti-trans sentiment occurred after Obergefell, Obergefell caused this sentiment and polarization). Still, as I will characterize herein, there is reason to believe that the chronological nature of these two (broadly characterized) events is more than mere coincidence.

Speaking personally, the post-Obergefell anti-trans offensive found my own social media feed full of sentiments by other trans persons expressing the notion of "I told you so," in the sense that "I told you that a ruling in favor of same-sex marriage would result in a vehement anti-transgender backlash." Noting the relationship between the Obergefell decision and the hundreds of anti-transgender policy initiatives in the years following the decision is one of the driving forces of this project. In this chapter, the Obergefell decision will be reviewed both with regard to the reasoning of the justices and also with regard to the ways that it may have sown the seeds of the anti-transgender offensive. Relatedly, I review the arguments of those who were opposed to the prioritization of marriage rights and the relationship of their reasoned opposition to what we now know, through the 2020 vision of hindsight, following the ruling. I hope to show that neither the Supreme Court decision itself nor the prioritization of marriage equality is a simple case of affirming the importance of love or the political equality of LGBTQ persons. There are, in fact, many reasons to critique the reasoning of Justice Kennedy, who wrote the opinion of the court, as well as the identification of same-sex marriage as the cause of the era that deserved so much backing and attention. My analysis, including both critique and congratulation, has ramifications for how we understand social justice movements, the institution of marriage, and theories of legal interpretation.

THE COURT'S ARGUMENT

Leaving aside for the moment a consideration of whether or not a prioritization of marriage equality above other social justice goals was justified, familiarity with the content of the Obergefell ruling is important to understanding the context of the ruling's aftermath. As I will explain, the Supreme Court's decision does explicitly value gay and lesbian couples as important members of society and as potential parents and caregivers. This is, indeed, revolutionary. Relatedly, the court is explicit in characterizing traditional marriage as a moral ideal on which the health of our society, even civilization itself, relies. While the first result is quite positive, the second is much more worrisome for those who reject the notion that respect requires assimilation into the current established practices of unearned and misused privilege. The conditional statement, "If opposite-sex couples are eligible for civil marriage and its benefits, then same-sex couples should be eligible for the same," is quite different from claiming that traditional marriage is of greater moral value or that it is somehow more able to produce flourishing individuals and compassionate societies than alternative care-taking configurations. As so many have argued, there is no reason to restrict marriage to two individuals who are of "opposite" sexes, but is there reason to restrict it at all when it is a choice among consenting adults? Indeed, given the multitude of options and the decidedly violent and oppressive history of traditional marriage, there seems to be little reason to believe that traditional marriage is superior to all other arrangements. The result of the Obergefell ruling is that those individuals who participate in marriage are now considered new members of an expanded and privileged class. For some, it is one privilege among many others; for others, it is one social privilege among relatively few.

In what can be seen as more than a nod toward traditional thinkers—perhaps more like a full concert standing ovation—the court's decision, written by Justice Kennedy, includes a section specifically devoted to the history of the institution of marriage. The history presented foregrounds European/colonial culture but makes somewhat half-hearted attempts to include examples of the importance of marriage across culture and time period. Tellingly, examples of nonheteronormative familial organizations go without mention. Here, the traditional institution of marriage characterized is untenably positive. Kennedy characterizes marriage not simply as a choice among different lifestyle options or a choice among many that might serve to fulfill human aspirations and needs. Instead, for Kennedy and the majority of justices, marriage is "transcendently important," it is "essential," and it rises "from our most profound needs and aspirations."[8] The court took pains to communicate that the petitioners in the case (originally sixteen same-sex couples) chose not to seek to change the meaning or status of traditional marriage, but simply to make it inclusive of same-sex couples. It is the enduring importance of marriage that was thought to underlie the petitioner's contentions: "Far from seeking to devalue marriage, the petitioners seek it for themselves because of their respect—and need—for its privileges and responsibilities. And their immutable nature dictates that same-sex marriage is their only real path to this profound commitment."[9] So reasons the court that, because the petitioners are gay and lesbian, they are unable to access this human good in any other form.[10]

The lynchpin of the court's argument rests with the use of the Fourteenth Amendment, both the Due Process Clause and the Equal Protection Clause. Using this as the basis of the argument, while not unprecedented, is controversial. Section 1 of the Fourteenth Amendment reads as follows:

> All persons born or naturalized in the United States and subject to the jurisdiction thereof, are citizens of the United States and of the State wherein they reside. No State shall make or enforce any law which shall abridge the privileges or immunities of citizens of the United States; nor shall any State deprive any person of life, liberty, or property, without due process of law; nor deny to any person within its jurisdiction the equal protection of the laws.[11]

The Due Process Clause of the Fourteenth Amendment is related to that of the Fifth Amendment, which identifies the rights of those accused of crimes; one such right is that of due process before any federally mandated imprisonment. The Due Process Clause is similar, but more expansive, and regarded as covering those rights listed in the Bill of Rights, as well as those rights that are not explicitly listed in that document but that are seen as fundamental.[12] Both the Fifth and the Fourteenth Amendment include reference to a prohibition against deprivation of "life, liberty, or property without due process of law." The Fourteenth Amendment follows these words with what is called the Equal Protection Clause, which reads, "nor deny to any person within its jurisdiction the equal protection of the laws." It is important to note that in this case, as in *Loving v. Virginia* (1967) that banned miscegenation laws, the Due Process Clause and the Equal Protection Clause are both used. Here, the Fourteenth Amendment is used in a two step process. First marriage is argued to be protected under due process, then that being the case, states must provide all equal protection for this right. Appeals to the Fourteenth Amendment have been instrumental in supporting the right for married couples to use contraception (*Griswald v. Connecticut*, 1965), the right to an "interracial" marriage (*Loving v. Virginia*, 1967), the right for unmarried couples to use contraception (*Eisenstadt v. Baird*, 1972), the right to an abortion (*Roe v. Wade*, 1973), the right for same-sex couples to participate in consensual sexual activity (*Lawrence v. Texas*, 2003, overturning *Bowers v. Hardwick*, 1986), and the case of interest here, the right for same-sex couples to marry. Indeed, while a changed social climate may make at least some of these decisions seem noncontroversial today, they were so in their own day and were dramatically transformative for the nation. Some remain divisive, most notably *Roe v. Wade*, which is both legitimately a wedge issue in contemporary politics and is also weaponized to drive such wedges broader and deeper for the purpose of amassing political power and influence.

Determining exactly what rights are fundamental to the Constitution and thus fall under the requirement of due process is no simple task. In *Poe v. Ullman* (1961), the court maintained that identifying such rights is not given by any "formula" but is contextual and up to the determination of the court. The Obergefell majority opinion, written by Justice Kennedy, refers to the Poe decision in the following passage:

> Rather, it [the use of the Due Process Clause] requires courts to exercise reasoned judgment in identifying interest of the person so fundamental that the State must accord them its respect. That process is guided by many of the same considerations relevant to analysis of other constitutional provisions that set forth broad principles rather than specific requirements. History and tradition guide and discipline this inquiry but do not set its outer boundaries. See *Lawrence*, supra at 572. That method respects our history and learns from it without allowing the past alone to rule the present.[13]

So, to employ the Due Process Clause in a way that is consistent with the history of its use, the court had the task of demonstrating that marriage, in this case for those of the same-sex assignment, was foundational to the Constitution. The court attempted to do so on the basis of the following four premises:

(P1) Marriage is a choice "inherent in the concept of individual autonomy."[14]
(P2) The right to marry is fundamental in its importance to its participants.[15]
(P3) Marriage is an institution that protects and supports families and children.[16]
(P4) Marriage is the "keystone to our social order."[17]

The assertion by the court of (P1) and (P3) is historically significant in the sense that same-sex couples are judged to be equally as valuable as heterosexual couples. This is indeed a step forward in recognizing the value and equal citizenship of lesbian and gay individuals. While the liberal and neoliberal emphasis on individual autonomy can be persuasively criticized, to assert that desiring to marry one's same-sex partner is related to autonomy and not mental illness is a positive step, especially given the historic and ongoing oppression of LGBTQ persons. The notion that lesbian women and gay men are equal citizens is light years away from their classification as mentally ill in the Diagnostic and Statistical Manual of Mental Disorders (DSM) from 1952 to 1973, as well as the criminalization of some intimate sexual activities until *Lawrence v. Texas* in 2003.

Similarly, the recognition that same-sex couples are parents and should be afforded the same protections as straight parents is a much more just legal position than having one's sexual orientation be the reason that one is barred from having any parental rights at all, a not-uncommon practice that kept countless parents from *coming out* as lesbian or gay for fear they'd be sacrificing their parental rights to their straight partner. Here, the court asserts that gay and lesbian parents are no less competent and nurturing caregivers to their children than are heterosexual parents: "As all parties agree, many same-sex couples provide loving and nurturing homes to their children, whether biological or adopted."[18] The court recognized the stigma that exists for children of same-sex parents whose commitments are deemed not equal to civil marriage at best, or an abomination at worst. At the same time, the court makes clear that while having children is sometimes a component to marriage and serves as reason for the court to support healthy unions, it is not a necessary ingredient.

As for P2 ("The right to marry is fundamental in its importance to its participants"), it seems undoubtedly true that many same-sex couples did and continue to desire to be married, and do so for a variety of reasons. For many, civil marriage is a sign of public and private commitment, of joining participants together as family with hopes of long-term security and acceptance. In the heteronormative dominant culture, few have not had encounters with traditional marriage, whether that be marriages depicted in the media or the marriages of one's parents, guardians, siblings, grandparents, neighbors, or friends. Whether one believes there is something objectively valuable in the practice of traditional marriage or one realizes that marriage comes with numerous material and nonmaterial benefits, it is simply true that many in the LGBTQ community see it as an important and valuable institution. The fundamental nature of marriage to the country is described by the court through a reference to *Griswold v. Connecticut* (1965), which asserts that the right to marriage is "older than the Bill of Rights":[19]

> Marriage is a coming together for better or for worse, hopefully enduring, and intimate to the degree of being sacred. It is an association that promotes a way of life, not causes; a harmony in living, not political faiths, a bilateral loyalty, not commercial or social projects. Yet it is an association for as noble a purpose as any involved in our prior decisions. (*Griswold v. Connecticut* at 486)[20]

This passage from Griswold supports the reading of this premise (P2) that an individual's desire to become traditionally married does not primarily, nor only, involve contemporary civil contracts but is instead pre-political. That is, it is not about a particular tradition of the United States, or even of societies in which heterosexuality and adherence to the gender binary is socially compulsory, but something that is central to being human. The court's recognition that the choice of individuals to seek marriage (or not) is an important aspect of autonomy is laudable; but claims regarding this rosy picture of marriage itself are quite a bit more suspect.

Now, let us turn to (P4), that traditional marriage is not just a lifestyle choice among many, but one that is normatively ideal and foundational to society. That the court regards civil marriage as the "keystone of our social order" makes clear that traditionally characterized marriage is a normative ideal, and those who participate in it hold a special place in our society. Echoing the colonial belief system at the time, the court in 1888 declared marriage as "the foundation of the family and of society, without which there would be neither civilization nor progress."[21] It is less shocking that such views would be offered as part of the court's reasoning in 1888 than that they would be in 2015. The court regards marriage as the social institution that is deemed valuable enough to the state's interests to support with the myriad of benefits that are awarded through state-sanctioned marriage. My own view on the political importance of championing same-sex marriage has been heavily influenced by Cheshire Calhoun and her essay "In Defense of Same-Sex Marriage."[22] Consistent with Calhoun's position, I believe it is noteworthy that the court recognizes that those engaged in same-sex marriages are worthy to fulfill this thought-to-be-special role in our society. Doing so is a step toward the affirmation that lesbian women and gay men are not outsiders of our own civic communities, towns, cities, states, or nation, but are valuable members of the same, and it is our presence *and* our affiliations, along with others, that bind our communities together. In other words, it is not the case that lesbian women and gay men are free-riders who leech off of the stability and community-making efforts of our straight community siblings, but that we together are valuable and foundational.

For Calhoun, the conception of marriage as the pre-political foundation of society has an important implication: if a social group can lay claim to being inherently qualified or fit to enter into marriage and found a family, it can also claim a distinctive political status. Members of the group can claim that they play an essential role in sustaining the very foundation of civil society. Conversely, if those of a particular social group are deemed unfit to enter marriage and found a family, that group can then be denied this distinctive political status.[23] This denial of social value has been the case for those in same-sex relationships until 2015. It is in this way that Calhoun's ideas served to force the discussion regarding what are thought-to-be differences between heterosexual and non-heterosexual persons. If one accepts the pre-political status of marriage and its foundational role, then the meaning of marriage itself falls into the background and, perhaps, the table is cleared to discuss the equal status of lesbian women and gay men relative to heterosexuals. A review of the ruling itself supports the conclusion that the kind of argument that the majority engaged in does consider marriage to be a pre-political institution. It is not just an option among many, but of particular social importance. In other words, if it is accepted that those who would form same-sex couples are shown to be capable of this special status, of upholding the very foundation of society, then the gold standard of acceptance and political equality has been achieved. Borrowing from the words of Liza Minnelli and her character's view of New York City, "If we can make it here, we can make it anywhere."[24]

There is, however, an obvious underside of the court prioritizing a certain kind of familial ideal above others. In the words of the court, "no union is more profound than marriage, for it embodies the highest ideals of love, fidelity, devotion, sacrifice, and family."[25] Not surprisingly, Calhoun and many others explicitly reject this kind of claim. The socially conservative argument that marriage is a "committed, monogamous, sexually faithful relationship [that] contributes to personal and social flourishing"[26] is, for her, one that is "fundamentally anti-liberal."[27] Like many who have criticized the prioritization of the marriage equality movement by LGBTQ rights organizations, Calhoun accepts that there are a plurality of family forms, and that the valuing of traditional marriage (complete with the notions of romantic love, monogamy, and the assumption of till-death-do-us-part partners) unnecessarily privileges one form of relationship. In her words, "marriage rights, so construed, ought not to have priority in a gay/lesbian political agenda."[28] Calhoun is right here. While it is noteworthy that lesbian women and gay men are seen by the court as suitable to play this foundational role in our society, it is important to recognize that this judging as *sufficiently competent* is from a heterosexual-cisgender lens and privileges those same-sex marriage applicants and participants who most closely approach the dominant ideal of being monogamous, employed, not-anarchist, family- and country-loving, non-BDSM, and otherwise conforming to the ideal plaintiff couples in this kind of case—white, long-term couples who are seen, because of these dominant and intersecting characteristics, as already poised to be the *standard-bearers of society*. That is, they are those who have significant societal privileges already, except access to legal marriage.

It is noteworthy that the plaintiffs include James Obergefell, whose relationship with his partner, John Arthur, spanned over two decades. Plaintiffs April DeBoer and Jayne Rowse both were working as nurses, and as a couple adopted three special needs children. For a third couple, Ijpe De Koe and his partner Thomas Kostrura, the court could cite DeKoe's military service in the Army Reserves as evidence of his worth and stalwartness. There is more than just a passing concern that those who are offered as ideal emissaries of the LGBTQ community strengthen the privileging systems already in place. This is certainly not a new issue, and many have brought attention to it in the last decade. It is not just the case that privileging those who have already amassed significant social privilege leaves so many people out, or that it fails to recognize the harms against BIPOC folks (Black, Indigenous, people of color) and those who are transgender or gender non-binary or non-conforming, but it also consolidates power for those who are white or cisgender or gender conforming.

Discussing what sociopolitical structures are foundational to the functioning and unity of US society has a different tenor as I write these words in 2021, than when written by the Supreme Court in 1888, Calhoun in 2008, or Kennedy in 2015. Since 2015, the word "disunity" comes to mind more than does "unity" or discussion of societal characteristics. Disunity is an ongoing experience of those who unjustly suffer from immensely harmful systemic racism and those who fail to recognize this harm. There was disunity in our political structures as the Trump administration refused to concede the election and as so many of us watched in horror as the US Capitol was stormed January 6, 2021. The COVID pandemic has, if anything, shown us that what binds a society together involves the virtues of compassion, understanding, and true caring for each other, and there is no reason to think that married couples, whether straight or lesbian, gay, or queer, are any more foundational to the practices of those virtues than is anyone else. Those who were in favor of spending the time, energy, and money on the campaign for same-sex marriage and those who believe that doing so simply supported systems and narratives that would be best dismantled might momentarily agree with the claim that if straight couples are seen as the foundation of society, then so, too, should lesbian or gay couples, but the latter may quickly add that supporting heteropatriarchal structures and myths is a kind of harm itself. Before considering those types of concerns, the next section is devoted to a review of the minority opinions voicing dissent to the majority's ruling. As will be obvious, these dissenting opinions shaped the 2020 Bostock ruling, the subject of chapter 8.

DISSENTING OPINION: ROBERTS, SCALIA, THOMAS, AND ALITO

One of the first things to understand regarding the dissenting positions of Roberts, Scalia, Thomas, and Alito is that the primary issue for these justices, at least that which is explicit in their written opinions, is not that gay men and lesbian women are unfit for marriage, are degenerate, morally unequal to straight persons, or mentally unwell. The commonality of their dissents involves the role of the Supreme Court and when it is appropriate or inappropriate for rulings made by the court to override state law. In their view, it is not the role of the highest court to rule in a way that could be construed as preempting a legislative solution or overriding otherwise acceptable legislation itself. To believe otherwise is to advocate, in their view, "legislating from the bench," a charge often on the lips of many conservative thinkers for decades and particularly popular with those who call themselves textualists.

Textualism is a theory of legal interpretation that has been made particularly popular by the late Justice Antonin Scalia. Textualists believe that the application of a law must be consistent with the meaning of the statute at the time of its authorship and must be consistent with the meaning that the original authors wished to convey. Recall that the majority of the court argued that same-sex marriage should be the law of the land based primarily on the Due Process Clause of the Fourteenth Amendment and the characterization of marriage that Kennedy, and others, present as a foundational right. The majority refer to the autonomy of the individual to have the liberty to make their own choices with regard to this most intimate and foundational of relationships. Kennedy, writing for the majority, explains:

> It is now clear that the challenged laws burden the liberty of same-sex couples, and it must be further acknowledged that they abridge central precepts of equality. Here the marriage laws enforced by the respondents are in essence unequal: same-sex couples are denied all the benefits afforded to opposite sex couples and are barred from exercising a fundamental right. Especially against a long

history of disapproval of their relationships, this denial to same-sex couples of the right to marry works a grave and continuing harm.[29]

On the question of whether the court should rule on this issue at all or leave the country, through its elected lawmakers, to resolve the matter, the majority is clear: "The dynamic of our constitutional system is that individuals need not await legislative action before asserting a fundamental right."[30]

It is disagreement on the role of the Supreme Court that is the primary dispute between the four justices who denounce this ruling and the five who believe justice was served. Chief Justice Roberts, and others, assert that since this right to same-sex marriage is not explicitly identified in the Constitution, it cannot be made so without the court acting as a legislature. In other words, if it is the case that choosing whom to marry, even if that be a person considered to be the same sex, is a fundamental right that should be enshrined by the Constitution, then it is up to the legislature to do so. To do otherwise is to usurp the power of elected officials and to allow a few "unelected lawyers"[31] to have undue, perhaps even dangerous, influence. From Chief Justice Roberts,

> But this Court is not a legislature. Whether same-sex marriage is a good idea should be of no concern to us. Under the Constitution, judges have power to say what the law is, not what it should be. . . . The fundamental right to marry does not include a right to make a State change its definition of marriage.[32]

Scalia's similarly dissenting point is dramatically penned,

> I join THE CHIEF JUSTICE'S opinion in full. I write separately to call attention to this Court's threat to American democracy.[33]

> This practice of constitutional revision by an unelected committee of nine, always accompanied (as it is today) by extravagant praise of liberty, robs the People of the most important liberty they asserted in the Declaration of Independence and won in the Revolution of 1776: the freedom to govern themselves.[34] . . . We have no basis for striking down a practice that is not expressly prohibited by the Fourteenth Amendment's text, and that bears the endorsement of a long tradition of open, widespread, and unchallenged use dating back to the Amendment's ratification.[35]

In a kind of argumentation that we will see again on display in the ruling of the Bostock decision, the dissenting Justices note that the authors of the Fourteenth Amendment did not foresee or intend that it would be employed to guarantee the right for individuals to marry the same-sex partner of their choosing. Similarly, the authors of Title VII did not anticipate that their statute regarding discrimination on the basis of sex would prohibit employment discrimination on the basis of sexual orientation or gender identity. Again, for Roberts, Scalia, Thomas, and Alito, the application of the law is constrained by a strict and precise application of the text according to the meaning of the language written by its authors.[36] Strict textualists argue that the court is inappropriately broadening, or even distorting, the law's meaning and application.

It can barely be denied that the prospect that a majority of "nine unelected lawyers," who hold lifetime appointments and who—especially in the age of Justice Amy Coney Barrett, whose nomination to the Supreme Court seemed particularly partisan—have broad powers to overrule the will of the people, is fear-inducing for some. It is also true that the prospect of holding our country too tightly to the attitudes of a small group of unelected eighteenth-century colonialists, whose morality was so askew as to support the enslavement and brutal treatment of thousands upon thousands of individuals, who attempted and supported genocidal actions against Indigenous North Americans, and who regarded women as unfit to participate in the political and professional sphere of society, is also, if not much more, worrisome. That said, the Fourteenth Amendment, the lynchpin of the majority's decision, was written in a post–Civil War America and ratified by two-thirds of the states to become law in 1868. The amendment's authors were focused on the injustices of the state-supported enslavement of millions of individuals over hundreds of years and sought to remedy those injustices and provide a foundation for a more just society going forward. Still, it certainly is not clear whether, with regard to LGBTQ rights, being held hostage by the ideologies of a collection of colonialist rebels is a whole lot different from being held so by a group of nineteenth-century Reconstructionists. This history of the treatment and consideration of LGBTQ persons in this country is abysmal, as this is a point of agreement of the majority and dissenting minority of the court. So, to trust the treatment of LGBTQ persons to the stale and harmful social norms of over a hundred years ago that regarded even the *existence* of a gay man, lesbian, bisexual, or trans person as a moral abomination is to perpetuate injustice and to recommit to the closed-mindedness of past lawmakers. Roberts writes that the right to marriage is not the right to a *same-sex* marriage, in essence supporting the idea that the institution itself becomes a different type of institution when nonheteronormative couples participate in it. I do not deny that this would be the view of those who originally wrote the Fourteenth Amendment, but I disagree that their views on LGBTQ equality should be seen as relevant in this case.

With regard to waiting for the federal legislature to fashion a kind of compromise proposal that would suit the tastes of marriage conservatives and others enough to get passed, there is reason to think that this represents a scheme to needlessly perpetuate injustice and harm. The question brings to mind the history of the Equal Rights Amendment, the legislation, first proposed in 1923 by Alice Paul, that would amend the Constitution to guarantee equal rights regardless of sex. My own 1970s childhood included listening to serious debates and the seriously harmful ridicule of the attempts to ratify this amendment. To this day, it has not become part of our Constitution. Biases, systemic injustices, and collective habits create a social inertia that makes change difficult. Having an Equal Marriage Amendment, like the Equal Rights Amendment, would be highly politicized and would, in the end, mean that those who are privileged to have benefited from being eligible for legal marriage before 2015 would be in a position to vote on the marriage rights of the not so privileged. I fear that a tradition of injustice would reproduce the same. Kicking the decision back to the legislature only because the Supreme Court justices believed themselves unsuited to understand and apply the concept of liberty seems more an abnegation of responsibility than an adherence to appropriately stringent judicial ethics.

As mentioned in a previous section, Kennedy, writing for the majority, speaks of the American institution of marriage as something wholly positive and noble. I believe few would accept this claim as uncritically true, and while the institution of marriage can serve as a context to practice the virtues of patience, commitment, love, and mutual respect, so too does a single lifestyle provide a context of important virtues, as does a polyamorous connection of three or more people. At best, marriage is one choice among many and should be a choice for all who are so interested, regardless of whom one wishes to couple (or triple?) up with. If the US embraced living wages, universal health care, guaranteed sustenance allowance, housing, and education as a right of all, not just a state-sanctioned privilege for some, then maybe any institution resembling civil marriage would simply become irrelevant and would cease to be the choice of all but a very few. Until then, it falls on the courts to do what they can to try to provide the context of equal rights and equal dignity for all by applying the relevant concepts of the law, even when those do not coincide with the original author's imagined applications.

Before leaving this section, there is one unique argument offered in Justice Thomas's dissent that is due some attention. Thomas focuses on the concept of liberty, which serves as the key idea in the majority opinion. That is, if marriage is a fundamental right (and they argue that it is) then the liberty of individuals to access that right should not be curtailed without due process. Thomas argues that the majority misunderstands the concept of liberty, and it is this mistake that leads to an erroneous ruling. Thomas states, "In the American legal tradition, liberty has long been understood as individual freedom from governmental action, not as a right to a particular governmental entitlement."[37] He takes issue with the majority's precedents and claims that they illustrate the original conceptual mistake just identified and this is why they are not as relevant to the case as the majority claims. For instance, consider the case of *Loving v. Virginia* that legalized interracial marriage. While this case is obviously about the right to marry, it also involved a criminal prosecution of the couple since they married in the District of Columbia but were living in Virginia. Imprisonment and a banishment from the state of Virginia was the punishment approved by the lower court that was under review. A second case identified as precedent, *Zablocki v. Redhail*, involved a law prohibiting men who were delinquent on their child support payments from marrying. Zablocki was also threatened with punishment if he did go through with his intended marriage. The last case, *Turner v. Safley*, involved a prohibition on the marriage of prison inmates without the expressed permission of the prison superintendent. Permission was only given in particular circumstances. Thus, Thomas concludes, "In none of those cases were individuals denied solely governmental recognition and benefits associated with marriage," instead they were also attempting to avoid punishment.[38] According to this view, in the first two cases the petitioners were not solely seeking government benefits but also to be free from state administered punishment. I assume that the third case does not involve all of the government benefits since the benefits of marriage would be inaccessible to the prison inmates anyway. In this way, Justice Thomas defends his position that, since liberty is primarily a freedom *from* governmental intervention into one's life, and not simply freedom *to* access government benefits, and since the Obergefell plaintiffs have been free from governmental intervention in nearly everything they have wanted to do (except to enjoy the benefits of legal marriage), the ruling is unjustified.

I find Thomas's treatment of this issue noteworthy for two very different reasons. First, it is shocking to recognize that while the majority of the court characterizes marriage as a foundational, ancient, and valuable institution of not just American but *human* society, the conservative Justice Thomas reduces it to a government benefit program for those who meet government eligibility requirements. While there is reason to be cautious of the rosy characterization of marriage as written by Kennedy, many would admit that it is an institution that, at least for some participants, has meaning above and beyond the collection of benefits that this government has decided was justified *based on the value* of the institution itself. On the other hand, if marriage really is only a collection of government distributed perks, common notions of fairness and equal treatment would find serious critique of such governmental benefit programs that provide benefits to some and not others without sufficient justification. Secondly, if, unlike Thomas, we accept an articulation of a different concept of liberty, a *liberty-to*, and not just a *liberty-from*, then new consequences present themselves. The collection of economic rights, as distinguished from political rights, all seem to be *liberty-to*. For instance, it could be persuasively argued that there is liberty to safe shelter, liberty to meaningful and fairly paid work, liberty to a sustainable and healthy environment, liberty to sufficient food and clean water, and liberty to an adequate amount of leisure and recreation. The concept of liberty *from* governmental intervention into one's life is important, but also seems to imply that being free from such intervention sets the foundation for a flourishing life. If marriage or a living wage, for example, is important or necessary for the flourishing of human beings, then, indeed, one's liberty is curtailed if either are restricted or prohibited. Liberty, far from only requiring an absence of intervention or restraint, requires the foundational necessities for mental and physical health, a sense of value and recognition from society, the time and space to wonder and to wander, to be curious, to be creative. An expansive liberty recognizes that a kind of obsessive individualism and emphasis on bootstrap pulling, which denies embedded systemic injustices, will never be a sufficient conceptual model for a just society. Of course, Thomas is not advocating for the kind of liberty that could serve as a foundation for human (and environmental) flourishing. Yet, when considered from a different light, many have argued that, far from being an object of criticism, an expansive sense of liberty is a concept with great possibility.

DISSENT FROM WITHIN: CRITICISMS OF SAME-SEX MARRIAGE PRIORITIZATION

We briefly reviewed Cheshire Calhoun's position on same-sex marriage earlier in this chapter, but she is not the only theorist who has weighed in on this matter, nor is she alone in her concerns that prioritizing one form of familial organization above others is problematic both in general and specifically in our contemporary context. The value and justifiability of marriage has long been a popular topic among philosophers and philosophical thinkers, and continues to be a vital area of study in this post-Obergefell era.[39] Notable in the ramp-up to the marriage equality debate was a piece entitled "Beyond Same-Sex Marriage: A New Strategic Vision for All Our Families and Relationships," signed by such academic and political leaders as Susie Bright, Charlotte Bunch, Judith Butler, Paisley Currah, Ann Fausto-Sterling, Leslie Feinberg, Jack Halberstam, Yasmin Nair, Dean Spade, Gloria Steinem, and Cornel West. Here, the signers made clear that not all LGBTQ individuals, nor LGBTQ thought-leaders and allies, believed that a prioritization of marriage was justified.[40] The authors include a long list of relationship types that provide stability, compassion, and love to those who participate. Caring unions including senior citizens living together, extended families, close friends and siblings who care for each other on a long-term basis, two or more queer couples who jointly raise a child but live in separate households, and others, make a prioritization of one form of assumed monogamous, heteronormative, two-spouse marriage seem exceedingly narrow, uninventive, and even unobservant. If one accepts that marriage is a civil right of heterosexual couples, then there are numerous persuasive ways of arguing why this is also a right of same-sex couples, but this, for these thinkers, is too constrained a conversation. Even if one does accept the conditional statement, this does not imply that the material benefits of marriage should only be regarded as a right of those forming these traditional conjugal pairs, or that other relationships of care might not produce the same benefits for society, and perhaps even without the well-documented abuses and historical injustices of traditional marriage itself. Indeed, outside of tradition, there seems to be no reason that a civil institution like marriage, that exists to support well-lived lives and economic and personal security, need have anything to do with assumptions of romantic love and sexuality. Seniors living together platonically and caring for each other should have no less *right* to visit each other in the hospital than I have to visit my wife, nor, if they so choose, a right to their friend's inheritance to support their continued economic security, or the right to be listed as surviving family members on death certificates. If the aim is to produce flourishing individuals and caring collectives, then the value of any social institution is based on its potential to improve the lives of its members and the collective as a whole. I agree that expanding marriage rights means a great deal to couples throughout the nation who benefit from the newly acquired rights and social status, but going from a rights view to one that is broadly inclusive of human flourishing makes obvious that it is just these kinds of benefits that many marriage-ineligible or -disinterested individuals need.

Among the dominant voices critical of the marriage equality campaign has been scholar and activist Dean Spade. For Spade, marriage is far from being an ideal relationship but is "a tool of social control used by governments to regulate sexuality and family formation by establishing a favored form and rewarding it" with certain benefits.[41] For this reason, the material consequences of civil marriage include an unequal distribution of resources that unnecessarily and unjustly privilege one kind of relationship over others for the benefit of the mostly privileged and to the detriment of the most unjustly created vulnerable. Furthermore, on this view, LGBTQ inclusion in marriage serves to "valorize" marriage, and its prioritization is unethical for the movement in that it uses this unjust institution to benefit the relatively privileged of our communities at the expense of those targeted by racial, economic, and other injustices. For Spade, a focus on gaining the recognition of civil rights is a key part of neoliberal strategies that do not benefit those labored with the multiple oppressions that are a consequence of our institution's systems. This point is, I believe, especially poignant now, when the stories of police brutality against persons of color have, for years, provided stark and horrifying evidence that civil rights legislation is impotent to protect individuals from the harm of systemic racism and internalized racist ideology. It is clear that even explicit equality under the law does not prevent the worst kinds of imaginable atrocities.

Through the years from 2015 to 2020, the rates of violence against trans and gender non-conforming individuals spiked, with 2020 being the deadliest year since such records have been kept. These kinds of outrages persist despite explicit hate-crime laws in some of the locales, civil rights legislation meant to value the lives of Black, Indigenous, and other people of color (BIPOC) who are targeted for this kind of abuse, and the obvious illegality of violent attacks themselves. Furthermore, income inequality causes real hardship, which adversely affects those with simultaneous combinations of identities that include being a person of color; being LGBTQ or gender non-conforming; being poor; being disabled; living in an area that is overpoliced; and being incarcerated, or having family members who have been incarcerated. It is not that civil rights legislation (including the right to state-sanctioned marriage) may not be part of the answer to building a more compassionate and just community, but, for many critics, it is certainly not the place to prioritize when other much more detrimental policies have persisted with the implied consent of those over-privileged enough not to feel their effects. I agree with Spade and Gayle S. Rubin that while the Obergefell ruling did affirm the equality of lesbian women and gay men for recognition and its corollary benefits, the game, as constructed, is one of arguing who is *special* enough for particular state recognition, who is *worthy* enough to be deemed the foundation of society. In Rubin's characterization, gay and lesbian relationships are now deemed part of the "charmed circle" of relationship types.[42] Again, this is best understood as the privileging capacity of privileging systems, not a court's recognition of an inherent need or desire based on one's human nature. Discussions regarding what kind of intimate relationship is the most noble and then awarding those who engage in that form of relationship is a very different conversation than that which focuses on what all individuals need to flourish regardless of the kind of relationship they choose or reject.

THE GENDER/SEX BINARY AND MARRIAGE

What has complicated the marriage debate, for so many, is that nearly all of us have at least some personal experiences and strong feelings about the institution itself. Whether our parents were never married (and then unjustly seen as lesser than others), commune dwellers, divorced, affected by imprisonment, or qualifiers for a Norman Rockwell portrait of the often-touted virtues of love and commitment, we all have been affected by this institution and its various legacies. My own experience with marriage is relevant to my views here. When my soon-to-be-wife and I applied for a marriage license while on a road-trip stop in Las Vegas in the summer of 2006, we did so as a (mostly) heterosexual-looking couple. I was one year into my gender transition and had gained the designation of "M" on my driver's license where there had been an "F" just some months before. As a trans person, even one with racial and educational privilege (among others), I was ready to be harassed by the Las Vegas court employees and denied the license. To my surprise, the license to legally marry in Clark County was in our hands in minutes. This experience made undeniably clear to me that the marriage restrictions in place at the time were unarguably asinine. The state deemed my relationship with my dyke-identified wife as wholly acceptable that day whereas just months before we would have been judged unfit for this special union.

Recall the brief mention of my argument in "Trans-Marriage and the Unacceptability of Same-Sex Marriage Restrictions."[43] In this essay I focused not on the status of gay men and lesbian women in society but on the institution's reliance on the sex/gender binary, which is itself bankrupt and leaves scores of human beings not just ineligible for certain privileges but unable to participate in society at even the most basic levels. My analysis in "Trans-Marriage" relied in part on the analysis of Jacob Hale in "Are Lesbians Women?"[44] Hale makes clear that any identification of thought-to-be necessary or sufficient conditions for sex and gender identification simply fail. The position that humans come in one of two sexes and one of two genders, and that gender identity (expression, role, etc.) somehow logically follows from certain biological facts identifiable at birth, is a lie that can only be maintained by denying the existence and experiences of transgender, gender non-binary, and individuals with intersex condition. The gender/sex binary is a myth that requires a disregard for epistemological privilege of one's understanding of oneself, the erasure of those whose bodies do not conform to binary expectations, as well as a misunderstanding of the power that unnecessarily privileges some while erasing or demonizing others.

The belief that all individuals come in one of these two varieties and that heterosexual pairings are the only acceptable romantic structure is ahistorical and colonial. Heteropatriarchal structures have been imposed upon Indigenous people the world over for reasons of control, amassing power, delegitimizing Indigenous cultural values, stealing land, and interrupting and delegitimizing ancient traditions. In "Heterosexualism and the Colonial/Modern Gender System"[45] María Lugones pulls from her own work, as well as the work of Oyéronké Oyewùmí and Paula Gunn Allen, to explicitly connect the conceptual dots between colonialism and an oppressive enforcement of heteropatriarchal marriage, gender norms, and an obsessive belief in and enforcement of a strict sex/gender binary. Oyewùmí explains,

> The imposition of the European state system, with its attendant legal and bureaucratic machinery, is the most enduring legacy of the European colonial rule in Africa. One tradition that was exported to Africa during this period was the exclusion of women from the newly created colonial public sphere. . . . The very process by which females were categorized and reduced to "women" made them ineligible for leadership roles. . . . In the West the challenge of feminism is how to proceed from the gender-saturated category of "woman" to the fullness of an unsexed humanity. For Yorùbá obinrin, the challenge is obviously different because at certain levels in the society and in some spheres, the notion of "unsexed humanity" is neither a dram to aspire to nor a memory to be realized. It exists, albeit in concatenation with the reality of separate and hierarchical sexes imposed during the colonial period.[46]

Colonization of North America imposed the same sorts of ideologies for the purpose of control and power acquisition. Lugones highlights and quotes from Allen's work,[47]

> Among the features of the Indian society targeted for destruction were the two-sided complementary social structure; the understanding of gender; and the economic distribution that often followed the system of reciprocity. . . . Gender was not understood primarily in biological terms. Most individuals fit into tribal gender roles "on the basis of proclivity, inclination and temperament."[48]

Colonization of North America and elsewhere can be understood as a gendercide as well as genocide. The gendercide of trans and non-binary identities means that cultural practices, rituals, and the language that was used to describe and affirm those identities and experiences in some cases became lost due to oppression of Indigenous cultures and ways of understanding. Scholar and teacher Saylesh Wesley in her essay "Twin-Spirited Woman" tells her story of researching her own Halq'eméylem language for a term like that of "two spirit" but found that it was lost to history.[49] Hers is not just a story of loss however, but of new beginnings, creative imaginings, and a process of nurturing a present that is consistent with and carries forward traditions and understandings of the past. In keeping with the traditions of the Stó:lō people of British Columbia's lower Fraser Valley, Wesley looks to her grandmother to assist in bridging the linguistic, cultural, and spiritual divide and is eventually gifted a new term that can be used to describe her and others' identity. The term *Sts'iyóye smesíyexw* translates as "two-spirited woman" or "twin-soul woman." Wesley writes, "I tell my story in order to isolate my specific 'queer' Sto:lo identity that makes space for other transfolk of my nation and subsequently for all queer indigenous people who remain unidentified and/or displaced from their home territory(s)."[50] In doing so, ways of being that are both historic and contemporary are affirmed and reaffirmed, asserted and reasserted, and decolonized gender identities are recognized.

In contrast to these more affirming belief systems, the court's decision in Obergefell is written assuming that humans only and always come in two and only two unambiguous varieties: one man and one woman whose identities as such are wholly consistent with their assumed-always-unambiguous identification at birth. This is evidence that the sex/gender binary is even more fully instantiated in our nation's collective psyche and institutions than belief in the special status of heterosexual marriage. The sex/gender binary is a foundational construction of the kind of marriage that Justice Kennedy so praised as foundational to society and, as such, ignores or redefines marriages involving gender transgressive individuals. The 1999 case of Christie Lee Littleton Van de Putte is particularly noteworthy because the court ruled that her marriage to her then husband, Jonathon Littleton, was fraudulent and illegal only due to her gender history of being assigned male at birth.[51] Her rights as Jonathon's surviving spouse hinged, the court argued, on the status of her sex assignment at birth, not her legal sex or her gender identification. This was the case despite undergoing a state regulated and wholly administratively approved gender transition and legal marriage. Assuming all else remains the same in this case except that same-sex marriage is legal, Littleton Van de Putte would not have had her marriage essentially nullified by the court and her spousal benefits withheld. This would have been a positive outcome. Still, her marriage would have been considered a gay marriage, despite the fact that this characterization was at odds with how she understood her life with Jonathon. Her marriage would not have been nullified, but nonconsensually re-characterized. The Supreme Court was correct in its Obergefell ruling, but its continued reliance on the universality of a binary sex/gender identity and experience would require one to exchange one's autonomy over gender identity and sexual orientation for the privilege of legal marriage. Littleton-Van de Putte passed in 2014 at only fifty-one years of age, but her courage to challenge the court system remains a legacy that has been replicated by trans and gender non-conforming persons to this day.

PRIORITIZATIONS AND PREDICTIONS

In a concern that was addressed by the Bostock Supreme Court decision in 2020, then vice president Joe Biden realized that the right to marriage was, if anything, the tip of the iceberg of injustices suffered by LGBTQ persons. Shortly after the Obergefell decision Biden remarked, "There are still 32 states where marriage can be recognized in the morning, and you can be fired in the afternoon."[52] Indeed, there are many instances where one can become married in the morning and be burdened by a variety of institutionalized biases and injustices in that same day. Some of these injustices may have to do with being perceived as gay, lesbian, bisexual, or trans, but those that are not tied to these identities are no less significant.

To be clear, identifying social justice priorities within the context of an imperfect and highly complex society is not an easy task. Arguments toward the conclusion that one must follow the political momentum where it leads so as not to miss opportunities to improve society when the context is ripe for change can be persuasive. There certainly was momentum behind the push for legalized same-sex marriage and it can be argued that gaining same-sex marriage had the possibility of severely damaging the heterosexist power structures and assumptions and thus lead the way for even more fundamental societal improvements. It can even be argued that the ruling of Obergefell paved the way for the ruling in Bostock that prohibited discrimination on the basis of sexual orientation and gender identity. This may be true but also exceedingly difficult to verify. Still, it is important to note that while the momentum behind same-sex marriage was in some ways organic, it was also nurtured and directed. The direction and force of any campaign is obviously related to who is generally listened to, who has societal clout, and who has a large bank account. Could the same kind of momentum have been created to pressure the government into a radically different schema of school funding that ensured educational equity across economic disparities? Could the same momentum for same-sex marriage be conjured and used instead to make homelessness unthinkable as opposed to what has come to be a nearly constant feature of our nation's cities?

Identifying which social justice endeavors should be given prioritization falls in the realm of nonideal theory. This is theory to be applied in the messy and radically imperfect society that we have, in which principles of justice, however articulated, are not always followed. The distinction between "ideal" and "nonideal" theories of justice was first articulated by Rawls in his own *A Theory of Justice*.[53] Rawls favored "ideal theory," which was to identify an ideally just society and the principles needed, assuming they are adhered to, to obtain that society. Nonideal theory, on the other hand, is to be employed under the conditions that we actually inhabit. These are conditions of noncompliance with principles of justice, in which biases, imbalances of power, marginalization, all regularly affect so many of our lives. Interestingly, even Rawls stated that we have a duty to "remove any injustices, beginning with the most grievous as identified by the extent of the deviation from perfect justice."[54] While I am not a Rawlsian, he may have been right in this sentiment, at least.

It is difficult to argue against the slogan "Love Wins," and it has not been my attempt to do so. The ruling in Obergefell is a clear and historic win for LGBTQ rights and should be celebrated. It signals a new and official recognition, that same-sex couples are recognized to have relationships of love and commitment, that they are part of the civic foundation of our societies, that their unions support families, and that their relationships are neither "sick" nor immoral is a positive outcome. It is also true that the ruling allowed many people to access the material benefits that were otherwise limited to persons who are non-disabled and in opposite-sex relationships. These materials benefits, for those that qualify, make lives better. There is certainly no reason that only some couples enjoy these benefits and not others. Still with all this, I have attempted though to challenge the premises of both the ruling and the campaign. That is, I believe it is important to question the "givens." The Obergefell decision is a historic victory, but one that supports these new privileges on the assumption of relationship ideals whose value, at the very least, does not seem unique. While the post-Obergefell world is still quite young, decades from now, young scholars will recount LGBTQ mobilization for marriage equality and what occurred after that goal was achieved. One possible future involves individuals with less social support, security, and privilege distancing themselves from the LGBTQ collective in hopes of finding campaigns devoted to their well-being elsewhere. Another scenario involves the LGBTQ movement actively supporting coalition-building campaigns that focus on the efforts and priorities of Black, Indigenous, and other people of color, those that are trans and gender expansive, those that are disabled, and those that are poor. The fight for "marriage equality" can lead the way for more broad-based support of LGBTQ folks of all backgrounds and experiences. History will tell which of these two options obtains, or if there are others not articulated here. I, for one, hope that continued coalition building is what is prioritized in the future—that would be the best possible legacy of the Obergefell ruling.

CONCLUSION

It is not my argument that the marriage equality movement *caused*, in a simplistic way, the anti-transgender offensive that followed, but as I argue in subsequent chapters, the anti-trans offensive had aspects of being a backlash to marriage equality. If we understand backlash as a kind of force, then it was the passion, dedication, and concern held by anti-marriage equality activists that had to go *somewhere* and directing this force against the transgender community was perhaps the most likely direction. Dog-whistling can help direct this force, especially if such directions promise successful elections by "turning out the base." For those wishing to amass political power in the post-Obergefell era, lists of email addresses of anti-marriage equality individuals were not difficult to come by, a ready army frustrated by a recent loss and all the more fearful of the next one. Scapegoating is, of course, an aspect of both backlash and dog-whistling; given the very small size of the transgender and gender non-binary population, it really is astounding what we have been blamed for. As we have seen, the arguments from the Supreme Court certainly did not mention how trans and gender non-binary individuals are affected by same-sex marriage restrictions, or even mention that non-binary and trans persons exist. Being made invisible, to being further marginalized, to being explicitly targeted is an unfortunate sequence experienced by many.

In the next chapter I present evidence of what I call the anti-trans offensive that just followed the Obergefell ruling of 2015. Across the country there were hundreds of explicitly anti-transgender pieces of legislation proposed, Title IV support for transgender students was rescinded, the recognition of transgender existence was scrubbed from federal government documents and web pages, and violence against trans persons increased dramatically. Whether incarcerated trans persons should receive health care, whether trans and gender non-binary students should have access to safe and affirming bathrooms, and whether transgender persons were fit to serve in the US military all became increasingly politicized issues. Whether the more conservative straight population surmised that allowing same-sex marriage would lead to the recognition of transgender persons—a step that some feared would usher in the moral and social demise of the nation—or whether the response to marriage equality can be understood as a kind of predictable backlash, or a more weaponized form of scapegoating used by some to maintain political power are topics of later chapters. Social conservatives' collective exclamation of "Enough is Enough!" seemed palpable not long after that summer day in July—just as scenes of joyous celebrations across the nation were shared from coast to coast. Perhaps such scenes only left marriage restrictivists feeling more insecure of their place in our country, more concerned that their vision of a morally upright society was being dangerously dashed aside in favor of political correctness and judicial activism. As a result, moral recognition of trans and gender non-binary persons became the "step too far" of LGBTQ equality. An intense five years of politicization and targeting of trans persons, following closely on the heels of the historic Obergefell ruling, had begun.

NOTES

1. *Obergefell et al. v. Hodges*, Director, Ohio Department of Health et al., June 26, 2015, http://www.supremecourt.gov/opinions/14pdf/14-556_3204.pdf, p. 3.
2. In much of this chapter I refer to lesbian and gay relationships being the focus of the Obergefell ruling. This is not because bisexual, queer, and transgender folks were not also importantly affected, but because the ruling itself and the rhetoric leading up to the ruling focused on lesbian and gay couples.
3. *Washington Post*, February 10, 2015.
4. Pew Research Center, Fact Sheet, "Same Sex Marriage Around the World," compiled by Senior Writer/Editor David Masci, Research Associate Elizabeth Sciupac, and Editorial Manager Michael Lipka, October 28, 2019, https://www.pewforum.org/fact-sheet/gay-marriage-around-the-world/.
5. Madison Alder, "Fact Check, Was the White House Lit in Rainbow Colors on Obama's Last Night in the White House?" *Republic*, https://www.azcentral.com/story/news/politics/fact-check/2017/01/20/fact-check-white-house-lit-rainbow-colors-obamas-last-night-office/96843594/.
6. By the word "trans," I mean to include all of those individuals who identify as such. There are no necessary requirements attached to this inclusion. There are also times in this work I use the term "gender non-conforming" or "gender non-binary," since the ramifications of the recent politicization affect individuals in all of these intersection groups and identities. Negative impacts have affected those who do not conform to social expectations of the gender binary, even though they do not perhaps identify as trans. The terms "gender expansive" or "gender transgressive" refer to all marginalized genders. As I am trans myself, I tend to use the plural "we" or "us" when discussing trans persons as a collective, but this should not be understood to imply that I believe that all trans experience is the same or conforms to my own experience.
7. Loren Cannon, "Trans-Marriage and the Unacceptability of Same-Sex Marriage Restrictions," *Social Philosophy Today* 25 (2009): 75–89.
8. *Obergefell et al. v. Hodges*, Director, Ohio Department of Health et al., June 26, 2015, http://www.supremecourt.gov/opinions/14pdf/14-556_3204.pdf, 3.
9. Obergefell, 4.
10. Ibid., 4.
11. United States Constitution.
12. This idea, that the Bill of Rights does not exhaust an individual's civil rights, is also reiterated in the Ninth Amendment.
13. Obergefell, 11
14. Ibid., 12.
15. Ibid., 13.
16. Ibid., 14.
17. Ibid., 16.
18. Ibid., 15.
19. Ibid., 13.
20. Ibid., 13.
21. Ibid., 16.

22. Cheshire Calhoun, "In Defense of Same-Sex Marriage," in *The Philosophy of Sex: Contemporary Readings*, ed. Alan Soble and Nicholas Power (Lanham, MD: Rowman & Littlefield, 2008), 206.
23. Ibid., 206.
24. John Kander, composer, Fred Ebb, lyrics, theme song for the Martin Scorsese film, *New York, New York*.
25. Obergefell, 28.
26. Calhoun, "In Defense of Same-Sex Marriage," 199.
27. Ibid., 200.
28. Ibid., 200.
29. Obergefell, 22.
30. Obergefell, 24.
31. A sentiment expressed both by Roberts and Scalia.
32. Obergefell, Roberts dissent, 2.
33. Obergefell, Scalia dissent, 1.
34. Obergefell, Scalia dissent, 2.
35. Obergefell, Scalia dissent, 4.
36. A small technicality, some textualists, particularly Justice Kavanaugh in his dissent of *Bostock v. Clayton County*, disagree with a "literal" interpretation of texts. One can interpret the law strictly, precisely, and within the context of its ratification, without being *literal*.
37. Obergefell, Thomas dissent, 7.
38. Obergefell, Thomas dissent, 13.
39. For two excellent volumes on this matter that have been written since the Obergefell decision of 2015, see Clare Chambers, *Against Marriage: An Egalitarian Defense of the Marriage-Free State* (Oxford: Oxford University Press, 2017) and Elizabeth Brake, ed., *After Marriage: Rethinking Marital Relationships* (New York: Oxford University Press, 2016).
40. See http://www.beyondmarriage.org/BeyondMarriage.pdf.
41. Dean Spade and Craig Willse, "Marriage Will Never Set Us Free," Organizing Upgrade: Engaging Left Organizers in Strategic Dialogue, September 6, 2013, http://www.organizingupgrade. com/index.php/modules-menu/beyond-capitalism/item/1002-marriage-will-never-set-us-free.
42. Gayle S. Rubin, "Thinking Sex: Notes for a Radical Theory of the Politics of Sexuality," 1984, http://www.feminish.com/wp-content/uploads/2012/08/Rubin1984.pdf.
43. Cannon, "Trans-Marriage."
44. Jacob Hale, "Are Lesbians Women?" *Hypatia* 11, no. 2 (Spring 1996): 94–121.
45. María Lugones, "Heterosexualism and the Colonial/Modern Gender System," *Hypatia* 22, no. 2 (Winter 2007): 186–209.
46. Oyéronké Oyewùmí, *The Invention of Women: Making an AfricanSense of Western Gender Discourses* (Minneapolis: University of Minnesota Press, 1997).
47. Paula Gunn Allen, *The Sacred Hoop: Recovering the Feminine in American Indian Traditions* (Boston: Beacon Press, 1986/1992).

48. Lugones, "Heterosexualism," 199.

49. Saylesh Wesley, "Twin-Spirited Woman: Sts'iyóye smestíyexw slhá:li," *Transgender Studies Quarterly* 1, no. 3 (August 2014): 338–351.

50. Ibid., 344.

51. *Littleton v. Prange*, 9 S.W.3d 223 (1999).

52. Tani Maxwell, "Joe Biden Just Gave a Rousing Gay Rights Address That Sounded a Lot Like a Campaign Speech," *Business Insider*, July 9, 2015, http://www.businessinsider.com/joe-biden-just-gave-a-rousing-gay-rights-address-that-sounded-a-lot-like-a-campaign-speech-2015-7#ixzz3hdGSgfXV.

53. John Rawls, *A Theory of Justice* (Cambridge, MA: Harvard University Press, 1971).

54. Ibid., 246.

Chapter 2

The Anti-Trans Offensive

The colonial institutions of the United States have explicitly legally and socially marginalized transgender and other forms of sexual and gender diversity and all those of non-European descent since the nation's conception. With regard to the former, laws against what was considered "cross-dressing" have given reason to incarcerate, bully, extort, over-police, harass, and physically and emotionally abuse individuals who did not conform to the dominant society's limited conception of appropriate gender expression and identity. Such regulations have been weaponized even further by racism and used against BIPOC folks with hateful and damaging vehemence. Many know the name and public fascination with the GI turned "Blonde Bombshell," Christine Jorgenson, who was lauded for her impressive transformation into the image of white-lady femininity, but the stories of Lucy Hicks Anderson, Carlett Brown, and Ava Betty Brown,[1] who were prohibited from making similar life choices, are less well known, perhaps outside of their own families or the police office mockery.

Then, as now, there are opposing societal influences attempting to characterize transgender persons, and this characterization is dependent on context and other factors. Do transgender persons represent the embodiment of heroic and authentically lived lives in the face of societal rejection? Fascinating stories of the incredible power of science to transform GIs into bombshells? Lived embodiments of pre- and anti-colonial understandings of the diversity of human expression? Alongside these more positive constructions has been the enduring one that transgender and other sex/gender transgressors are sick, abhorrent, evil, pedophilic, and as laughable as the overused and damaging "man in a dress" character. Unfortunately, still, nearly always an image that will entice a few non-self-reflective laughs. Like the nearly required "drunk Irishman" of nineteenthth-century English playhouse, the tactic of expressly using public ridicule of the already marginalized both brings a smile to the privileged and strengthens oppressive structures.

Yet, even with this history in which so many have lost their lives, have been ostracized from society, and have shown resilience against forces that sought the erasure and eradication of their type of difference, the years between 2015 and 2020, between the Obergefell and Bostock decisions, can be characterized as a relentless legal and social assault on the rights of transgender and gender non-binary persons. As attention was paid to proposed legislation that would ban us from using public restrooms, changing our identification documents, adopting children, participating in sports, accessing health care, or serving in the military, our identities and right to social participation became a topic of debate across the country. Aspects of our social participation became something to have a position about, an open question to consider. *Just how much should society be expected to* tolerate *us*? Supporting the flourishing of transgender persons came to be seen, by some, as a harmful consequence of damaging ideology. Perhaps by design, the politicization quickly resulted in providing those who wished to energize ties both to fundamentalist/evangelical Christianity and conservative politics, with a hot and contemporary social wedge issue. Transgender and gender non-binary persons' biological need to use the bathroom became indicative of the end-of-society-as-we-know-it. Many were convinced that same-sex marriage would usher in the moral degradation and ultimate demise of "civilized" society, but found the state of marriage, and the country, oddly none-the-worse after Obergefell. Instead, the fears of societal disintegration were transferred to the question of transgender affirmation and social participation, just when justice for trans and gender non-binary persons was finally receiving some positive publicity.

As I discuss herein, much of what I take to be response from the Obergefell ruling that legalized same-sex marriage across the nation has come in the form of proposed legislation to severely limit the social participation and well-being of transgender persons. The breadth and depth of the proposals give evidence that, while Obergefell itself was mute regarding the humanity and civil rights of transgender persons, we are seen as part of the LGBTQ collective and thus an appropriate target for those who feel that their worldview and belief system is eroded by LGBTQ equality in general. As mentioned in the previous chapter, I do not deny that persons of all genders have benefited from the marriage equality ruling. Of course, many trans persons are also gay, lesbian, bisexual, fluid, and may desire to engage in same-sex marriage and should be able to do so and incur all the benefits thereof.[2] This is indisputable. However, in many other ways, the years between 2015 and 2020 have been extremely difficult for trans persons across the nation, a difficulty only increased by the relative optimism of 2015.

In this chapter my focus will be to describe a number of ways transphobia has presented itself in the first five years of the marriage equality era. This includes proposed and, in some instances, ratified, anti-transgender legislation and increased trans-directed violence. With regard to the latter, the rates of trans-directed violence have been rising since 2015, with the year 2021 being the most violent since the statistic first came to be compiled. This points to the obvious conclusion that the political goals of marriage equality and transgender acceptance and safety are distinct enough that the Obergefell ruling certainly did not reduce, but instead increased, the steady drumbeat of murders of trans individuals, mostly trans women of color. Secondly, I present my thoughts on five different kinds of proposed legislation that have sought to erode the social participation and well-being of transgender and gender non-binary individuals. This transphobic quintuple includes five different kinds of proposed statutes: (1) those used to carve-out exceptions to just and fair treatment, (2) those reducing or prohibiting health care access for transgender persons, (3) those reducing one's ability to correct the gender designation on personal documentation, and (4) the notorious bathroom bills whose debates have demonized and disregarded the well-being of trans women, "invisibilized" and disregarded the existence and safety of trans men as well as gender queer or non-conforming individuals, and effectively ostracized trans participation in a number of different kinds of public spaces. The last type of legislation (5) is that which has attempted to legalize certain definitions of generally gendered terms to reinstate the sex-gender binary and thus to present barriers to transgender inclusion across contexts.

After five years of nearly relentless targeting of transgender persons, trans societal participation had become so politicized that public ridicule and hatred of trans persons was even used to help enrage and weaponize the January 6th insurgency mob to storm the nation's Capitol Building searching for elected lawmakers who were executing the duties of their office. Why did Donald Trump Jr. demonize trans women in his speech before the "Stop the Steal" rally on January 6, 2021? Perhaps because those individuals had been effectively taught that trans persons, unlike violence, racism, sexism, income inequality, the grinding effects of poverty, or having a president who continually lied, were the *real* national problem. In a few short years, the lives and experiences of trans and gender non-binary persons went from something that few discussed to a topic used to illicit ardent disgust and ridicule, especially at particular types of political or religious events.

TRANS-DIRECTED VIOLENCE

Partly due to national vigils on Transgender Day of Remembrance, it has become practice in communities of transgender and gender non-binary folks to acknowledge and show respect for those who have lost their lives to anti-transgender violence by memorializing those lives stolen due to this hateful violence and honoring all those touched, including the victim's families, friends, coworkers, and community, by this ongoing national tragedy. "Rest in Power" is a typical response when yet another story of a transgender or non-binary individual whose life was unjustly cut short due to their identity is shared on social media. Since 2015, there has been an increase in the number of reported murders of transgender and gender non-conforming persons. According to GLAAD, 2016 surpassed 2015 in the murders of transgender persons with a total of twenty-seven reported murders. Those at GLAAD reassert something that is now becoming well known: "The victims of this violence are overwhelmingly transgender women of color, who live at the dangerous intersections of transphobia, racism, sexism, and criminalization which often lead to high rates of poverty, unemployment, and homelessness."[3] In the years from 2015 to 2020, the number of reported victims of anti-transgender bias grew to forty-four. The highest number ever reported. Bonaire (Bonnie) Black, a nineteen-year-old Black transgender woman whose death was originally thought to have involved no "foul play," may have been the last individual to lose their life to transgender violence in 2020. Bonnie had moved to Atlanta, Georgia, at age seventeen due to being rejected by her birth family and experienced the trials of racism and financial and housing insecurity.[4] Like so many of the individuals lost, there is often little will or commitment to fully investigate these crimes, and misgendering in police and newspaper reports is still common. Due to these factors, any statistic regarding the number of souls lost is under-representative of what is actually the case.

In 2018, I attended the Trans Thinking/Thinking Trans conference, held that year in Washington, DC. One presentation, entitled "Mapping and Contextualizing Black, Queer, and Trans Resistance in North Carolina," began with an explicit recognition of the lives lost to the racist, misogynistic, transphobic violence that touches so many in our communities.[5] An altar was created in the conference space, to remember and respect those lost. Honestly, this form of recognition was foreign to me. I had never gone to a philosophy conference in which the spirits and memories of the lost played such a role. It was both touching and appropriate. Partly as a result of this experience, I find it difficult to discuss statistics of violence without a commitment to humanizing and contextualizing the statistics. Discussions of statistics without stories is dehumanizing and, I fear, tends to approach a kind of self-serving practice. Just as the result of economic injustice provides middle-class jobs for multitudes of social workers, career counselors, and Medicare benefits analysts, so too does transgender-directed violence and oppression come to provide a collection of thought-to-be-trendy new topics for sociologists, psychologists, criminologists, and others who wish to earn tenure, be seen as sufficiently "woke" by their colleagues, or simply engage in a fascinating set of academic questions and answers. As a trans academician myself, I would much rather have nothing to write about in this section than to have to report about the at least 155 individuals who, between 2015 and 2020, were gunned down, stabbed, burned, or found lifeless in trash cans, who were violently killed because the racist, sexist, and deeply transphobic society of the United States fails to recognize the humanity and moral value of all of our citizens. Each of these individuals, now lost, had stories and dreams and family (chosen or otherwise) and shared with all of us the vulnerability of being a human in an unjust society. I share with them the experiences that are generally common to trans persons, but my privileges have resulted in me being the one to write about this ongoing moral atrocity, and not be a victim of it.

The harm of terrorism extends beyond that experienced by its direct victims. Terrorism has far-reaching effects on the community being terrorized because each individual in the community knows that they could become, at any time, a victim of assault, homicide, or other kinds of attacks. Transgender women have been shot while walking their dogs (Quartney Davia Dawsonn Youchum, 2016), swarmed and brutally murdered by assailants while walking with a friend (Shante Thompson, 2016), murdered while at a homeless encampment (Amos Beede, 2017), and killed by police (Sean Ryan Hake, Kiwi Herring, Scout Schultz, 2017). Many experience violence by an intimate partner (Christa Leigh Steele Knudslie, 2018), possibly the result of being known for doing trans advocacy work (Viccky Guierrez, who was brutally tortured and killed in 2018), or while under police custody (Layleen Cubilette-Poblanco, 2019) or in ICE detention (Johanna "Joa" Medina, 2019). Terrorizing a community means that the credible threat of violence is always there, a mile away, a block away, a step away, in one's own home, when traveling, when celebrating holidays. I am in agreement with Claudia Card, who, in "Recognizing Terrorism," argues that the concept of terrorism itself is not limited by the images that might result from thinking of former president Bush's declaration of a "War on Terror."[6] Home-grown terrorists and their tactics persist within the United States, and the ongoing targeting of trans women of color is rightfully seen in this light. The immense moral harm relevant to these murders involves a loss of life, opportunity, dreams, relationships, and also the harm that is experienced by those transgender and gender non-conforming persons who are left behind to carry on in a society that has proven to be anything but safe, let alone affirming and edifying. It is appropriate to honor the resiliency of those who resist this threat of actualization of violence, but not without supporting a transformation of our society in which such resilience is not necessary.

I believe it vitally important to recognize the violence directed at women who are BIPOC and also trans. I also realize that forms of abuse and victimization take many different forms, some which are more or less documented.

Recent investigations of intimate partner abuse point to the concerningly high rates among trans men and trans masculine persons and illustrate how norms of masculinity and the targeting of transgender identities together create serious crisis.[7] The transgender advocacy organization FORGE reports that trans men and trans masculine persons experience intimate partner abuse at higher rates than even cisgender women. A number of different factors are relevant here. First, norms of masculinity of not wishing to seek help come into play, especially when trans masculine persons are attempting to newly navigate a society that has particularly strict rules for expressions of vulnerability. This is coupled with the fact that trans masculine persons are often raised and acculturated as girls, which can mean that abusive behavior can be so ever present that it becomes and expected part of the norm. If a trans masculine person does seek help, this is complicated by the fact that domestic violence shelters are reticent to accept trans men or make any efforts to keep them safe. All of these factors combine as a perfect storm of trans masculine domestic abuse. For obvious reasons, information of this kind is difficult to compile, and it is difficult to say whether rates of domestic abuse have increased proportionately to other forms of violence. It seems unfortunately true that, with regard to the trans community generally, if abuse isn't found, one is probably not looking hard enough.

Taking a broader view, according to the FBI, hate crimes have increased considerably during the Trump administration. Multiple analyses suggest that the former president's rhetoric as well as the occurrence of hateful events and rallies both increased the rates of violence and harassment to those of marginalized identities.[8] A leader's rhetoric can create a climate that condones atrocities and generally antisocial behavior. So too can events like the white supremacist march in Charlottesville, Virginia (2017), affect one's attitude regarding what is permissible or what one, with enough privilege, can get away with. With regard to anti-transgender violence from 2015 to 2019, hate crimes against transgender persons increased 106 percent. Specifically, the FBI reports that hate crimes against transgender persons numbered 73 in 2015, 105 in 2016, 106 in 2017, 142 in 2018, and 151 in 2019. The rate of increase of such crimes against those with more than one marginalized identity is even worse. For the years 2015–2019, in order, the report identifies 32, 58, 69, 84, and 211 for the number of hate crimes reported in those respective years—a staggering increase of 559 percent.

Attempting to provide a causal analysis for this rise in violence is difficult, for it involves a degree of speculation into the motivations of individuals in our present white supremacist and anti-transgender context. One might begin by considering that those whose identities and worldviews were threatened by the Obergefell ruling, and who are prone to violence, are likely to target the most economically and socially vulnerable of those affiliated with the loose collection of letters and identities that make up our "community." Numerous empirical studies verify that trans folks, particularly those with multiple marginalized identities, are economically oppressed, highly discriminated against, and socially devalued. Still, while many are convinced that the Obergefell ruling and trans inclusion generally were going to catalyze the end of "civil society" as we know it, and may have been murderously motivated for this reason, the connection between Obergefell and trans-directed violence is probably more nuanced. Fear and frustration that one's way of life may be coming to an end certainly may have been a factor, along with the far-from-nuanced social construction of trans persons as sick, dangerous, and unwanted, combined with an already deadly racism. In the last two years, we have witnessed and participated in some of the largest demonstrations in our country's history against systemic racism and police brutality. It is obvious (if indeed there was any doubt) that the United States continues to struggle with its legacy and contemporary practices of racism, sexism, ableism, and classism, along with transphobia, biphobia, and heterosexism. Given that the victims of such violence are overwhelmingly women of color, seriously addressing this problem requires addressing the racism, sexism, classism, and transphobia that combine to form murderous tendencies in the over-privileged.[9]

Indeed, as I have argued elsewhere, being effectively trans-inclusive *requires* one to be anti-racist. Attempting to be trans-inclusive without recognizing the harm that racism plays in the lives of so many trans and gender non-conforming is not to be trans-inclusive at all. George Fredrickson's *Racism: A Short History* is relevant here.[10] Fredrickson characterizes racism as a "scavenger ideology" that attaches itself to whatever contemporary beliefs support the racist action. For instance, at different times in history non-white people have been thought of as spiritually inferior due to the distortion of the meaning of certain religious texts, and at other times pseudo-science has been employed to attempt to justify racist practices and policies. More contemporaneously, assumed differences in culture have been used in a similar way. Just as religion, science, and classism can be used as tools of racism, so can anti-transgender animus. Understanding and responding to these harms requires recognizing that transphobia exists as a separate source of oppression and also that it combines with and magnifies the oppression of multiple other vectors. While single-issue proposals, like the right to marry, are thought to lend themselves to focused arguments, improving the well-being of those who are oppressed along multiple lines requires a different kind of approach. Barriers to flourishing include discrimination in housing, employment, health care, and in some areas police oversurveillance and profiling. While the Transgender Day of Remembrance serves an important role in bringing attention to this disgraceful level of violence, as does the practice of memorializing murdered individuals on social media sites, this mournful counting and naming is not sufficient to change the lives of those who are so often the focus of this violence and, unsurprisingly, neither is marriage equality.

LEGISLATIVE OVERVIEW

My own recognition of the quantity of proposed anti-trans legislation began in the spring of 2016 when I was teaching the first funded trans theory course on my campus. As with many courses, I included a "current events" type of module on the web-supported course page. I noted and posted the news of the anti-bathrooms bill, North Carolina's HB 2 in March of that year. Soon, it was obvious that this general noting of current events was documenting an avalanche of anti-transgender proposals that were being proposed across the nation. This list eventually grew to three hundred proposed bills that specifically targeted transgender, gender non-binary, or LGBTQ persons in general. The class discussion went from "Let's discuss what is happening in North Carolina," to "Let's discuss the recent legislation in . . . Alabama, Alaska, Arkansas, Arizona, Colorado, Florida, Georgia, Hawaii, Kentucky, Illinois, Idaho, Indiana, Iowa, Kansas, Kentucky, Louisiana, Maine, Massachusetts, Maryland, Michigan, Minnesota, Mississippi, Missouri, Montana, Nebraska, New Hampshire, New Jersey, New Mexico, New York, North Carolina, North Dakota, New Hampshire, Nevada, Oklahoma, Ohio, Pennsylvania, South Carolina, South Dakota, Tennessee, Texas, Virginia, Washington, West Virginia, Wyoming."

From my count, at least forty-five states introduced anti-trans legislation between 2015 and 2020. Most of the states mentioned above attempted to pass more than one bill limiting the rights of transgender persons and even our basic social participation.

These bills were wide ranging in their attempted, and sometimes effective, curtailment of civil rights. Taken together, the result of this proposed legislation is the politicization of trans persons and, when the proposals were successful, moderate to severe reduction in opportunities for positive and respectful social participation. If the majority of these proposals were to find their way into state law, it would be nearly impossible to participate in society as a trans person or gender non-binary person in certain locales. It is a legal onslaught seemingly meant to cleanse public spaces of all those who are neither cisgender nor gender conforming. The National Center for Transgender Equality (NCTE) originally produced an analysis of the proposed legislation that involves the use of six different categories:[11]

1. Carve-out bills that identify *carve-outs* that allow discrimination of trans folks as exceptions to already enacted laws,
2. Limit health care coverage of trans individuals,
3. Limit trans individuals from changing identity documents,
4. Prohibit trans individuals from using facilities consistent with their chosen gender,
5. Mandate certain policies in school bills (usually also involving restroom and locker room use),
6. Preempt the passage of bills that protect LGBTQ individuals from discrimination.

Since NCTE developed this list, we can add at least two more categories: 7. Limiting health care coverage specifically to youth, and 8. Prohibiting athletic competition to transgender athletes. The sheer quantity of proposed legislation prohibits me from considering each one in specific detail, but in what follows I will highlight aspects of those I believe to be the most potentially harmful or rhetorically dangerous. The following sections will delve more deeply into the categories of carve-out bills, health care discrimination, prohibitions in updating personal identification, bathroom bills, and language mandates.

CARVE-OUT BILLS

With regard to the overall aim of civil rights advocacy in general, what stands out as particularly egregious are those bills designated as "carve-outs," which specifically identify whose rights can be legally ignored in particular contexts. "Carve-out" bills are those bills that are meant to "carve out" certain civil rights, that is, prohibit transgender or other LGBQ persons from exercising those rights. Some of those carve-out bills were specific responses to the Obergefell ruling and same-sex marriage. For example, in Missouri, SJR 39 was proposed in 2016 and aimed to prohibit the exercise of certain rights to same-sex couples using an argument involving religious freedom. Specifically, this bill involved a constitutional amendment that prohibits state penalties on religious organizations that refuse to solemnize same-sex marriages or on individuals who decline to provide certain goods and services for same-sex marriages on the basis of their "sincere religious belief concerning same-sex marriage."[12]

Other carve-out bills focused on other aspects of civil engagement. For instance, Oklahoma's HB 2426 (2016) prohibited retribution for LGBTQ discrimination on the part of the child welfare agency.[13] This bill, and others, allows such agencies to deny placement of children into otherwise safe and nurturing homes when the would-be guardian(s) are transgender or LGBQ. Similar bills were introduced in Tennessee, Alabama, Colorado, Georgia, Kansas, Hawaii, and other states. Other carve-out bills were written to allow businesses in general to discriminate against LGBTQ individuals, such as Virginia's HB 1667 and HB 2011 (both in 2017), which specifically exclude transgender persons from protection under any anti-discrimination law. Wyoming (2017) and West Virginia (2018) proposed similar legislation. All of these bills, numbering more than one hundred, whether targeting transgender individuals or LGBQ folks more generally, function to identify a specific class of persons not eligible to the same collection of civil rights as those not in that class. "All men are created equal"—except for those of a certain assumed or actual sexual orientation or gender history. Perhaps there is some solace to be found in the fact that these bills are so blatantly discriminatory rather than underhandedly so, but it is rarely the case that those who are marginalized do not know the source of such marginalization. Whether the sponsoring lawmakers were attempting to demonstrate their right-wing credentials to would-be voters and do not believe the anti-trans political rhetoric, or if they do believe that trans inclusion represents such a grave harm, the effects are the same.

STATE-SANCTIONED HEALTH CARE DISCRIMINATION

The second category of proposed legislation includes those bills meant to decrease access to adequate health care. This kind of legislation may come in the form of prohibiting gender-affirming surgeries in state prison (Arizona HB 2293), prohibiting such surgeries for those on Medicaid (Arizona HB 2294), allowing medical insurance to specifically exclude trans-related care (Minnesota HF 1183), or so-called "religious freedom" bills such as Arkansas HB 1628, that allow medical providers the option of refusing treatment to trans individuals due to their religious beliefs. It has been well established that access to gender-affirming medical interventions, including surgery and hormone replacement therapy (HRT), is medically necessary for many trans individuals. To deny this kind of medical care is in direct conflict with the recommendations of the American Medical Association, the American Psychological Association, the World Professional Association for Transgender Health, and other health professional organizations. In fact, to deny medically necessary health care to trans individuals in this way is to send the message and instantiate a policy that the health and well-being of gender non-binary and trans persons is of no moral importance. Targeting those in prison, who already face trans-directed violence and discrimination, and the poor, whose health and well-being face challenges at every turn, targets the already severely marginalized. Lastly, so-called "religious freedom" bills encourage discrimination by medical providers, adding to the already serious problem of trans health care access. The data gained for nearly a decade has been consistent: nearly one in three trans persons already experience health care–related discrimination, often to the point of having the provider refuse treatment or having the trans person simply give up on receiving respectful and appropriate health care.[14] If enacted, this "weaponization" of health care (in)access, in an attempt to bolster a transphobic and heterosexist ideology, will make this problem considerably worse. More substantially, providing government support for denying medically necessary health care to targeted groups is a form of state-sponsored violence. The potential consequences of being denied health care are well known, but for advocates of these policies, the harmful effects are simply seen as less important than attempting to maintain and bolster their threatened worldview.

While the focus of this project was originally intended to span from the Obergefell ruling in 2015 to the Bostock ruling in 2020 (and creeping into the 2020 election), it is noteworthy that a number of bills have been proposed in the year 2021 that specifically focus on health care for transgender youth. In early 2021, eleven states (Alabama, Arizona, Indiana, Iowa, Mississippi, Missouri, Montana, New Hampshire, Oklahoma, Texas, and Utah) have proposed bills prohibiting medically necessary and medically approved care.[15]

It is well known that puberty can be the most difficult time for some transgender persons. For those of us who come to suffer from differing forms of gender dysphoria, puberty, when our bodies begin to change in ways that are distinct from the way we see ourselves, can be nearly nightmarish. In my own personal case, I often described it as the feeling that I was on a train towards an identified destination—all of my school friends were celebrating the eventual arrival of that destination, while I feverishly looked for a way off the train. How does one jump off the train and avoid killing oneself in the process? The feelings of confusion are made that much more difficult to attend to when nearly all forms of dominant popular culture celebrate this coming-of-age when youth become young adults of two keenly specified varieties. It is a kind of socio-cultural gaslighting for nearly all those on the LGBTQ spectrum. For many trans youth, the changes that come from puberty are less celebratory than nightmarish; the gifts of coming-of-age (breasts, a larger penis, hips, muscles, attention by those others witnessing these changes) are unwanted and can be the source of deep depression, shame, or worse. Puberty simply *can't leave well enough alone.* This is as true for those assigned female and also male at birth. For the latter, the relatively permanent changes of testosterone (facial hair, voice tone) can be unwanted.

For some, these changes, combined with aspects of our misogynistic culture that constructs acceptable femininity as only existing within strictly narrow and mostly unattainable parameters, may mean that living safely as a woman is more difficult. Legislation of the sort of AZ SB 1511, which makes gender-affirming treatment with the use of temporary and harmless puberty blockers a felony with a punishment of up to twelve years in prison, usurps the authority of parents, youth, and their doctors to make decisions that alleviate harm, both during puberty and into adulthood. A recent study in the journal *Pediatrics* found that these kinds of treatments reduce the alarmingly high rate of suicidal ideation among those who are treated. Their conclusion makes clear what is at stake:

> There is a significant inverse association between treatment with pubertal suppression during adolescence and lifetime suicidal ideation among transgender adults who ever wanted this treatment. These results align with past literature, suggesting that pubertal suppression for transgender adolescents who want this treatment is associated with favorable mental health outcomes.[16]

PROHIBITIONS ON UPDATING IDENTITY DOCUMENTS

The fourth category of anti-trans legislation—such as Indiana HB 1361 and Arkansas HB 1894 (both in 2017), as well as more recent proposals like HB 1076 (2021) of South Dakota—involves limiting trans individuals' ability to change personal identification documentation.[17] While this kind of legislation obviously disregards the identity claims of trans persons requesting such changes, it can also couple with so-called "bathroom laws" that restrict access to the gender identified on their birth certificates. Idaho, Kansas, Ohio, Tennessee, and South Dakota have put up the most vehement fights in attempting to prohibit trans persons from changing the assigned sex on their birth certificate. The law in Tennessee was challenged by lead plaintiff Kayla Gore, who has been an advocate for change in that state. She said of her experience being unable to secure accurate identification: "People would make comments about my previous gender, about not being a complete woman. There was just a lot of bullying."[18] Another plaintiff in the case, Jason Scott, testified that having mismatched documentation put his college career and scholarship at risk.[19]

In some states (Alabama, Arizona, Arkansas, Colorado, Florida, Georgia, Kentucky, and others) changing identification, especially the birth certificate, can require serious medical procedures that are neither medically necessary nor desired by the individual.[20] Not all gender transitions require the same procedures. Additionally, even if the medical intervention is required for the individual's health, it may be inaccessible for at least two reasons. First, these kinds of procedures are not always paid for by health care insurance or Medicaid, and these benefits, especially in the years between 2015 and 2020, were in danger of being decreased by the repeal of the Affordable Care Act or by the kinds of anti-trans legislation discussed above. In addition, a lack of access may prohibit treatment for individuals in rural or otherwise geographically remote areas due to a lack of skilled and/or unbiased medical professionals. In cases such as these, correcting the birth certificate becomes practically impossible.

Changing identity documents, birth certificates, driver's licenses, social security cards, and even types of membership cards to designate one's name and gender may seem trivial for many whose own documents have always been reflective of their identity. Having these documents aptly reflect one's identity is not trivial, but is a very material, tangible sign of societal acknowledgment, a congruency between internally experienced selfhood and that of the state. For many, this sense of societal affirmation is much less materially crucial than simply having some chance of participating in society without risking one's life or well-being. Just as discussing transgender violence needs to be acknowledged for the personal, traumatic, often racist offense it is, one that is not reducible to descriptive statistics of those lost, so too should anti-transgender threat and harm be humanized and not simply quantified. What follows is a firsthand account offered by CL," which highlights the very often justified anxiety that can accompany otherwise mundane experiences.

> My name is CL and I would like to share a story of my most frightening experience as a trans woman. Since I was not out yet in my hometown, I traveled to San Francisco as my male self. I had a wonderful time there as my "authentic self for a few days." As I was preparing to return home, I decided to stay as a female for the trip home, some seven hours away. I crossed the Golden Gate Bridge and felt so comfortable. Within a few miles, my car's radiator exploded and thank goodness I was able to get the car stopped part way down the off ramp. My level of anxiety was immeasurable. Here I was dressed as CL, yet my AAA card had only my male information. The AAA representative on the phone said she would get a tow truck to me very quickly because I was not completely off the freeway. When I hung up I realized I was in a dress, nylons, and dress shoes. Panic set in! So I changed back into my male clothes inside my small car, got most of my make up off and then remembered that I had enjoyed a manicure at a nail salon in San Francisco. I looked down and saw my beautiful pink acrylic nails. I had no remover . . . "Oh my God. Can this get any worse?" . . . I looked around the car and found my pocket knife. You can only imagine what my hands looked like when I got the nails pried off. I was sobbing when the tow

truck pulled up. This was the most frightening experience in my entire life, but I survived it. For weeks I found pieces of pink acrylic on the floor of my car.[21]

Those unfamiliar with the threats of being gender non-conforming might wonder why my acquaintance went through all the trouble to appear gender normative to the driver. Perhaps one might arrive at the notion that "She should be proud of who she is!" and not attempt to transform herself as the tow truck driver approached. This attitude illustrates an ignorance about the real threats that trans and gender non-conforming persons face every day. Quite frankly, navigating and preparing for these types of situations are time consuming, emotionally draining, and can have life or death consequences. To believe that CL should proudly present herself as the woman she knows herself to be in such a context is to mistake the virtue of Aristotelian courage for the vice of being foolhardy. It would be a mistake that could very well have dire consequences. While it is logically possible that the tow truck driver would not have been disrespectful, uncooperative, or violent, statistics tell us that the risk was real. CL knew that her AAA had the designation of "M" rather than "F," and that this would make her a target on that empty rural road. Presenting this kind of identification puts the individual in extreme risk. To be sure, this story is not meant for the reader to infer that anti-trans violence is a rural phenomenon; this violence is found in our largest cities as well as our smallest towns. Without appropriate documentation, transgender persons are prohibited from participating in such otherwise mundane activities as traveling between cities, airplane travel, international travel, buying alcohol or cigarettes, voting, and virtually any other activity that requires identification.

Correcting some documents, especially a birth certificate, can lead to more easily changing other documents (e.g., driver's license, social security card, voter registration, military identification, immigration paperwork, housing/employment forms) and can make a person less vulnerable to transphobic violence, harassment, or discrimination due to being unnecessarily outed as a result of uncorrected gender designations. Yet, in addition to these serious yet practical concerns, having correct documentation is terribly significant in its own right. The importance and meaning of documentation is not limited to that which identifies gender, but also that which is related to other aspects of one's personhood. Carlos Alberto Sánchez's essay "On Documents and Subjectivity: The Formation and Deformation of the Immigrant Identity" focuses on the meaning of immigration documentation and its relationship to SB1070, an anti-immigrant bill passed in Arizona in 2010.[22] Sánchez gives a phenomenological account of identity documents, such as those allowing one to work and reside in the US, and what they can mean to one who has obtained them and to those who wish to do so. His work has relevance here. As he explains, the meaning of a piece of documentation far exceeds that of the material or physical existence of the document itself. Instead, documentation, whether it certifies a worker's or immigrant's legal status, or, I would add, the gender marker on one's driver's license or birth certificate, has a relation to identity, belonging, and narrative. His focus was on Arizona SB 1027 (now somewhat revised), which required Arizona law enforcement officers to ask for the documentation papers of any individual they suspected of being in the country illegally. It also required that such documentation, for those who *look undocumented* according to common racist stereotypes, be on one's person at all times. The effect of the bill was that those who *looked like* the current social construction of an undocumented worker—in this case, having brownish skin, speaking Spanish, etc.—were likely to be approached and questioned by police whether or not they possessed official permission to reside and work within the US. Undocumented workers who appeared white were not targeted by the bill or by the police. This is why the bill, in essence, required racial profiling. Those who did fit the profile were targeted to such a degree that simply participating in society, by driving, walking, shopping, recreating, etc., was likely to attract negative attention from police officers and result in detention or worse. As Sánchez explains, to obtain permission to work in the US cannot be reduced simply to obtaining a certain kind of document like a green card. Instead, it can signify the end of a long journey in which security for oneself and one's family, dignity, and belonging are the goals, and a sense of a kind of identity is part of the result.

> Having a green card is socially, culturally, politically, and existentially significant. It is significant in the first three senses because, obviously, to be given one is to exist within the space of the law; it is significant in the last sense, because to be given one is to be given the security of living freely within one's own existential possibilities.[23]

Because this bill required police to stop all those who might have brown skin or a certain accent or a certain "being-in-the-world," the promise of gained identity documentation proved a lie: one's narrative changed from one of a successful journey to one of always being Other, a narrative in which social participation, meaningful recognition, and even many aspects of agency itself become impossible. Indeed, it was a similar kind of lie as when Christie Lee Littleton Van de Putte's marriage was essentially nullified after the death of her husband, due to her gender history, despite her gender transition and marriage completely obliging all legal requirements. (Recall this story was also mentioned in chapter 1.)

Many of the ways that documentation is relevant to the life, narrative, and identity of an immigrant (whether cisgender or not) that Sánchez describes are also relevant to the experiences of many trans and gender non-binary persons (immigrant or not). Attaining a driver's license; immigration status paperwork; a social security card; voter, military, or employment ID; or a birth certificate with one's appropriate gender marker and name is a reason for celebration, often in ways that memorialize the day that the name-change court order was given or the new identification card was first handed over. From my own perspective, being pleased with this kind of event is not so much because the issuing office is seen as an authority on one's identity, but it is instead an outward sign of a certain kind of social recognition. It is, especially with the birth certificate, a way of setting the record straight so that one's life, and the human artifacts that are used as a physical representation of the seen and unseen characteristics of that life, tells a story that is consistent with one's own experience. Indeed, the birth certificate records the first moment of physically being seen and recognized as oneself, of first experiencing this world as an individual human; it is a record of the most significant and defining moment of one's life. Sartre, in *Being and Nothingness*, wrote that "'Being-seen-by the other' is the truth of 'seeing-the-Other.'"[24] That is, to note that one is being seen is to understand that the seeing Other has the capacity to have a subjective point of view. The viewer is not a mere object. But what of the content and veracity of any such being-seen? To be misrecognized—that is, to be seen as a subject, but one who is arrogantly judged in a way that is at odds with one's subjective experience—is a distortion of a more meaningful recognition. To be regarded as something other than what one knows oneself to be, and to find that one has no authority to respond to the distortion, is a psychological and moral harm. Feminist philosopher Marilyn Frye in 1983 called this kind of perception "arrogant perception"—to perceive another only through one's own lens without consideration of who the person is for themselves. Going back to Sartre, it is a kind of denial of the other's subjectivity, their point of view.[25] In response, María Lugones, also a feminist philosopher, furthers Frye's ideas but argues that *true* recognition, the kind of recognition so many are denied, comes not from just a loving perception (from Frye) but stresses understanding and acceptance through an acknowledgment of interdependence that rejects the individualistic assumptions of Frye. Lugones writes from her perspective as a Latina woman who, along with others similarly positioned, has felt an arrogant perception from white women.

> I am not particularly interested here in cases of white women's parasitism onto women of color but more pointedly in cases where the relation is characterized by failure of identification. I am interested here in those many cases in which white/Angla women do one or more of the following to women of color: they ignore us, ostracize us, render us invisible, stereotype us, leave us completely alone, interpret us as crazy. *All of this while we are in their midst.*[26]

Such arrogantly distorted judgments occur all the time to cisgender and transgender persons alike, and Lugones is, of course, correct that those practices of ignoring, ostracization, stereotyping, and invisibilizing follow from this lack of recognition and, to Lugones's point, lack of connection of our shared humanity and interdependence. As a result, those distortedly seen are not "at ease in the world."[27] Having appropriate identification is, by no means, the final step to the respectful recognition of another, of having an open mind to consider another's lived experience. It can, however, provide some "ease" in a world that is generally hostile to one's experiences, can reduce or at least hopefully put a check on some of those distortions. At the very least, it gives authority to one's own understandings of self.

Thus, documentation, and having the ability to change it, is of crucial importance. With regard to this issue, it is the State of Idaho that particularly demonstrates how the politicization of trans identity has resulted in the devaluing of transgender lives being used by some to score political points. It was in 2018 that US magistrate Judge Candy Dale ruled that the Idaho law prohibiting transgender persons from updating their documentation violated the Constitution's Equal Protection Clause. Judge Dale asserted, "Any new rule must not subject one class of people to any more onerous burdens than the burdens placed on others without constitutionally appropriate justification."[28] Just a year after Judge Dale's ruling, the Idaho Department of Health and Welfare passed a temporary rule that put barriers into place regarding ID revision, and then in 2020, HB 509 has again made it impossible to update identity documents. This will undoubtedly be settled in court. (At the time of writing this chapter, the Idaho District Court has mandated that the State of Idaho cannot prohibit individuals from changing their documentation. It remains to be seen if this is the last chapter in this story.)

While the legitimacy of HB 509 will be legally challenged, this does not offset the harm that has already been, and continues to be, exerted upon Idahoans. Assuming sound legal decision-making, HB 509 should be struck down for the reason that Judge Dale originally ruled in 2018. The fact that SCOTUS's Bostock decision used similar reasoning to prohibit discrimination on the basis of gender identity, and to see such discrimination deemed unconstitutional under Title VII, will only bolster the case against it. Still, it is crucial to note that at issue here is the well-being of a *certain class* of individuals. The well-being, legitimacy, moral and social value, even the right to basic self-determination and identity of a certain class of individuals is being debated by those unaffected by the outcome of their votes/rulings, except possibly to garner favor or disfavor with certain voting constituencies. Being unable to change documentation puts individuals at risk of violence and discrimination, limits freedom of movement, and instantiates a second-class status for those who simply wish to live a flourishing life. The stated justification for HB 509 is that the government requires a certain kind of data: "The purpose of documenting factual information on vital records is to help the government fulfill one of its most basic duties: protecting the health and safety of its citizens."[29] To be consistent with the ramifications of this bill, it seems that the lawmakers in Idaho are only worried about the health and safety of their cisgender citizens and wish to erase evidence of anyone who is not in that category. Data is power, indeed, and can be used to support the state citizenry in a variety of ways. Knowing how many people petition to change their birth certificates would provide helpful information regarding the need for transgender health care in Idaho hospitals and the need for transgender recognition in K–12 schools, as well as colleges and universities; such data would make clear that homeless shelters in Idaho need to make sure they are welcoming to trans and gender non-binary persons. Instead, Idaho attempted to make sure that transgender existence goes unacknowledged and to prevent Idahoans from exercising many basic rights. One Idaho trans woman puts it this way,

> To be honest, it's disheartening how they justify the reasoning behind it as a deep concern for the welfare and health of Idahoan citizens, justifying it by needing correct data and so in good faith can't let trans people change their sex—it's all about the data. The problem is that they can't imagine trans people as actual citizens or [that they] could benefit from having demographic information reported in order to better understand the health and welfare of trans people . . . it seems more of an excuse of their myopic transphobia, but it isn't fear—it's terrorism.[30]

BATHROOM BILLS

In so many ways, the legislative frenzy began with North Carolina's HB 2, passed on March 23, 2016, which restricted individuals in schools, including postsecondary education, and government facilities to use only those multi-occupancy restrooms that are consistent with the gender designated on their birth certificate. It also made it illegal for any local municipality in the state of North Carolina to pass nondiscrimination policies barring discrimination on the basis of sexual orientation, gender identity or expression, which the city of Charlotte had recently done. On the face of it, the Charlotte bill served as the "Enough is Enough!" moment in which the heterosexist and cisgender assumptions of the presumed majoritarian culture were so severely threatened that lawmakers felt that drastic and immediate action was necessary to avoid the fictionalized slippery slope into a state of queer-sponsored heretical immorality. While this bill and its revised version are both clearly unacceptable in all aspects, it is the restrictions on public bathroom use that made North Carolina the subject of massive national boycotts. Backlash against the bill was swift and significant. Some estimate that boycotts cost the state upward of $400 million.[31] Indeed, whether or not economic boycotts are the best way to respond to such legislation, the economic backlash may have dissuaded some other states (Georgia, Indiana, Texas, South Dakota, and others) from following in the steps of North Carolina.

Despite the boycotts, the public shaming, and the ousting of Governor Pat McCrory, anti-trans legislative proposals regarding the use of bathrooms and locker rooms continued into 2017 and beyond. In 2017 alone, dozens of separate bills were introduced in legislatures across the country seeking to make using the restroom a crime in public spaces and schools. Such states include Alabama, Arkansas, Illinois, Kansas, Kentucky, Minnesota, Missouri, Montana, New Jersey, New York, North Carolina, Oklahoma, South Carolina, South Dakota, Tennessee, Texas, Virginia, Washington, and Wyoming. While the bills all target the same population of individuals, there are some differences. For example, some bills stipulated that one may only use facilities (e.g., multi-use restrooms, locker rooms) that correspond with the gender identified on one's birth certificate (South Dakota, New York, North Carolina), while others instead stipulated that one's chromosomes and birth genitalia were of relevance to legal bathroom use (Kansas, Kentucky). Of course, few such proposals ever seem to consider exactly how chromosomal tests could be administered, funded, and the test results policed, for obvious reasons. Still other states attempted to prohibit *policies* that are supportive of trans individuals using facilities consistent with their identity (Texas, North Carolina, South Carolina), while others specifically allow businesses to restrict trans bathroom use (Washington) or attempt to make it easier for individuals to sue schools that allow transgender individuals using a bathroom consistent with their identity (Virginia). Unjust proposed legislation of this kind has continued into 2021. One noteworthy example is HB 1182 in Tennessee that Governor Bill Lee signed into law in May of 2021. This law would require that buildings open to the public post signs if they allow trans persons safe and appropriate bathroom use. The sign is to read, "This facility has a policy of allowing the use of restrooms by either biological sex, regardless of the designation on the restroom."[32] It is not difficult to imagine how such signage will be stigmatizing to trans and gender non-conforming/non-binary persons and would result in the targeting of folks who use the facilities in signed locales. This bill, as with many others, faced legal challenges; as of this writing, it has been blocked by federal court.[33]

The idea that one's "real" sex (wrongly assumed to correlate with gender identity) is determined by chromosomes has been used in bathroom legislation as well as in legislation which attempts to mandate an official meaning of "sex" based on chromosomes (i.e., Tennessee's HB 1111 [2017] and South Carolina's SB 4949 [2018]). As I have elsewhere argued, there are no necessary and sufficient conditions for the designation of male or female, let alone man and woman. Believing this to be so, it is clear that in the first case the proposal erases the lives of those of numerous intersex conditions; in the second case, the position erases the lives of those who are transgender or gender non-binary. But, for the sake of argument, let's assume for a moment that one's chromosomal status would be a matter of government interrogation and surveillance. Frankly, few are aware of their own chromosomal status and at least a few of us might be surprised to find out these details. Assuming that every individual's chromosomes came to be checked (at birth?) and then used to proscribe appropriate and inappropriate activities, would we not then need some sort of outward sign so that government regulators would be able to ascertain whether we were breaking the law in using any bathroom facility? Perhaps arm bands with XX or XY or other formulations might be helpful to those wishing to police our activities. Under this scenario, wouldn't those that forgot their arm band on any given day probably be given a "pass" if they look acceptable enough (via gender, race, class, etc.) to access needed facilities? Racism and sexism could use this as a tool as well. This increase in police surveillance and monitoring would predictably result in the targeting of Black and Brown bodies for real and fictionalized infractions of the law. If not this scenario, then we would need bathroom monitors to do the chromosomal test as we are waiting to relieve ourselves. Either way, laws prohibiting bathroom access based on certain chromosomal structures put us into a dystopian reality that approaches that of the film *Gattaca* (1997) in which individuals' genetics are tested at birth and the results determine their life outcomes. To maintain the genetically determined class structure, constant testing is required. "But in a place where any cell on any part of your body can betray you, how do you hide, when we all shed 500 million cells a day."[34] Bathroom laws, restrictions on changing identification, and proposals that mandate that language be understood only to include explicit cisgender meanings, and a full instantiation of the false inferences of the gender binary, all weaponize an individual's past and physicality against them, simply due to irrational fears of cisgender persons or the political aspirations of those who see their path to success paved in the demonization of others.

Still, amid this anti-trans legislative frenzy, it is helpful to remember that of the numerous bathroom bills proposed, few were actually passed into law. It seems that it is far easier to propose anti-transgender legislation than to actually get it passed. Is it simply anti-transgender posturing that is desired here? Perhaps some politicians engage in vehemently anti-transgender rhetoric to get elected by their right-wing and/or evangelical base, and propose the legislation to be consistent with their political promises, knowing all the while that it is just a performance? I will consider some of these questions in subsequent chapters. For instance, North Carolina becomes a key player in this story once again, years after the original bill passed and the controversy ensued. North Carolina's replacement for HB 2 (HB 142) was passed one year after the original controversial bill. HB 142 prohibited local ordinances from mandating equal restroom access and put into place a three-year moratorium on local ordinances of LGBTQ nondiscrimination policies. It is noteworthy that North Carolina's HB 2 was a primary motivation for this book project, and that some four years later, the LGBTQ population in North Carolina is free to propose and pass pro-LGBTQ legislation once again. HB 142 expired December 1, 2020. This bill, like so many discussed in this chapter, has its own history and unique trajectory. Allison Scott, a North Carolina resident, trans woman, and policy director for Campaign for Southern Equality, rightly regards HB 2 and HB 142 as "bills of trauma."[35] She and others attest that HB 142 did not stop the harassment or targeting of trans persons in the state. When the status of a group of persons becomes politicized to the degree that being "for" or "against" those of the group is seen as part of one's identity or required by other social groups of which one is a part, the harm continues regardless of what laws are on the books. Scott describes the harms of the increased stigma: "In some ways people in the community wish it hadn't been in the public eye, because at least then there wasn't awareness," before the fight over bathroom bills, she said. "Now people yell at you for walking in a public space. They threaten you for trying to go to the bathroom. It's gotten much worse. I have to give GOP leaders credit," she added. "The compromise didn't deal with the stigma but continued the hateful part right underneath the public's eye."[36]

The fact that bias, unjust discrimination, and physical and psychological harm continue independent of passed legislation is glaringly true when discussing the harms of systemic racism, sexism, transphobia, and other forms of injustice. Anti-discrimination laws have been "on the books" for over fifty years, yet rights violated by crimes like those against George Floyd, Breonna Taylor, Sandra Bland, Philando Castile, Tamir Rice, Michael Brown, and so many precious others, went unprotected. Social demonization sets the stage for harm regardless of the legal context relevant to that harm, which is why I believe that the onslaught of anti-transgender legislation herein described is noteworthy even if most of the statutes were not voted into law. Additionally, anti-transgender legislation (or legislation that specifies any group as being less than full and equal participants in society) fan the flame of bias and invite many to participate who otherwise might have resisted doing so. On the other hand, legislation that prohibits discrimination is far from being a *cure-all* or even a *cure-most*, but, charitably speaking, may form the foundation of still required social transformation.

LANGUAGE MANDATES

I mentioned above proposals regarding language use, and it would be instructive to consider at least one such bill with some specificity. Tennessee's HB 1111, passed in 2017, broadly mandates that all terms used in the law be interpreted "by their natural and ordinary meanings" and became law in that state. The history of this bill (earlier proposed as HB 33, which failed) attempted to mandate that terms like "mother," "father," "husband," and "wife" must be interpreted in legal contexts according to biological distinctions. The intent of this bill seems clearly to lay the foundation for discrimination against those in same-sex marriages and families, but it could also be used to interpret the terms "boy," "girl," "man," and "woman" according to traditional cisgender meanings, thus encouraging restrictions on bathroom use, sports participation, access to gendered educational institutions, and anything else restricted by gender category. The psychological and social harm here, too, is grave. The passage of such legislation constructs a world in which transgender men and women, as well as those who are gender fluid, gender non-binary, or Two Spirit, are literally mischaracterized by legal mandate. Talia Mae Bettcher influentially and insightfully explained how transgender folks are often socially constructed as either "evil deceivers" or "make believers."[37] Statutes like HB 1111 put this damaging dichotomy into sharp focus. It is a denial of self-knowledge, of epistemological privilege regarding this kind of understanding, a gaslighting measure that not only regards the state as authority over identity but regards some identities as so dangerous as to require state control. As discussed in the previous section regarding the harm of politicization itself, regardless of laws passed or rejected, public knowledge of the law and its intents provide ammunition to those harboring anti-trans sentiment by encouraging harassment and a denial of self-understanding. "You aren't who you say you are" is one way the law's presumptions can be weaponized on the sidewalk, or the bus, or the classroom, thereby making the one harassed appear deceitful (and thus morally blameworthy) or delusional.

CONCLUSION

What began as a short "current events" portion of my trans theory class grew into what I called the "Spreadsheet Project" in which myself and two research assistants continued to log and track anti-transgender legislation across the country. Both the legislation and the anti-trans propaganda in support of the legislation (here remembering the 2018 advertisements for Massachusetts's "No on 3," which would roll back protections for transgender use of gendered accommodations) were of focus. Notably, 2017 had the most anti-transgender legislative proposals, followed by 2016, then 2018. Texas has the dubious distinction of being the state that posed the most such proposals, far exceeding even other states in the south, and having twice as many proposals as its neighbor Oklahoma. While there was a flurry of "bathroom bills" following North Carolina's HB 2, such bills became the exception rather than the rule. This is certainly related to the economic and political and economic costs of HB 2, and the fact that few other states wanted to risk the same response, although fears of an economic backlash may not be the only reason that few politicians had the stomach for such proposals following the North Carolina controversy. The Republican House speaker in Texas, Joe Straus, was reported as having identified the high suicide rates in the transgender population as reason to deny his own state's "bathroom bill."[38] I can at once attest that transgender persons are more than just the numbers that come to define us by description (suicide rates, murder rates, rates of unemployment, rates of health care discrimination, etc.) and at the same time I am glad that the Texas bill was unsuccessful in making the lives of Lone Star trans and gender non-binary folks even worse.

Herein, I have offered an overview of the recent anti-trans backlash from 2015 to 2020, beginning with the marriage equality ruling of 2015. The quantity and content of the bills proposed support the judgment that trans and gender non-conforming individuals are an obvious target of those who feel threatened by a changing world that includes greater acceptance of LGBTQ individuals, especially those that are trans or gender non-binary. I have not commented on so-called "religious freedom" bills that target transgender individuals as well as lesbians, gay men, and bisexual and queer folks. These may be a significant threat to LGBTQ equality in many locations and will lead to more court cases and more contested decisions. Nor have I delved into how the policies and practices of the Trump administration have harmed, erased, and disregarded the lives and experiences of transgender Americans. Even as I type these lines, many of these Trump administrative policies are being reversed by the Biden administration. My focus here has been on anti-trans legislation because the sheer quantity of the proposals and the potential to decrease the well-being of trans persons does warrant more attention. In the minds of some, trans persons represent the most egregious deviation from the cisgender heterosexist norm. We represent *what the world is coming to*, and thus society must be protected from our very existence and participation in society. *Time* magazine's article "The Transgender Tipping Point," which featured Laverne Cox on the cover, now feels more like an optimistic moment in history before the post-Obergefell onslaught that would happen just a few years later. While there has been a great deal more visibility of trans individuals (especially those who are otherwise gender normative and wealthy), the legislative history between 2015 and 2020 makes it clear that such visibility has not translated into acceptance, or a life free from discrimination and violence, especially for those most marginalized.[39] The next chapter focuses specifically on the morality of anti-transgender bathroom bills. Given the ongoing fear and misunderstanding regarding this issue, it needs to be addressed.

NOTES

1. C. Riley Snorton, *Black on Both Sides: A Racial History of Trans Identity* (Minneapolis: University of Minnesota Press, 2017).

2. The ruling only affected same-sex relationships by extending the right to marriage to all citizens regardless of gender. The ruling said nothing regarding trans individuals that may be in heterosexual relationships and/or identify as gay, lesbian, bisexual, pan/omnisexual, etc.

3. Alex Schmider, "2016 Was the Deadliest Year on Record for Transgender People," November 9, 2016, https://www.glaad.org/blog/2016-was-deadliest-year-record-transgender-people.

4. Juwan J. Holmes, "Black Trans Teen Found Dead in Parking Garage Could Add to a Record Year of Anti-Trans Violence," *LGBTQ Nation*, February 2, 2021. https://www.lgbtqnation.com/2021/02/black-trans-teen-found-dead-parking-garage-add-record-year-anti-trans-violence/?fbclid=IwAR0jveorFVxpzEdHQkuN79bk1NqPliBCvSRhLllTt1n-gWL63X1FML-dKPc.

5. Ash Williams and co-presenter, "Mapping and Contextualizing Black, Queer, and Trans Resistance in North Carolina," Trans Thinking/Thinking Trans Conference, Washington DC, October 5–6, 2018.

6. Claudia Card, "Recognizing Terrorism," *Journal of Ethics* 11 (2007): 1–29.

7. Orion Rodriguez, "There Is a Hidden Violence against Trans Masculine People," Daily Kos, August 9, 2019, https://m.dailykos.com/stories/2019/8/9/1877651/-There-is-a-hidden-epidemic-of-violence-against-transmasculine-people?fbclid=IwAR0sMneE0BxTnMCFSZ_YLfSxCyzHJU2KNBla53yiAuIh60EbbYntA4BuDEM.

8. Michael Kunzelman and Astrid Galvan, "Trump's Words Linked to More Hate Crime? Some Experts Think So," Associated Press, August 7, 2019, https://apnews.com/article/7d0949974b1648a2bb592cab1f85aa16.

9. I should mention here that, in using the term "vulnerable," I do not mean to suggest that trans persons or those of other marginalized identities are inherently physically or psychologically unfit, but rather that they are made vulnerable by the cultural conditions that relentlessly target individual and collective efforts to flourish.

10. George M. Fredrickson, *Racism: A Short History* (Princeton, NJ: Princeton University Press, 2016).

11. See http://www.transequality.org/action-center.

12. See http://www.senate.mo.gov/16info/BTS_Web/Bill.aspx?SessionType=R&BillID=28205321.

13. See http://webserver1.lsb.state.ok.us/cf_pdf/2015-16%20SUPPORT%20DOCUMENTS/BILLSUM/House/HB2428%20INT%20BILLSUM.PDF.

14. My evidence for this claim comes from one of the first studies regarding the transgender experience, titled "State of Transgender California, Results from the 2008 Transgender Economic Health Survey," by the Transgender Law Center, https://transgenderlawcenter.org/pubs/the-state-of-transgender-california, and, a more recent publication, "Report of the 2015 Transgender Survey" by the National Center for Transgender Equality, http://www.ustranssurvey.org/report.

15. Alex Bollinger, "31 Anti-Transgender Bills Proposed in 20 States as the GOP Target Transgender Children Nationwide," *LGBTQ Nation*, https://www.lgbtqnation.com/2021/02/31-anti-transgender-bills-filed-20-states-gop-targets-schoolchildren-nationwide/.

16. Jack L. Turban, Dana King, Jeremi M. Carswell, and Alex S. Keuroghlian, "Pubertal Suppression for Transgender Youth and Risk of Suicidal Ideation," *Pediatrics* 145, no. 2 (February 2020), e20191725, DOI: https://doi.org/10.1542/peds.2019-1725, https://pediatrics.aappublications.org/content/145/2/e20191725?sso=1&sso_redirect_count=1&nfstatus=401&nftoken=00000000-0000-0000-0000-000000000000&nfstatusdescription=ERROR%3A%20No%20local%20token.

17. This bill was voted down in committee on February 5, 2021. The bill stood little chance of becoming the law of the land in South Dakota since such bills were already deemed unconstitutional.

18. Travis Loller, "Transgender Plaintiffs Sue Tennessee, to Change Birth Certificate Gender," NBC News. https://www.nbcnews.com/feature/nbc-out/transgender-plaintiffs-sue-tennessee-change-birth-certificate-gender-n997996.

19. Ibid.

20. Again, the American Medical Association's position on this issue is that genital or sex-reassignment surgery should not be required for a person to receive corrected documentation.

21. Firsthand account of CL's experience. Shared to author on July 24, 2021, and included here with permission.

22. Carlos Alberto Sánchez, "On Documents and Subjectivity: The Formation and Deformation of the Immigrant Identity," *Radical Philosophy Review* 14, no. 2 (2011): 197–205.

23. Ibid., 201.

24. Jean-Paul Sartre, excerpt from *Being and Nothingness*, in *Being Ethical: Classic and New Voices on Contemporary Issues*, ed. Shari Collins, Bertha Alvarez Manninen, Jacqueline M. Gately, Eric Comerford (Peterborough, ON: Broadview Press, 2017), 106.

25. Marilyn Frye, *The Politics of Reality: Essays in Feminist Theory* (Trumansburg, NY: Crossing Press, 1983).

26. María Lugones, *Pilgrimages, Pregrinajes: Theorizing Coalition against Multiple Oppressions* (Lanham, MD: Rowman & Littlefield, 2003), 83.

27. Ibid., 90.

28. Keith Ridler, "Correction, Transgender Birth Certificates, Idaho Story," Associated Press, October 25, 2019, https://apnews.com/article/dc535a4b404c447c96b7328c54a08e72.

29. Legislature of the State of Idaho in the House of Representatives, House Bill 509, https://legislature.idaho.gov/wp-content/uploads/sessioninfo/2020/legislation/H0509.pdf.

30. Interview with an Idaho-born Latina woman who is transgender and living out of the state. She wished to stay anonymous. January 29, 2021.

31. Mark Abadi, "North Carolina Has Lost a Staggering Amount of Money Due to Its Controversial Bathroom Law," *Business Insider*, September 21, 2016, http://www.businessinsider.com/north-carolina-hb2-economic-impact-2016–9.

32. Bill Browning, "Businesses Will Now Be Forced to Post Signs Announcing They Serve Transgender Customers in Tennessee: The Tennessee Governor Has Signed the Cruelest Anti-Trans Law in the Nation," *LGBTQ Nation*, May 18, 2021.

33. L.A. Blade Digital Staff, "Judge Blocks Tennessee Anti-Trans Restroom Sign Law; Kye Sayers and Bob Bernstein Objected to the Stigmatizing Message They Would Be Required to Display—Said the Law Violates the First Amendment," *Los Angeles Blade: Southern California's LGBTQ News Source*, July 9, 2021.

34. *Gattaca*, Official Trailer, Written and Directed by Andrew Niccol, Produced by Danny DeVito, Michael Shambert, Stacey Sher, Gail Lyon, 1997, YouTube, https://www.youtube.com/watch?v=W_KruQhfvW4.

35. Ben Avery, "LGBT Rights Fight Reignited Four Years After N.C's 'Bathroom Bill' Controversy," NBC News, December, 8, 2020, https://www.nbcnews.com/feature/nbc-out/lgbtq-rights-fight-reignited-4-years-after-n-c-s-n1250390.

36. Ibid.

37. Talia Mae Bettcher, "Evil Deceivers and Make Believers: On Transphobic Violence and the Politics of Illusion," *Hypatia* 22, no. 3 (Summer 2007): 43–65.

38. Paul J. Weber, Associated Press, "Texas House Speaker Didn't Want Suicide Over 'Bathroom Bill,'" ABC News, July 3, 2017, http://abcnews.go.com/Politics/wireStory/texas-house-speaker-suicide-bathroom-bill-48419478.

39. Katy Steinmetz, "The Transgender Tipping Point," *Time*, May 28, 2014.

Chapter 3

The Case against Anti-Transgender Bathroom Bills

In the previous chapter, HB 2, the notorious North Carolina "bathroom bill," was discussed along with other anti-transgender legislation. Given that HB 2 was eventually rejected and other states did not pass their own similar versions, one might reason that there is little reason to be too concerned that these kinds of bills will be crafted and passed in the future. I disagree. The concern surrounding trans, gender non-binary, and gender non-conforming persons participating in society alongside our non-transgender fellow citizens is encapsulated and expressed in the bathroom debate—a debate that is at once about societal participation, bodies and their functions, scapegoating and demonizing, and political opportunism. In this chapter I present sufficient evidence that these kinds of bills, like HB 2 and others that have been proposed during the anti-transgender legislative frenzy from 2015 to 2020 and beyond, are morally inappropriate. Anti-transgender bathroom bills unjustifiably impose moral harms on transgender and gender non-conforming persons in the form of risk of physical and psychological harm, social ostracism, severe curtailment of opportunity, and lack of moral recognition. As I will explain, the opposing faulty logic relies on essentialist arguments and harmful social constructions of bodies.

BATHROOM BILLS: NO LONGER A THREAT?

I disagree that "bathroom bills," the likes of which were proposed in many states from 2015 to 2020, are unlikely to be proposed again in the future. I believe this is true because the concerns some have about trans and gender non-binary or non-conforming persons accessing public bathrooms did not originate with North Carolina in 2016 but stem from a fear, ripe for stoking by politicians, for decades. Given the hyper-politicization of trans and other gender transgressing people in the last five years, it is a fear still on many people's minds. Being actively anti-transgender still remains an aspect of far-right Republican political orientation. Some of these far-right individuals, disgruntled with the results of the 2020 election, are likely to identify even more resolutely with these ideologies. During the election itself, anti-transgender sentiment was used to attack Biden by alleging he supported "sex changes for kids,"[1] and anti-trans scapegoating was also used in Kelly Loeffler's run-off election in Georgia. Despite the efforts of the Biden administration to explicitly support trans rights, the same political partisanship and fear-mongering will likely be used again in the midterm elections in 2022.[2] The far-right has been successful in making transgender societal participation a social wedge issue, even to the extent of it becoming part of one's core beliefs and identity, setting the stage to galvanize voters through scapegoating and fear-mongering.

The concern some have about relieving themselves in the same public restroom as a trans person is not new, just newly weaponized. Many years ago, I was volunteering with the nonprofit organization GLSEN, which works to keep LGBTQ students safe in school and supports alliances between LGBTQ high school students and their straight allies. My participation in the group was not extensive, but I did help out with a few school staff trainings in the early 2000s. At the time, I was generally regarded as gender non-conforming and it was right at the beginning of my own gender transition. These kinds of trainings discussed the challenges of LGBTQ students in the K–12 setting, but, now nearly twenty years ago, we stayed far away from the issue of bathroom use for trans youth. The common wisdom at the time was that it was "just too controversial," or "don't mention that; you don't want them to freak out." Until the US dominant culture comes to accept trans bodies, I fear this issue will continue to arise, if not in legislation then in terrorizing violence.

In many ways, however, I am glad that things have changed enough so that we can, and do, mention these biological needs, and how bathrooms and gendered spaces are sites of harassment or worse, but this deep-seated and irrational fear bears mention in itself. In a sense, the cisgender fear of trans persons seems to be focused on the physical body of the Other. It is as if recognizing that we, too, need to relieve ourselves in ordinary ways goes a step too far in normalizing our bodies and our kind of difference. As will be discussed in the context of scapegoating, it is difference in the context of the familiar or "normal" that can elicit the most violent and harmful reactions. As an example, there is a sense in which LGBTQ kids are rejected by their parents not for their difference alone, but for their difference in the context of similarity, sameness, and unity. The differences of trans bodies, real or imagined, have resulted in them being the subject of fascination, curiosity, repulsion, fetishization, demonization, and fantasy for many. Whether we are thought to embody a rejection of god's plan or an exotic sexual toy, these attitudes allow an othering that refuses to recognize the realities of our lives, whether they be experiences of joyfulness, oppression, or the mundane necessities of being human. The need to relieve ourselves is a function of our human-mammalian physiology, a multiple-times-a-day activity that does much to normalize our existence, which perhaps is the reason for such massive non-transgender discomfort. Thus, while I would like to think that bathroom bills will soon be merely a strange footnote in legislative history, I am not confident in this kind of optimistic position. Bathroom use is still a highly contentious topic.

BATHROOM BILLS AND HARM

While my intent here is to argue against these "bathroom bills" in the general case, it is important to recognize that details of these proposals can vary with regard to how the "correct" gendered bathroom facility is defined. Factors thought to be relevant include one's assigned sex at birth, the sex designated on one's birth certificate, the shape and configuration of one's genitals, or even one's chromosomal status (a status unknown to all but a very few individuals). While these details are important, my initial focus here is on typical anti-transgender bathroom bills (ATBBs) that have roughly the following form:

General anti-transgender bathroom bill (ATBB): Individuals are prohibited from using gendered bathrooms (locker rooms, changing facilities, etc.) except those that correspond with their assigned sex at birth. Those assigned male at birth (AMAB) are prohibited from using facilities designated for girls or women and those assigned female at birth (AFAB) are prohibited from using facilities designated for boys or men.[3]

Enacted anti-transgender bathroom bills (ATBBs) put trans and gender non-conforming persons at risk of predictable physical and psychological harm. While so much of the rhetoric in favor of ATBBs has centered around the safety of cisgender bathroom users, there is no mention of the harm that will predictably come to trans and gender non-conforming persons when/if these proposals are adopted. First let us consider the risk of probable harm for trans women and trans feminine persons. While the common rhetoric regarding "keeping women safe" is often employed as a means to instill sufficient fear to gain support for these proposals, the concern for safety seems only applicable to cisgender women. Consider how ATBBs *require* trans women to use men's facilities, putting them at considerable risk. It is predictable that her presence in the men's restroom will be met with a variety of responses, some of which will be menacing. There are those who would regard her presence in the restroom as an invitation to verbal or physical harassment or violence; this would be the case for both trans and cisgender women. Proponents of ATBBs mistakenly argue that such measures increase safety while mandating that women who are trans regularly put themselves at serious risk. In the context of a municipality that enforces ATBBs, a woman in a men's bathroom will likely be thought to be there because she is trans. As such, she is at risk of harassment and violence that is sourced in misogyny and anti-trans animus and often further strengthened by other marginalizing biases and structures. If the woman is not read as a white woman, she is yet more vulnerable to the violence inherent in racism and the deadly results of the triad of sexism, anti-trans bias, and racism. This threat of violence is not merely possible; it is predictable. As discussed in the previous chapter, the rates of violence against trans women, especially trans women of color, have regrettably only increased in the years since the passage of marriage equality.[4] While the rhetoric of these kinds of legislative efforts cloaks itself in a concern for safety towards women, the result is, essentially, to place a target on the backs of women who are otherwise the most vulnerable to violence and harassment.[5]

Trans men are likewise put at risk for harm by requiring them (us) to use women's facilities. It is singularly ironic that, in the name of protecting women from men in restrooms, ATBBs *require* men to use women's facilities where they/we will be seen as a dangerous threat. The negative attention that my own appearance would receive if I were to attempt to use a woman's facility is as predictable as it is unpleasant, and this is true for many trans men and trans masculine individuals. Trans masculine individuals will find that our attempt to abide by the law will result in being yelled at, harassed, assaulted, shoved or kicked out of the room, and perhaps even being reported to the police for a violation of the law. It is important to note that the threats to one's safety include more than those individuals *using* the facility at any given time. Consider the actions of guardians waiting outside a restroom for their young daughters when they believe that a dangerous man has entered the same bathroom. Given the social constructions that persist in portraying boys and men of color as violent and menacing,[6] consider again what might happen to the Black trans man who enters a women's restroom in his attempt to abide by a local ATBB when those awaiting outside have internalized these racist stereotypes. Imagine that the group of white men who are waiting for their daughters outside the restroom have internalized these ubiquitous stereotypes and are also armed. In considering the harm of these statutes we need to consider the full ramifications. Who, as a result of the bill, becomes targeted, harassed, or terrorized?

Of course, a trans man or a masculine appearing gender non-conforming person may simply refuse to abide by the law and use men's facilities, but doing so puts them/us at risk of civil prosecution if they/we are found to be breaking the law. Given anti-trans sentiment generally, if the individual is thought to be assigned female at birth, or "really a woman," they will be vulnerable to harassment and violence. Thus, ATBBs put trans men and trans masculine individuals at risk and create a context in which many need to choose to either be *seen* as breaking the law (and thus face potential harassment, violence, and police intervention) or *actually* break the law (which if discovered leads to prosecution, potential harassment, and violence).

The double bind just referred to, that ATBBs force individuals to choose between two unacceptable options, is a defining feature of systemic oppression and exists for all trans and gender non-conforming persons. In these cases, both abiding by the law and breaking the law put the individual at risk of violence, harassment, police intervention, and even criminal prosecution. The idea that the experience of such double binds indicate oppression was clearly articulated by feminist philosopher Marilyn Frye when she wrote, "One of the most characteristic and ubiquitous features of the world as experienced by oppressed people is the double bind—situations in which options are reduced to a very few and all of them expose one to penalty, censure or deprivation."[7] I referenced Talia Bettcher's work in the previous chapter and how her formulation of the double bind for many trans persons is being seen as a deceiver or a make believer. This particular double bind is relevant in this context as well. It is not uncommon for a trans person to be regarded as a deceiver if they/we do not continually make our gender history public. That is, if we do not correct those that might read us as cisgender or clarify our full gender history for those that may find our bodies and styles difficult to place within their limited understanding, then we are at fault for deceiving those individuals. Of course, this kind of personal disclosure is not seen as required in most cases of cisgender or gender conforming individuals. Alternatively, if one is quite public about one's gender history, others are apt to believe that the individual is "make-believing" that they are a woman or a man and essentially asking others to go along with the pretense.[8] Being cast as a deceiver is particularly relevant to those trans individuals who may, for the sake of their own safety and well-being, choose to use a gendered space consistent with their gender identity (as opposed to that assigned at birth) and are eventually "found out" by official or self-appointed gender police. Being cast as a make believer is condescending and presumes that trans and gender non-binary persons are childish or deluded about their own identities. ATBBs essentially require trans individuals to make their/our personal histories public each time we need to use the loo, an imposition that results in an infringement of privacy and increased risk of harm.

It is important to recognize that while ATBBs target transgender persons, they negatively affect individuals of various gender identities and histories. Assuming that neither original birth certificates, chromosomes, hormone levels, nor physical genitalia will be officially inspected before using public restroom facilities, enforcement of ATBBs will be on the basis of appearance. In other words, whether one is in the "wrong place" or not will be determined by how a person appears and how this appearance compares to certain societal standards of what women and men *should* look like. Given that passage of ATBBs is usually supported by fear of nefarious restroom intruders, surveillance, especially in women's restrooms, will only be increased in order to spot such intruders as they enter the facility. This heightened scrutiny, in the form of judging and policing others' gender expression, will not affect just trans individuals, but all individuals who express themselves in ways that are not resolutely within strict bi-gendered categories. Nearly any woman or gender non-binary person who at times presents her/themselves in what is thought of as "masculine" will have a "bathroom story" to share. A recent report from England supports the idea that increased anti-trans sentiment has negative effects on gender non-conforming persons who use women's facilities. England is presently undergoing their own heated debate regarding the degree to which trans persons will be supported in their need and desire to participate in society at the same level as non-transgender persons. As in the US, the effects of these debates are predictable. In "Butch Lesbian Opens Up about 'Increased Harassment' She Faces When She Uses Public Toilets," reporter Jasmine Andersson interviews a woman, Ms. Stonborough, the Associate Director of Policy and Research at Stonewall, who has been increasingly a victim of harassment. Stonborough, like many, has experienced ongoing gender harassment in gendered spaces. Andersson reports,

> I have barely left my house in the last ten months, and one of the handfuls of times I've had to use a public toilet, a woman challenged me when I was quietly standing in line to use the facilities in a park. . . . One of the worst times was in an art gallery, where a man started screaming that there was 'a f****** man going into the toilet' at the top of his voice, and started following me around the gallery once I'd left the toilet.

It is important to understand the ubiquity of this kind of harassment, in all locales in which transgender persons have been politicized, and also that it affects all gender non-conforming persons who use women's restrooms, whether they be trans, non-binary, or cisgender. Andersson continues to report that Stonborough is not the only gender non-conforming person to experience this harassment, but that restrooms have "become a prominent site of conflict and a focal point for gender-critical feminism."[9]

Norms of expression, especially for women, have come a very long way in just a few decades. It is no longer a travesty for a woman to wear trousers, and while masculine gender norms are much less accommodating, there has at least been some recognition of a widening variety of expression. To turn our gender accommodations into spaces of extreme gender investigating, policing, and enforcing is to narrow our understanding of human expression, a turn that is both unnecessary and harmful. For gender non-conforming persons, such increased social monitoring and regulating of gender norms means that virtually no public place is free from harassment.

As explained above, ATBBs put gender non-conforming and trans individuals at risk of verbal harassment and physical violence. Enacting legislation that results in putting persons at risk of predictable harm, for no demonstrable good, is wrong. But I am not merely offering a consequentialist argument, for the harm incurred is not unrelated to the right of trans persons to at least a minimal level of moral respect. Indeed, the harm of physical assault is an obvious expression that the perpetrator does not recognize the full moral worth of another. The work of Axel Honneth is particularly useful here, in that he recognizes that blows to one's body are also blows to one's sense of self, one's autonomy, and are acts of disrespect. At the most basic level, respecting another means to, at the very least, respect that they have authority over their physical bodies. According to his view, "Those forms of practical mistreatment in which a person is forcibly deprived of any opportunity to dispose freely over his own body represent the most fundamental type of personal degradation."[10] This message of disrespect includes also the psychological harm of being humiliated and of not even being recognized as having authority over what happens to one's body.[11]

Even if a transgender or a gender non-conforming person escapes physical violence, being harassed when simply using a bathroom is not a trivial harm and likewise represents a form of moral disrespect. To be glared at, yelled at, and/or kicked out of a restroom facility conveys the message that the individual is unacceptable, out of place, unwanted, and unwelcome. Repeated and/or particularly harmful cases of such harassment have been shown to lead to PTSD, to "holding it" and thus risking damage to one's urinary tract, or simply isolating oneself from public spaces to avoid the harassment altogether.[12] In the end, such harassment conveys the message that an individual is unfit to participate in public life itself. Encouraged by ATBBs, targeted individuals find that their moral worth is suspect or explicitly denied; one is harassed or criminalized for inhabiting a condition of social impossibility,[13] as one's personhood and personal history are regarded as sufficient reason for ostracism. Whether one is denied social participation due to being seen as personally unacceptable or because one belongs to a group who are socially devalued, the result is the same: It is a denial of full moral status as an individual and social participant.

However, as we each plan our days, we know that being any place more than a few hours requires us to acknowledge and attend to our physical being. Humans are urinating, defecating, menstruating, teeth-brushing, sometimes medication-needing, handwashing, hair-and-clothes-adjusting kinds of beings. To the extent that we are expected to do these activities in privacy and under somewhat hygienic circumstances, using bathrooms is a necessary part of social life. Given the identified ramifications of ATBBs discussed herein, gender non-conforming and trans individuals are essentially barred from public spaces subject to these laws. To deny one the ability to attend to one's physical needs is to infringe on one's opportunity to participate in society—whether that be to pursue an employment opportunity, protest one's government by picketing the state capital, or take one's child to a public zoo. Being offered a job, accommodation, or even an education that denies one's basic physical needs and puts one at risk of harassment or violence is to deny that job, accommodation, or education. It is to explicitly deny any semblance of a right to equal opportunity, a notion thought to be sacrosanct by many, and famously supported by philosopher John Rawls.[14] As Honneth explains, it is not just the *content* of the denial that encompasses the harm, but the resulting lack of moral recognition that is just as significant. He contends, "The distinguishing feature of such forms of disrespect, as typified by the denial of rights or by social ostracism, thus lies not solely in comparative restrictions on personal authority but in the combination of these restrictions with the feeling that the subject lacks the status of full-fledged partners to interaction who all possess the same moral rights."[15] Enacting legislation that puts certain members of society regularly at risk of physical harm, harassment, and social ostracism is to condemn those individuals to lives of increased marginality, isolation, and moral injury. As aptly conveyed by Richard M. Juang, "Despite its unquantifiability, recognition's importance can be measured by the consequences of its absence: an unvalued person readily becomes a target or a scapegoat for the hatred of others and begins to see himself or herself only through the lens of such hatred. An existence restricted to purely private expressions of the self, to the closet, becomes corrosive."[16]

As I have argued above, ATBBs put trans and gender non-conforming persons at risk of serious harm, and this constitutes a lack of recognition of moral worth and a denial of equal opportunity. Now, it is conceivable that one might agree with the argument presented thus far and yet believe that ATBBs are legitimized through the need to keep certain society members safe. Indeed, the rhetoric surrounding ATBBs predictably cites protecting (cisgender) girls and women against sexual assault, so one might question whether this is a situation in which, due to the presence of serious threats, certain civil liberties are justifiably curtailed. After all, it is not unusual to consider security and liberty as having an inverse relationship. In times that are thought to require increased security, citizens are often willing to forgo certain liberties—for example, in WWII when London was being regularly bombed by German forces, Londoners accepted being in blackout periods at which times they agreed not to use electricity. To consider an example closer to home, many can remember when airline travel did not include increased security screening in which certain liberties are curtailed and new procedures enforced. I remember the freedom of walking right up to the gate to welcome friends and family directly off their plane. This has been regarded as too dangerous and is now an experience of the past. Thus, it might be argued that there are times in which certain liberties need to be curtailed for the added security of all and that ATBBs are acceptable as response to a grave security threat.

The problem with an attempt to justify ATBBs due to a kind of trade-off of liberty for security is that there is no security threat posed by trans or gender non-conforming persons who wish to use public facilities. In fact, there is no evidence that gender non-conforming individuals pose a threat to anyone using a public bathroom. As discussed before, statistically it is trans and gender non-conforming individuals who face violence and harassment at the hands of cisgender individuals, not the other way around. Thus, limiting access to gendered facilities based on one's sex assignment at birth is a solution without a problem, and a "solution" that does grave moral harm to otherwise innocent individuals. I recognize that one might argue that a cisgender man might "dress up" like a woman in order to gain access to women's facilities for the purpose of carrying out an assault, but there is little evidence supporting this fear either. As one chief records clerk of a police district without ATBBs recently asserted, there is no evidence that there is an increase in restroom sexual assaults in such locales: "We track our sex offenders very carefully and we haven't seen any instance of sexual predators assaulting in bathrooms."[17] It has been known for decades that most sexual assaults are committed by individuals who are at least acquaintances of the victim, not by strangers in public restrooms.[18] Yet, even supposing this was not the case and cisgender men are waiting in the wings of trans inclusion to express themselves as women and enter gendered spaces for the reason to commit assault, it would still not be justified to restrict bathroom access to those who are not using the restroom to perpetrate such crimes. It is as if one were banned from owning a car because someone might steal the car and use it to perpetrate a crime, or from working as a physician because someone might pose as such for disreputable purposes, or from dressing in women's clothing because someone thought they'd be more likely to get away with a crime.[19] Indeed, the examples can be multiplied nearly without end. Simply put, it is unjust to non-trivially and harmfully limit someone's liberty only for the reason that there is a slight chance that another may perpetrate a crime by attempting to capitalize on that liberty. We all deserve to live lives that include safe and meaningful social participation and taking this seriously does not include the social ostracism of trans and gender non-conforming persons.

BATHROOM EXCLUSION OF BODIES

There are many ways to argue against the adoption of anti-transgender bathroom laws. The argument above focuses on the harm that trans and gender non-conforming persons, and society in general, will be subject to when such laws are in place. This non-trivial harm is not one that exists to avoid a worse harm, but one that is wholly unjustified and unneeded. A different kind of analysis is one which critiques the social phenomenon of the popularity of such restrictions. It is to this second topic that we now direct our focus. The beginning of this chapter offered a brief discussion and questioning of why bathroom exclusion tactics would be seen as acceptable or needed. What is it about gendered bathrooms and other such facilities that leads some individuals to be so easily persuaded that trans persons and other gender transgressive persons are dangerous predators when statistics so obviously indicate otherwise? There are several ways to attempt to answer this question, including consideration of social norm adherence or denial, the prudential decisions of some politicians in their efforts to amass power, and the stoked and directed fear of certain collectives. In this last section of this chapter, however, the focus is on bodies and body parts. Given the ubiquity of belief in the sex-gender binary system and its control over our lives, bathroom and other restrictions are restrictions against those who have certain kinds of *bodies*, those who have bodies with certain histories, and those who have bodies that may have certain futures of adornment, modification, or what others see as incongruity. Bodies, and of particular concern here body parts, are constructed to have *meaning* beyond merely being types of wanted or wanted bits of flesh. According to the most conservative and binary thinking, certain body parts dictate who we should love, how we should feel about ourselves, what societal role we should play, how we should have sex, what pronouns to use, what hobbies to enjoy, and what spaces we are allowed to inhabit. In chapter 2, Lugones's work on arrogant perception was cited as relevant to our study here. Such perception regards another's knowledge-making experiences as irrelevant to one's own arrogant judgment on the identity and subjectivity of another. The fact that white supremacy reduces Black individuals to simply Black bodies remains true and is relevant to this context. The fact that sexism reduces women's bodies to usual parts also remains true and is relevant to this context. In addition, trans exclusion often reduces trans and gender expressive bodies to body parts that are seen as either appropriate or inappropriate, depending on what kind of body those parts are attached to and where that body is located.

FEMINISM, MICHIGAN MUSIC FESTIVAL, AND BODY BITS

The proponents of bathroom-use restrictions, and the related proposals that spread across the county like a contagious plague, have always focused on a concern for cisgender women. The assumption seems to be that creating a society in which trans and gender non-conforming persons can participate freely and without harassment or violence would put cisgender women at risk. The commercials for such proposals make use of ominous music and innocent, young white women who are surprised by a bathroom intruder. As trans men have pointed out time and time again, there is no comparable voiced concern that trans men and trans masculine persons using the women's facilities are equally as dangerous, or even a recognition that such legislation would mandate trans men and trans masculine persons to use the women's facilities, in which we'd be most certainly subject to harassment. It is quite obvious that it is trans women and trans feminine persons who are being explicitly demonized here, and the well-being of trans men and trans masculine persons are conveniently ignored or simply disregarded as unimportant. The framing of the narrative as that of keeping cis women safe from dangerous trans women has found purchase in some radical feminist communities for decades, and predictably laid the foundation of the debates regarding access to the Michigan Womyn's Music Festival. This conflict raged for years, dividing the loyalties and trust of the thousands of lesbians, women-identified-women, wimmin, wemyn, dykes, gender non-binary persons, trans men, gender non-conforming people, women-born-women (always a strange image since no one is born as an adult), trans women, and others. The issue, like that of bathrooms, was who was allowed access, in this case, to "the land."

Michfest is relevant here due to the long controversy surrounding the festival's policy of explicit exclusion of trans women. The first year of the festival was 1976 and it persisted until 2015, when their trans-exclusion policy and the position of festival organizer Lisa Vogel that "the land" would always be "womyn-born-womyn" space contributed to its closing. In the years leading up to is closure, "Camp Trans," located just outside "the land" of Michfest, was created as both an alternative and a protest for those who objected to the trans-excluding policy. Despite the fairly well-known debate regarding excluding trans women from the event, the "word on the street" was that, despite the "womyn-born-womyn" policy, trans men and trans masculine individuals were often accepted into the space. This is consistent with many lesbian and feminist spaces of the era, that a more masculine gender expression was seen as acceptable for persons assigned female at birth generally, and that trans men were not really taken terribly seriously in our gender identification. In a way that is also seen in Sheila Jeffreys's unfortunate *Gender Hurts: A Feminist Analysis of the Politics of Transgenderism* (2014)[20] and the more recent *Irreversible Damage: The Transgender Craze Seducing Our Daughters* by Abigail Shrier (2020),[21] while trans women and trans feminine persons tend to be demonized, trans men and trans masculine folks tend to be seen as vulnerable victims in the worrisome patriarchal devaluing of women or in the "transgender epidemic" that is fooling girls and women into thinking that they are gender non-binary or men. In keeping with Janice Raymond's monumentally disastrous *The Transsexual Empire* in 1979,[22] trans women are seen as directors and perpetrators of patriarchal violence whereas trans men are seen as victims of the same or, according to Jeffreys, simply selfish in our desire for male privilege and uninclined to join our feminist sisters to eradicate sexist systems.

Of all the ink and tears spilled over Michfest's exclusionary policies, the most insightful piece written of the controversy was Emi Koyama's "Whose Feminism Is It Anyway? The Unspoken Racism of the Trans Inclusion Debate." In this piece, Koyama critiques the "no penis" policy that was advocated at one time during the years-long controversy. This "compromise" was advocated for by some cisgender festival leaders as well as a group of post-operative trans women who would qualify for inclusion under the policy. Notably, Riki Wilchins, then executive director of GenderPac, was against the policy, and instead defended one that allowed inclusion of all those who live as women, a policy that would include women who are trans and have not had genital surgery. Decades ago, dividing trans persons into "pre-op" and "post-op" descriptors was common; it is, thankfully, less so now. This is an improvement, since certainly not all individuals wish to have, or can afford, the costs of such surgeries, or even have the privilege of a caretaker whose presence is so needed after the procedure. Wilchins, and a few brave others at the time, publicly asserted that being a woman or man is not reducible to the configuration of genitalia and rejected the notion that identity should be essentialized to bits of historically gendered flesh.

Koyama, a grassroots activist out of Portland, begins her piece with admitting that she had "never been interested in getting myself into the mud wrestling of the whole 'Michigan' situation."[23] She decided, though, to join the fray due to the "no penises" policy and her repeated exposure to middle-class and middle-aged white feminist spaces that refused to take responsibility for racist, ableist, classist, and transphobic policies and practices. Koyama writes,

> Speaking from the perspective and the tradition of lesbians of color, most if not all rationales for excluding transsexual women are not only transphobic but also racist. To argue that transsexual women should not enter the Land because their

experiences are different would have to assume that all other women's experiences are the same, and this is a racist assumption. . . .To suggest that the safety of the Land would be compromised overlooks, perhaps intentionally, ways in which women can act out violence and oppressions against each other. Even the argument that "the presence of a penis would trigger women" is flawed because it neglects the fact that white skin is just as much a reminder of violence as a penis. The racist history of lesbian-feminism has taught us that any white woman making these excuses for one oppression have made and will make the same excuse for other oppressions such as racism, classism, and ableism.[24]

Koyama believes that the "no penis" policy is racist since it implies that BIPOC women experience the world just as do women who are white, and it is also classist in that it gives privileges to those who can afford an expensive surgery (it was not ever paid for by insurance at that time), which would tend to favor those who are middle class and relatively wealthy. Given the ongoing generational economic injustices against those of Black, Indigenous, and other communities of color, as well as those who are disabled, this policy favored those who are white and able-bodied. While Koyama does not explicitly articulate this idea, the fact that the privileged position is essentialist regarding physical characteristics is also ableist. A person's worth or value is not reducible to their body parts, regardless of what part they are being reduced to. Koyama cites the position of the Combahee River Collective, who at the time rejected the white feminist calls for "lesbian separatism" as a function of white privilege. The collective, made up of Black women, wrote, "Although we are feminists and lesbians, we feel solidarity with progressive Black men and do not advocate the fractionalization that white women who are separatists demand."[25] White women, especially many who would call themselves "radical feminists," regard sexism as the most "pervasive, extreme, and fundamental of all social inequalities"[26] and view other forms of oppression, including racism, as less fundamental, thus advocating for a separatism by assigned sex at birth, which would result in fragmentation of Black families and communities and reduce their ability to respond to the racism that they face together. It is important to understand that this fragmentation of Black families would be to further (white) feminist goals, goals that, especially at that time, did not prioritize anti-racism. According to Koyama, the white women of Michfest, despite assertions to the contrary, prioritized their own experiences as white cis women (by rejecting those raised as boys, assuming a kind of "taintedness" with male privilege despite the common experience of harassment and violence against non-masculine boys) and white transgender "post-op" women (by assuming all have access to the funds for surgery despite the fact that centuries of economic oppression against communities of color have made this all but impossible for many).

The essentialism of white feminism does not only essentialize their experiences; it also fails to acknowledge how their privileges have been both taken for granted and at the same time assumed to be universal.

The Michigan Womyn's Music Festival decision makers accepted the need for spaces in the festival to be designated for women of color only. Arguments for the "no penises" policy, or a policy of no trans women in general, was argued by the organizers of the festival, particularly Lisa Vogel, to be comparable to the need for white-excluded places in the festival. Yet, the idea of having a "womyn-born-womyn" section of the festival to serve a similar function was never seriously considered, because the essentialist reasoning failed to see trans women, especially trans women of color and/or poor trans women, as belonging at all.

Interestingly, Michfest ended in 2015, the year that marks the temporal beginning of this study. The anti-trans offensive that followed would surely have reverberated in that expansive, mosquito-laden campground. Perhaps the obvious amount of harm caused by the anti-trans offensive would have led the leaders of Michfest to be more allied with women of differing experiences and physicalities, or perhaps it would have strengthened their own position. What is important to note now is the racism and essentialism that are still at play in anti-transgender bathroom bills and the politicization of trans identities. While the arguments for such policies pretend to be about protecting young girls (nearly always depicted as white), the predictable results will be that gender non-conforming and trans persons of color will be the individuals who are policed, harassed, and targeted for violence because of the policies. Quite literally, the safety of trans and gender non-conforming persons, especially those who are persons of color, is being regarded as unimportant to this essentialist ideology of "cis women only" spaces.

Most significantly, Koyama makes clear that white skin can be as much of a "reminder of violence" as a penis. Indeed, a moment of thought might produce a long list of images that could, in the eyes of another, bring back memories of violent encounters. Fists, raised voices, or types of voices, boots, weapons or household items used as weapons, sneers, white skin, a particular hair style, the sound of car tires arriving home or of a door opening—all of these could trigger the reliving of a violent experience. Violence is rampant in our society and takes on various forms. Still, to say that nearly anything could elicit a triggering response of reliving past trauma does not mean that all, or any, such images or things need be essentialized as violence or a kind of weapon, including genitalia types.

It has been the possibility of having a penis "on the Land" or, since the folding of Michfest, "in the bathroom" or other gendered space that has been the often unnamed concern driving trans exclusionary policies. Much has been written about the social construction of the ideal woman's body, of femininity and masculinity, of the white social construction of Black and Brown men and boys as violent, the false narrative which Trump attempted to capitalize on with regard to immigrants, especially those from Latin America. Much less, I believe, has been written about the social construction of men's bodies, although I am glad to see that this is slowly changing. Of the characteristics of some men's bodies that are the most storied are the penis and also the presence of testosterone. Despite the radical feminist construction of penises as essentially a weapon, thus painting penis-bearers as rapists in waiting (especially those who are trans women, a construction originating with Janice Raymond), penises are, actually, simply a variety of human organ, but one that has taken on differently social constructed meanings throughout history and across culture. In *A Mind of Its Own: A Cultural History of the Penis*,[27] David M. Friedman identifies how the social construction of the penis has changed depending on social context—from the admiration of small-sized penises in ancient Greece, to the "demon rod" of the European Middle Ages, to the "icon of creativity," by many pre-Christian pagan societies.[28] Discussion of penis size even asserted itself in recent politics when Republican nominees for the GOP ticket in 2016 felt it necessary to bicker with each other about the size of their hands—thought to correspond to the size of their penises. The construction of the penis as a "demon rod" (as opposed to a "gear shift," "measuring stick," "cigar," "battering ram," or "puncture proof balloon"—the names of Friedman's other chapters) was tied to the belief that witches would generally swoon over Satan's own member and that intercourse with Lucifer himself was the most exciting of "nearly every witch's confession."[29] The witch trials were irredeemably sexist, anthropocentric, and unjust, and they relied on a "demonization" of a body part that is no more demon than so many human and nonhuman attributes.

It is uncontroversial to suggest that the meaning of penises are today also socially constructed, and even that this construction may be different in different contexts and for different penis-owners. Unlike the history of Michfest, discussions of bathroom access generally do not include explicit reference to penises, but it is unrealistic that these social constructions are not at play. In the past forty years, and up to the present, we have seen the penis constructed as synonymous with violence and penises belonging to women depicted as worthy of disgust, as demonstrated in *The Crying Game*, when Dil's naked body is enough to cause Fergus physical illness and anger. To accept and propagate such harmful constructions of trans bodies is to support a narrative that makes personal body acceptance difficult for many, reduces chances for acceptance by intimate partners, increases risk of harm, and, as we see in the case of bathroom bills, ostracizes individuals who are trans or otherwise gender transgressive from even basic social participation. This negative construction of the penis has a legacy in feminist writings, particularly of a certain era.

From Raymond's claim that all trans women are essentially rapists to Andrea Dworkin's position that any woman who engages in sexual intercourse with a penis (yes, including consensually) is essentially participating in her own oppression, being a person who has a body with a penis, or a body that used to have a penis, or a body that may desire a penis in the future, has been reason for unwarranted bias. These ideas, first made popular in the 1970s and 1980s, have been refashioned for the twenty-first century, but their essentialization of gender and of body parts remains the same.

The essentialist position that genitalia are necessary markers to gender identity and expression sets the stage to unnecessarily evaluate some bits of flesh as positive or negative, sometimes depending on what kind of body those bits are attached to. Contrary to popular and sometimes contradictory constructions, women and persons with wombs and related physiologies are neither essentially reproducers nor sex objects; men and persons with penises are not essentially sexual predators; men without penises are no less men than those that do have them, and no generalization can be made on the basis of the presence, or belief of such presence, of any type of genital package for any human being. Similarly it should be noted that while women have been harassed, demonized, and thought to be inherently predatory due to having a penis, this member for a cisgender man can be a testament to his power and virility. It is as if such positive attributions could not be equally descriptive of a woman, transgender or not.

CONCLUSION

Bathroom bills are unethically exclusionary for the multiple reasons given herein. They cause harm to all trans and gender non-conforming individuals in the form of harassment and the threat of violence, and make moral recognition and safe social participation nearly impossible. Since these measures predictably put BIPOC persons at particular risk, they are racist, and to the extent that they reduce individuals to body parts and physical histories, they are both essentialist and ableist. The essentialism at the conceptual heart of such measures does not only produce an injustice to all individuals concerned but relies implicitly on social constructions of human body parts. Trans women or trans feminine persons who may have a history or presence of a penis are deemed dangerous. Trans men and trans masculine persons who have a different relationship to this storied organ are often regarded in light of this physical attribute, whether seen as insufficiently manly, forever impotent, or if one has a surgically constructed penis, as duped-by-the-patriarchy, or even dangerous. While I have restricted this project to discussing politicized events between the years 2015 and 2020, it seems clear that 2021 will be the year of record legislation against trans youth and also trans athletes who wish to compete in their respective areas. With regard to the latter, the focus is again on trans girls and women, as an uncomfortable toleration of trans men and boys, especially as long as the individual doesn't use hormone replacement therapy or surgery, persists. In this way, like the social construction of the penis, testosterone is socially constructed to be perhaps not "Satan's rod" but his weaponized potion. We need to be cautious that our childish notions of testosterone (whether the substance is produced within oneself or is by prescription) do not result in regarding the hormone as an angry hulk-producing elixir that results in superhuman strength and violent personality traits. This same kind of flawed thinking is behind disallowing some cisgender women from participating in international athletic competition and for attempting to disallow athletic competition by trans women, whose testosterone levels are comparable to typical cisgender women. Both unreasonable concerns illuminate the dominant culture's lack of scientific literacy on the subject. What is important here is safe social participation for all and not mythology. What is crucial is real inclusion that nurtures humans and human communities and not scapegoating and dog-whistling tactics that have been used to direct the energies of those threatened by Obergefell into a dangerous backlash. Conceptual analyses of the notions of backlash, scapegoating, and dog-whistling and applications of those ideas to the politicization of trans persons are the topics of chapters 4 through 7.

NOTES

1. Tom Kertscher, "Conservative Group That Claims Joe Biden Backs Sex-Changes for Kids, Is False," PolitiFact, The Poynter Institute, October 27, 2020, https://www.politifact.com/factchecks/2020/oct/27/american-principles-project/conservative-groups-claim-joe-biden-backs-sex-chan/.

2. Nico Lang, "Anti Trans Facebook Ads Target Georgia Voters Ahead of Critical Run Off Election," Them, January 5, 2021, https://www.them.us/story/anti-trans-facebook-ads-target-georgia-runoff-election-voters?fbclid=IwAR1ru5stQDRFqh7jf6 I7Bq4pnz6PDQbJmGU-dyE1oPGD7VuebRC5zQUDgHM.

3. I will be attending to arguments centered on bathroom use, since it seems the most controversial, but these arguments are readily transferable to other gendered spaces with limited revision.

4. Various studies and news reports support this claim.

5. Jody L. Herman, "Gendered Restrooms and Minority Stress: The Public Regulation of Gender and Its Impact on Transgender People's Lives," *Journal of Public Management and Social Policy* 19, no. 1 (2013): 65–80. (The incidents of harassment or assault experience by people of color were reported at a "much higher"

rate than white respondents as were problems experienced by those who were trans feminine rather than trans masculine [77].)

6. Tommy J. Curry, "Michael Brown and the Need for a Genre Study of Black Male Death and Dying," *Theory and Event* 17, no. 3, supplement (2014), https://muse.jhu.edu/article/559369.

7. Marilyn Frye, *The Politics of Reality: Essays in Feminist Theory* (Trumansburg, NY: Crossing Press, 1983), 2.

8. Talia Mae Bettcher, "Evil Deceivers and Make Believers: On Transphobic Violence and the Politics of Illusion," *Hypatia* 22, no. 2 (Summer 2007): 43–65.

9. Jasmine Andersson, "Butch Lesbian Opens Up about Increased Harassment," *Inews*, UK, January 19, 2021, https://inews.co.uk/news/uk/butch-lesbian-public-toilet-women-abuse-government-review-gender-neutral-facilities-833787?fbclid=IwAR3Ne6JYqGGL9FC5jF0-INlZZrDoh8PT7ScFGKxVOMKaHEdAVgTJzbgsIkE.

10. Axel Honneth, "Integrity and Disrespect: Principles of a Conception of Morality Based on the Theory of Recognition," *Political Theory* 20, no. 2 (1992): 190.

11. Ibid.

12. Herman, 76.

13. Dean Spade, *Normal Life: Administrative Violence, Critical Trans Politics, and the Limits of the Law* (Brooklyn, NY: South End Press, 2011).

14. John Rawls, *A Theory of Justice* (Cambridge, MA: Harvard University Press, 1971).

15. Honneth, 191.

16. Richard M. Juang, "Transgendering the Politics of Recognition," in *Transgender Rights*, ed. Paisley Currah, Richard M. Juang, Shannon Price Minter (Minneapolis: University of Minnesota Press, 2006), 242.

17. Emanuella Grinberg and Dani Stewart, "Three Myths That Shape the Transgender Bathroom Debate," CNN, March 7, 2017, https://www.cnn.com/2017/03/07/health/transgender-bathroom-law-facts-myths/index.html.

18. According to the Department of Justice, Dru Sjoden National Sex Offender Website (NSOPW), only 25 percent of female victims are assaulted by strangers (2010) and only 10 percent of perpetrators are strangers when the victim is a child, https://www.nsopw.gov/en/Education/FactsStatistics.

19. The presently popular movie *Ocean's 8* comes to mind here. In this story eight women pull off a diamond heist through the enactment of a highly complex plan that involves posing as women attending a star-studded fashion gala. The leader of the group, played by Sandra Bullock, states she only wants women to participate in this criminal scheme since in this context, "women are invisible," and less likely to be detected. Using the arguments that some use to support ATBBs, perhaps to avoid diamond heists we should make it a crime for anyone to appear as a woman, or, perhaps women should be barred from star-studded galas?

20. Sheila Jeffreys, *Gender Hurts: A Feminist Analysis of the Politics of Transgenderism* (New York: Routledge, 2014).

21. Abigail Shrier, *Irreversible Damage: The Transgender Craze Seducing Our Daughters* (Washington, DC: Regency, 2020).

22. Janice Raymond, *The Making of the She-Male* (New York: Teachers College Press, 1979).

23. Emi Koyama, "Whose Feminism Is It Anyway? The Unspoken Racism in the Trans Inclusion Debate," in *The Transgender Studies Reader*, ed. Susan Stryker and Stephen Whittle (New York: Routledge, 2006), 698.

24. Koyama, "Whose Feminism," 702.

25. Combahee River Collective, "A Black Feminist Statement" (1977) in *This Bridge Called My Back*, ed. Cherríe Moraga and Gloria E. Anzaldúa, quoted in Koyama, "Whose Feminism," 701.

26. Koyama, "Whose Feminism," 701.

27. David M. Friedman, *A Mind of Its Own: A Cultural History of the Penis* (New York: Free Press, 2001).

28. Friedman, *A Mind of Its Own*, 4.

29. Ibid., 2.

Chapter 4

Backlash

The last chapter dealt with the morality of socially excluding trans persons and the flaws of the arguments that are thought to justify such exclusion. This chapter takes a different focus. Instead of a moral analysis, this chapter focuses on the collective, that is, the political landscape that has supported and legitimized trans-exclusionary legislation, policy, and practice. This chapter will focus on a conceptual analysis of the term "backlash" and will apply this idea to the political climate of anti-trans sentiment and policy. This analysis will continue into later chapters, in which the concepts of scapegoating and dog-whistling will be employed to deepen the understanding of what has led to the politicization of trans identity. It is not my intent to claim that one of these ideas is primarily explanatory or that one phenomenon obtains to the exclusion of the other two, but rather that each interdependent concept is applicable to the recent wave of anti-trans policies and proposed legislation.

BACKLASH

The term "backlash" is used in a variety of ways. Generally, the term is used to characterize a response that is thought to be unprogressive and unacceptable. While in this way the term can be regarded as normative, it is important to note that this normative nature is contrary to the origination of the term itself. "Backlash" was originally meant to describe the movement of machinery, a "recoil" or "back-lash" that was dangerous, automatic, and unintentional. Consider how a rifle recoils after it is fired. The forward momentum of the bullet produces a backward thrust—sometimes painfully sending the butt of the rifle into the shooter's shoulder. In what is generally considered the "Industrial Era" of Western Europe and some of its most *industrious* colonies, workers found themselves laboring in close proximity to unsafe machinery that could literally kill or maim them in the course of a workday. This threat of bodily harm was not to be taken personally or intentionally. At least before union organizing against such conditions empowered workers, neither the machine, nor often the employers who profited off of the labor of the workers were seen as responsible for the machine backlashes, regardless of the degree of danger.

From this origin, the term has come to explain a type of response, a response of disfavor toward proposed or newly adopted attitudes, laws, policies, or norms. A search of the academic literature on the subject brings many examples from disparate contexts. For instance, the term has been employed to explain that Nixon's successful 1968 campaign was the result of racial backlash against the civil rights era.[1] The conservative turn of the 1980s and 1990s has also been described as a sexist backlash,[2] and, according to Sherry Vint, certain films (for example, the Hollywood reprisal of the 1970s sitcom *Bewitched* and the film *The Stepford Wives*) can be seen as part of that same backlash response.[3] There are even events characterized as backlash within the confines of academic disciplines such as the ontological backlash against analytic philosophy.[4] Indeed, even superficial investigation will support the claim that the idea is employed in many disparate contexts and across cultures.[5]

A close analysis of the idea of backlash reveals that it involves at least four different elements. I will explain each of these elements in turn. First, a backlash response is *collective* in nature. Any action by an individual must be tied to that of a collective to be seen as part of the backlash response. Second, the response is a *directed* response, and as I will argue herein, the direction it takes can vary widely. Third, the backlash response can be analyzed with regard to its *normative* character (in content and direction). This analysis involves considerations of responsibility that is, in turn, related to that of intentionality. Fourth, and most obviously, a backlash response can be analyzed with respect to its *scope*. The scope is often related to the direction element, i.e., to whom or what the response is directed.

THE COLLECTIVITY REQUIREMENT

First it is important to note that backlash is a collective, not merely an individual, response. I take this to be a necessary characteristic of any response deemed backlash. Individual negative responses in the form of, for example, a disrespectful remark, a robbery, or a single case of tax evasion would not be generally seen as acts of, or part of, backlash. We respond to our own conditions in a variety of ways as individuals, but these responses are not always or usually tied to a kind of collective wave of similar reactions. Still, even the above-cited examples could be part of a backlash response under specific circumstances. For instance, if the disrespectful remark were one that illustrated a dogmatic attachment to the belief that the former president Obama was born in Kenya, even in the face of persuasive evidence to the contrary, then the remark could be related to the racist backlash to the election of this country's first Black president. A robbery could be seen as a kind of backlash, if it were directed toward business owners of a certain social group (in the case of racial, ethnic, or sexist backlash) or perhaps against a certain kind of company with newly adopted policies. Failing to pay one's taxes can be an individual intentional choice to be a "free rider" and thus benefit from tax-funded social goods, or it could be a part of a collective response against, say, funding an unjust war (nods toward Thoreau). Thus, whether or not one can produce a persuasive argument that a discrete action is part of a backlash response depends on how well it can be tied to a collective countermovement to a change or proposed change.

To agree that backlash is essentially collective is not to claim that individuals do not often "lash out" in a variety of ways that might be reminiscent of the idea of backlash, in that the lashing out contains an element of plurality of instances, but not collectivity of agents. Consider the case of the woman who absorbs the harm of both off-handed and pointedly cruel sexist remarks while at work and does this for years, if not decades. Consider the individual who takes the courageous step to announce that they are using different pronouns than before, only to have individuals regularly and often intentionally use the pronouns that individual has rejected. Persons in these kinds of situations can "lash out" when the cost to self becomes too high to accept such treatment without objection. These cases, which are unfortunately not uncommon, are instances of what is generally called "pile-up" rather than "backlash." There is an element of plurality—in this case, the plurality of *instances* in which the individual was faced with dealing with disrespectful treatment, not a plurality or collective *of individuals* responding to an event or proposal. Individuals often and understandably respond negatively to disrespectful behavior that they have tolerated in the past, especially when the pile up of instances becomes so obvious to make it clear that a pattern of disrespect has been established.

Given the sheer quantity of anti-transgender legislation and the rise in trans-directed violence described in chapter 2, there is little question that this response has been national, and thus collective in scope. This remains true even if the actors in question—politicians, religious leaders, and others—are not orchestrating their responses together. Not only is the anti-transgender response collective, so is the effect this has on trans persons across the country, as demonstrated by increased experiences of anxiety, depression, suicidality, etc.[6]

DIRECTIONAL CONSIDERATIONS

Secondly, as backlash is a kind of collective *response*, that response needs to have a certain direction, one that can be reasonably seen as a counter to the event, proposal, or proposed change that is regarded as objectionable. For example, vigorously washing and waxing one's car in 1965 to express anger at the passage of the 1964 Civil Rights Bill would *not* be seen as part of the backlash to that legislation, although joining the Ku Klux Klan could be seen as such. Now, it may be the case that a racist may be angry, depressed, or anxious at the passing of the civil rights legislation and may wash his car out of his efforts to "keep his hands busy" in dealing with the emotional response. Yet, it is otherwise difficult to argue that his washing his car is a response *directed* toward the civil rights legislation in a way to express his disfavor or even change it. The car-washing is more clearly a response directed toward alleviating emotional distress, not toward changing or challenging the legislation. Furthermore, even if there were a kind of collective car-washing by angry, frustrated, or fearful suburban whites organized for the first Saturday of the month, this would not constitute backlash. The collective element obtains but the directional element does not. I take these first two characteristics, that the response must be collective and directional, to be necessary to the concept of backlash. If they were not to obtain in a given case, a different term would be more aptly descriptive.

Backlash has a vector-like quality in that it is both directional and quantitative. With regard to the direction, the backlash response can be directed in various ways. First, it can be directed against those who are thought to be responsible for initiating or championing the change which is ill-regarded (either those responsible for bringing about the change or responsible for not countering the change effectively). Second, it can be focused toward those who are paradigmatically representative of the change itself or stand to benefit from it. Third, backlash can be aimed at those who are merely tangentially representative of the change, but who are vulnerable to the "lash" of the backlash due to either being socially marginalized and/or being an opportunistic and discernible public target.

In this work, I have presented the thesis that the anti-transgender backlash can be seen as related to the US Supreme Court ruling in 2015 in favor of same-sex marriage and to a greater acceptance of LGBTQ individuals generally. Before we consider the directed backlash against transgender persons, it is helpful to reflect on other aspects of the backlash to same-sex marriage equality. Certainly, some negative responses to the ruling did not implicate transgender persons at all. The most obvious and well publicized of these responses includes the case of Kim Davis, who refused to issue marriage licenses to same-sex couples in Kentucky based on her conviction that doing so would compromise her religious convictions. Here, Davis, while acting as an individual agent, is emblematic of a larger social response. While I have no way to know the thought processes of Davis, it is plausible that she staged her refusal with at least some knowledge that she was not the only one to disagree with the legal legitimization of same-sex marriage. That is, she believed that she'd be supported, and she was, by the Family Foundation of Kentucky and such notables as Mike Huckabee and Ted Cruz, both vying to be the Republican candidate for president in 2016. The attempts by numerous states to pass legislation that allows *carve-outs* of this basic right, in the form of religious exemption, as was discussed at length in chapter 2, obviously bear similarities to Davis's action. Similarly, the case of the Masterpiece Cakeshop in Colorado can be seen as backlash directed toward the primary origination of the change to legitimize same-sex marriages: the US Supreme Court. This case, which was originally seen as a potentially effective counterpunch to the original ruling, centered around the claim that the owner of Masterpiece Cakeshop, Jack Phillips, was not unjustly discriminating against the same-sex partners, Charlie Craig and David Mullins, who requested him to bake a cake for their wedding. In many ways, this case failed to be an effective pushback to the original ruling since, while the Phillips's team "won," they did so in a limited way that is not generalizable to all similar cases.

To claim that the above cases of Davis and Phillips are part of a broader backlash against marriage equality, or the changing social norms supporting a greater degree of acceptance of LGBTQ persons and relationships generally, does not count against the claim that the wave of anti-transgender legislation and even anti-transgender violence is part of the same backlash response. This is true for at least two reasons. First, it can be argued that the SCOTUS ruling of 2015, while unpopular with some, was seen as a *done deal*. That is, many individuals may reasonably conclude that the US Supreme Court may have the last word on this issue, at least domestically, and the best thing to do now is not to spend any more effort attempting to counter same-sex marriage but to make sure that the country does not slide further into a kind of cultural and thought-to-be moral morass of more extensive LGBTQ acceptance. Indeed, many may regard the Obergefell ruling as the tip of a dangerous iceberg whose unseen yet societally destructive base includes thought-to-be atrocities of group marriage, the end of "family," or traditional understandings of fatherhood and motherhood. The bottom of this slippery slope is often thought to include the acceptance and normalization of trans individuals, an idea that is often understood to include state support of physical "mutilation," the end of men and women and the traditional family structure, the invasion of all girl/women-centered spaces by dangerous men in dresses, etc. Examples of extreme claims are not difficult to find. The American Family Association, designated as a hate group by the Southern Poverty Law Center (SPLC), is just one source, among many, of anti-LGBTQ fearmongering. Their rhetoric includes: "The homosexual movement is a progressive outgrowth of the sexual revolution of the past 40 years and will lead to the normalization of even more deviant behavior,"[7] and "As with smoking, homosexual behavior's 'second hand' effects threaten public health. ... Thus, individuals who choose to engage in homosexual behavior threaten not only their own lives, but the lives of the general population."[8] The rhetoric targeting transgender persons is even worse, of course. Tom Gilson, author of *A Christian Parent's Guide to Discussing Homosexuality with Teens*, claims, "The world has never seen any movement so obviously damaging, so plainly irrational and so evil gain so much power so quickly."[9] Another noteworthy remark made in the same vein is from Ohio lawmaker Candice Keller, who attempted a causal analysis of the country's mass shooting problem. Her long recitation of the conditions responsible for the problem are numerous and include cannabis use, athletes taking a knee during the national anthem, and a culture that does not sufficiently prioritize god and the church. In this list, she includes the "breakdown of the traditional American family (thank you, transgender, homosexual marriage, and drag queen advocates)."[10]

The targeting of trans persons, or otherwise rejection of greater degrees of trans acceptance, can be seen as a response to what the Obergefell ruling *represents*, a dangerous degree of societal acceptance of deviance away from what are thought to be traditional, binary sex and gender norms supporting a patriarchal, heterosexual, cisgender society. This is true even though the ruling did not mention trans or gender transgressive persons nor were the plaintiffs characterized as having those identities. Not only is the acceptance of transgender persons seen as a challenge to the cisgender and heterosexual dominated society (and thus that which requires the most vehement refusal), but trans persons, as a collective, are some of the most socially vulnerable compared to their cisgender LGBQ counterparts. It should be noted that when I use the term "vulnerable" above it is not to suggest that transgender persons as a broad group, or any one of the subgroups of transgender persons that share a common social reality, are in any way weak, incapable, or otherwise underdeveloped in comparison with cisgender individuals or collectives. Indeed, it is the resilience of trans persons of color that erupted against police brutality in the Compton Cafeteria Riots, that spearheaded the LGBTQ Rights Movement at Stonewall Inn, and who, with various degrees of acceptance and oppression, daily assert their identity, expression, and value in ways that challenge the cis/het hegemony and white supremacy of our society. By "vulnerability" here, I mean only to refer to certain empirically verified facts: transgender persons are more likely to be unemployed or underemployed, homeless, be denied adequate health care, be rejected by their families of origin, experience verbal or physical harassment by others, and suffer from the hopelessness and suicidality that so often accompanies this kind of multifaceted oppression. Many trans persons bear the brunt of multiple oppressive structures, including racism, sexism, xenophobia, classism, ableism, homophobia, etc.

The social vulnerability just described and the fact that trans acceptance is seen by many as the extreme and unacceptable result of the efforts of LGBTQ acceptance and equality combine to make trans and gender non-conforming persons targets of a backlash response. This kind of vulnerability will be explored in the next few chapters since it is also related to scapegoating and also dog-whistling.

A consideration of historical examples underscores how backlash can and often does target the vulnerable or already marginalized. Elizabeth Barnes, in her essay, "Justice, at What Cost?," describes how one aspect of the backlash against emancipation was directed at recently emancipated Black women.[11] According to Barnes, "White supremacist groups rampaged across the South, using sexual violence as their primary weapon against formerly enslaved women."[12] The sexist and racist targeting of Black women by white supremacists is both an example of targeting an already marginalized group of individuals and also one of targeting a group of individuals that is representative of the proposed change. As Barnes explains, emancipation meant that formerly enslaved individuals were to be granted equal protection under the law, which meant that Black women could legally press charges against white men for the crime of rape and sexualized assault. This part of the backlash for Emancipation was directed toward Black women as a marginalized group due to racist sexism, but the sexualized assault was also the violent embodiment of the perpetrator's assertion that Black women are essentially non-persons and that thinking otherwise was a "step too far" that white supremacist men could not accept.

The 1992 LA riots, which are generally seen as a backlash response to the acquittal of the police officers who needlessly and unmercifully beat Rodney King, provide us with a second example. Many have written about how Korean-owned businesses were heavily damaged in the riots and seemed to be the target of the backlash response by the rioters. On one level of analysis, it is clear that the Korean business owners of Koreatown had nothing to do with the beating of Rodney King, nor the controversial acquittal of those responsible. Targeting the Korean-owned businesses was opportunistic in the sense that the areas of the riots included many such small markets and also that the Koreans were a marginalized community themselves and thus vulnerable to harm. On the other hand, the relationship between the Korean and Black populations of these areas is also relevant. That relationship was strained when, just two weeks after the King beating, Soon Ja Du, a liquor store owner, shot Latasha Harlins, just fifteen years old, after Du accused Harlins of attempting to steal a bottle of orange juice. While Du was convicted of voluntary manslaughter, her sentence involved only a $500 fine with no jail time.[13] The relationship between the African- and Korean-American communities of Los Angeles in the early 1990s is both complex and nuanced, and is beyond what is required for my analysis here.[14] It stands, however, as an example of backlash that was catalyzed by one event and then fueled by simmering tensions and injustice, and that was directed at a population that had little to do with the catalyzing event.

Thus, in this way, backlash can be seen as opportunistic in terms of its directional orientation. That is, those targeted may have less to do with the original concern of the backlashers but may be opportunistic targets which are representative of the new paradigm thought to be proposed or accepted. Both of the above examples involve racism. This is not surprising. In fact, in a search of academic literature on the subject of backlash, most of the work involves either racist or sexist backlash against more inclusive policies and practices.

Acknowledging the opportunistic nature of backlash is consistent with the analysis of racism by Stanford historian George Fredrickson.[15] Fredrickson's work was first mentioned in chapter 2 and is relevant here since backlash often involves aspects of racism and, conversely, racism often employs backlash. On this view, the false justifications for racism—from those focusing on the archaic notion of "blood," to the racist pseudoscience of the nineteenth century, to invalid arguments of cultural inferiority—change through time because racism *scavenges* on the cultural aspects of the era to produce the most believable justification *for those of that particular era*. So, while alleged commiseration with Satan may rile the masses of Medieval Christians against the resident Jewish population in the year 1350, a *different kind* of justificatory structure tends to be offered in the year 2020.[16]

Fredrickson's position that racism is scavengeristic, or opportunistic, is relevant to an understanding of backlash in at least two different ways. First, just as racism is opportunistic with regard to ideology, backlash is opportunistic with respect to targeted victim and direction. Backlash can be directed at those who are already marginalized, especially when the lashers are those with more privilege, as is often the case. This is true since often the catalyst for the backlash involves efforts to decrease marginalization and increase equity, which serves to challenge the status quo. In this way, backlash is less like a sophisticated guided missile and appears to manifest as something more like mob violence.

A discussion of opportunism should not lead one to infer that those most negatively affected by backlash are simply in the "wrong place at the wrong time" and that their marginalization is an accepted "given" of the social context as opposed to something that is a criticizable and noteworthy part of a structurally oppressive society. C. Riley Snorton's analysis of the story of Brandon Teena offers great insight here.[17] While the killing of Brandon Teena came to signify violence against trans and gender non-conforming persons, especially those on the trans-masculine spectrum, the death of Lana Tisdel's sister's boyfriend, Phillip DeVine, was left out of the popular movie dramatization of the events in the 1999 movie *Boys Don't Cry* as well as the story's popular retelling. When the killers John Lotter and Tom Nissen entered the Tisdels' home, DeVine (the boyfriend) was in the living room and was summarily shot before the murderers found Brandon Teena and Lisa Lambert. As Snorton notes in leaving out the story of DeVine, *Boys Don't Cry* is emblematic of the way in which the radical erasure of Blackness makes queer stories queerer."[18] The murder of DeVine was regarded by many as opportunistic, and he was said to have been in the "wrong place at the wrong time." Many considered it almost inevitable that the young Black man would be killed, even to the extent that his murder was problematically accepted as *normal*. Snorton quotes Anna Mae, Lambert's mother's, description of her walk through the household post-murders as follows: "[At] first I think I denied there was anything wrong. I just seen this Negro sitting on the floor with a coffee table over his lap. And I thought, this is strange, but yet you know, I knew then there was something there wrong, but yet, I just kept telling myself there wasn't and I just walked right on through the house."[19] To regard this senseless killing as "predictable" or "understandable," to be enough not to check on Phillip, to regard his killing as insufficient evidence that "there was something there wrong,"[20] and to deem it not part of the story of these murders, or so mundane as to barely deserve mention or attention, is to normalize racism and to misunderstand the nature of the relationship between anti-Blackness and anti-trans violence.

With the above ideas in mind, we can regard backlash as opportunistic with regard to accepted justificatory strategies (Frederickson's point) and often opportunistic as far as its direction. The direction being toward the already marginalized group that is representative of the change being proposed or actualized. This is not to claim that this is a necessary condition. Backlash against the over-privileged is not impossible, but rare enough that if it is effective, it is historically noteworthy. There is also a sense that backlash scavenges on the oppressive structures already in place. Given that anti-trans bias affects persons of color and particularly those who are women to a much greater extent than it does white individuals who are men, racism and sexism become a vehicle or perhaps a kind of steering mechanism for that backlash. Racism, sexism, and other oppressive structures *direct* the animus and moral disregard in ways that are both predictable and morally abhorrent. Indeed, in many ways, anti-trans animus becomes a tool of both white supremacy and toxic masculinity, just as racism and sexism become tools for heterosexual-cisgender supremacy. They are mutually reinforcing and sustaining structures, and the justice and flourishing of transgender and gender non-conforming individuals requires the dismantlement of all such oppressions. Indeed, any oppressive structure remaining in place will serve to direct backlash responses to the still marginalized.

The above discussion has focused on an explanation of how anti-trans bias, animus, legislation, and violence can be rightly seen as backlash against LGBTQ acceptance and as related to the Obergefell ruling of 2015. Trans and gender non-conforming persons are seen by some as the extreme and unacceptable edge of the radical LGBTQ agenda, perhaps taking the place of the previously imagined "Gay Agenda" that was never about corrupting the young, but more about living one's life free from violence, harassment, and to recognize the demands of health care justice. (Even the criticizable response of the US government to the COVID-19 pandemic is a far cry from the deadly apathy expressed by those who could have acted more resolutely in the face of the AIDs pandemic.) Furthermore, trans and gender non-conforming persons are targets of opportunity given certain social vulnerabilities. Being representative of an unwanted change and an opportunistic target can both occur at once, and in a variety of ways. One way for this to occur is when a member of the oppressed group, or one thought to be representative of the group, publicly asserts their advocacy for social justice, or, especially for those who are trans or gender non-conforming, simply asserts their identity.

A recent and timely treatment of the concept of backlash was recently offered by philosopher George Yancy. In 2018, Yancy published his short book *Backlash* on the response he received to his *New York Times* op-ed, "Dear White America."[21] The opinion piece itself, published in 2017, was described by Yancy as *a gift*. It was a gift of self-disclosure as Yancy transparently admits to being sexist, this despite his efforts to avoid this character trait and his familiarity with the costs and harm of oppression through his experience of being a Black man. The gift here is not just his radical public honesty, but his invitation to white Americans to be similarly self-critical with regard to their own racism. Yancy invites White America to "listen with love, a sort of love that demands that you look at parts of yourself that might cause pain and terror, as James Baldwin would say."[22] As he models public vulnerability, openness, and trust, he asks his white readers to do the same:

> If you are white, and you are reading this letter, I ask that you don't run to seek shelter from your own racism. Don't hide from your responsibility. Rather, begin, right now, to practice being vulnerable. Being neither a "good" white person nor a liberal white person will get you off the proverbial hook. I consider

myself to be a decent human being. Yet, I'm sexist. Take another deep breath. I ask that you try to be "un-sutured." If that term brings to mind a state of pain, open flesh, it is meant to do so. After all, it is painful to let go of your "white innocence," to use this letter as a mirror, one that refuses to show you what you want to see, one that demands that you look at the lies that you tell yourself so that you don't feel the weight or responsibility for those that live under the yoke of whiteness, your whiteness.[23]

It is important to understand the *kind* of gift that was given to his white readers in the form of this letter. His letter is more an invitation than a condemnation; the vulnerability requested is offered to his readers in the form of his own admitted culpability for sexism. He offers understanding to the racist when he admits that "every day of my life I fight against the dominant male narrative, choosing to see women as subjects, not objects. But even as I fight, there are moments of failure."[24] He appeals to both the rationality and the shared human experience of those whom he addresses in his letter in his efforts towards healing. This healing is one for the collective of white Americans whose sense of self and morality have become distorted by the racist systems that serve to privilege those with white skin.

Yancy's letter results in him being seen as representative of the "problem" itself, and therefore as a target for backlash. Indeed, as Du Bois asks, "How does it feel to be a problem?"[25] What I mean by saying he is representative of the "problem" of attempts of racial equality is that he is a Black man with a PhD teaching at one of our nation's universities (Emory). His education and position mean that he is a public intellectual and an individual who has personally experienced the harms of racism. As such, he is in a position to offer this letter, but to those who are incapable of engaging in the self-reflection he asks for, it is seen more as evidence of the negative consequences of "uppity-ness" that result from his esteemed position. Secondly, his public gift, and his book about the response that followed, mean that he is now an opportunistic target for all those who wish to deny the racism that manifests itself in nearly every aspect of US society and which exists in the character and intellect of nearly every white person living in the US. In his chapter entitled "Dear N***r Professor," he describes the content of the letters, emails, and voicemails he receives from white readers who not only wholly reject his gift but reject his humanity and moral worth. The epitaphs are as predictable as they are tragic and heinous. This chapter is titled with explicit use of the N-word to reflect the language used against him. (It should be noted that Yancy spells the offending word fully, and he explains why he does so.) The term is used to dismiss his education, his ideas, his worth. These individual responses can be seen as a backlash to his original letter to the *New York Times* (thus the title of his book), but they are also tied to a broader collective attitude of racism within the United States, a collective sentiment that has become increasingly emboldened in recent years.

I use the example of the backlash against George Yancy to demonstrate how individual actions (those of white people sending him racist hate mail) can together form a backlash, especially to those targets that are both representative of a certain cause or paradigm shift and are also opportunistic by way of vulnerability, public access, or both. In addition to targeted violence and legislative attempts to curtail our rights, trans and gender non-conforming persons are often the target of vitriolic, hateful language, especially on social media or in the comment section of any article that conveys a trans person's narrative. A case quite parallel to Yancy's is that of philosophy professor and professional cyclist, Veronica Ivy. Dr. Ivy is the first transgender athlete to win a world championship track cycling event with her performance at the UCI Masters World Track Cycling Championship for women in the 35–44-year age group in October 2018. News of her win brought Ivy opportunities to inform the public on the ethics of transgender participation in sport, but also caused a mountain of backlash against not only her participation, but her identity as a trans woman and philosopher. Her philosophical work on the acronym "TERF" (Trans-Exclusionary Radical Feminist) had already put Ivy on the radar of individuals who see participation by trans women in society as a threat to cisgender women. The cycling win and Ivy's public and stalwart support of trans women athletes only increased the animus that she already experienced, in terms of social media bullying, attempts to get her fired from her university, and attempts to prevent her work from being published. Ivy's academic and athletic career meant that she, like Yancy, was both representative of a paradigm change (accepting trans women as women, as academicians, and athletes with full participation rights in society) and also an opportunistic target for those who wished to lash against the paradigm change given the publicity of her cycling victory.

While Ivy's case is unique, nearly any online publicity regarding trans persons generally elicits a barrage of negative comments attacking the trans person in question. Fred Dreier, a reporter for *Velo News* who wrote on Ivy's win, reported that after the announcement, "Our Twitter feed became a firehose of offensive comments aimed [at Dr. Ivy] from the dark and toxic dregs of the internet." He follows up by saying that previous stories he has written regarding trans athletes have garnered similarly hateful responses:

> In each instance, I saw a familiar scenario play out. Those few transgender athletes participating in sports were met by the torch-and-pitchfork-toting masses. Those athletes who raised serious concerns over fair play and equality were either lumped in with the bozos or completely drowned out by the chorus of

angry tweets and offensive chants. In all cases, intelligent and nuanced conversation was overshadowed by hate.[26]

My intent on describing the cases of both Yancy and Ivy is not to claim that they are similar in all respects. While both Yancy and Ivy are philosophy professors of a marginalized identity, anti-trans animus is not the same phenomenon as racism, although as oppressive structures they have some similarities and combine in targeting trans people of color. The racist epitaphs directed at Yancy cannot be seen as exactly similar in content or effect from those that are regularly directed at Ivy and other trans individuals whose lives bring public attention, scrutiny, and abuse. What is similar between the two cases is that both individuals are subject to a form of directed backlash due to their capacity for representation and for an opportunistic show of hatefulness. As such, backlash is directed towards them just as it can be directed toward others who are thought to be socially vulnerable in relation to other potential targets. The legislative backlash that was discussed in chapter 2 is just one form of backlash, which can be seen as directly targeted against transgender inclusion and/or as a backlash against same-sex marriage and greater LGBTQ acceptance, and yet targeted at those individuals and groups who are the most vulnerable and socially marginalized.

CONSIDERATIONS OF INTENTIONALITY, RESPONSIBILITY, AND MORALITY

In this chapter thus far, it has been determined that backlash is a directed collective response that can take a variety of forms. It is now time to turn to clarifications of the relationship between backlash and morality, both in the general conceptual case and also in the given applied context.

Recall that in the first section of this essay I introduced the example of how withholding one's taxes could be either a purely individual action or part of a collective response against an unpopular war effort, depending on context. This example is helpful in recognizing the contextual difference between an individual action and a collective response, but it is also instructive when considering the relationship between backlash and normativity. In "Analyzing Backlash to Progressive Social Movements," Ann E. Cudd presents a conceptual analysis of backlash that opens this volume on the backlash to the feminist movement and its fought-for social changes.[27] Here, Cudd characterizes backlash as "at once both descriptive and normative."[28] The normative aspect, if accepted as a constitutive part of the term, means that instances of backlash are best understood as collective response against *progressive*, as opposed to *regressive*, movements or proposals. In other words, while backlash certainly involves a sentiment of disapproval and perhaps even resentment, Cudd's claim is more substantive in requiring the catalyst of the backlash to be of a particular moral quality. This requirement does complicate identifications of backlash, as Cudd admits:

> The other kind of problem is that some periods might indeed oppose the social movements of a previous era, but the previous era was not itself a progressive social movement. For example, let's suppose that the current opposition to affirmative action were overcome and affirmative action programs, perhaps in altered forms, were reinstituted. Then we might imagine those who oppose affirmative action on grounds that it violates the rights of Whites and men would say that there is a backlash occurring in the reinstitution of affirmative action.[29]

In the above example, Cudd does not think that the reinstatement of affirmative action programs should be seen as backlash since it is a response to a regressive, not progressive, change. Thus, for Cudd, if my previous example of refusing to pay taxes to fund a US war effort involved a plan for the US to invade and eventually annex certain areas of Mexico for the purpose of gaining access to oil reserves, then a collective response against the war would not be seen as a backlash, assuming that such military action by the US government would fail any litmus test for progress or justice. In short, the overall context matters.

While I agree with Cudd that the use of the term "backlash" is *generally* directed at changes thought to be progressive and not regressive (at least by those using the term), restricting the term in the way she does leads to arguments about what is and is not backlash, based solely on the moral quality of the catalyzing event or proposal. Contrary to Cudd, I believe if the collective and directional conditions are met, there is no reason to restrict the concept further. In other words, the collective and directive aspects of the concept are crucial, not the moral content. As a result, it can be reasonably argued that one might use the term in a way that implies no particular moral content of the original catalyst. For instance, the weekly PBS news program *Washington Week* offered an analysis entitled "Widespread Backlash to Donald Trump's Proposed Muslim Ban."[30] I see no reason to challenge the extremely competent moderator, the late Gwen Ifill, nor the others at PBS, in their choice of terminology. The focus of that episode, which first aired on December 11, 2015, was a collective and directed response against Trump's proposed ban, a response fitting with the characterization presented here. Thus, using the term "backlash" was not inappropriate, even if, contrary to Cudd's formulation, Trump's Muslim ban was certainly a regressive, not progressive, proposal.

Thinking broadly, the term "back" in "backlash" does imply movement in an opposite direction, as in the example of the rifle recoiling into the shooter's shoulder. Similarly, consider the action of a spring when released after being stretched; it will spring back, traveling in the opposite direction to that in which it was stretched. The original direction need not be designated. If traveling northward, "going back" involves a southward direction, whereas the opposite would be true if the original direction was southbound. In this way, Cudd is correct that some normative content obtains since backlash is a movement of disfavor.

Lastly on this topic, an identification and analysis of collective directed responses is a worthwhile endeavor and need not be unduly complicated by disagreements as to whether the catalyst to the response was *progressive* or *regressive* in nature since, in general use, the term "backlash" is used for both. After all, a normative analysis of the response can, and often is, dealt with secondarily to determine whether and in what ways the response is morally appropriate, morally inappropriate, morally required, or morally neutral. For instance, might there be a backlash against the trend of "man-buns" that favors men's short hairstyles? Perhaps this would be an example of a morally neutral response, despite the intense passion of many man-bun objectors. At issue here, the anti-transgender response to greater LGBTQ acceptance does constitute backlash and is morally inappropriate. It is a directed collective response to a, in this case progressive, change of greater LGBTQ equality. In the following section, I argue that since there is no reason to believe that backlash responses in question are unintentional, responsibility is not mitigated (or is at least not so in the typical case), and the agents are thus morally responsible for their actions. First the collective then the individual case will be considered.

Responsibility: The Collective Case

Because backlash is a collective response, it is important to consider intentionality on the level of the collective. Admittedly, this kind of inquiry can lead us into very murky waters involving the existence (or non-existence) of collective minds and an account of collective action. Perhaps, thankfully, we won't need to delve too deeply into the finer theoretical points of this issue, but just a bit of background will be helpful. In 1987, Steven Sverdlik wrote "Collective Responsibility" and argued that in cases of collective action, say in the example of individuals joining forces to push a car off of a cliff, the notion of collective responsibility is "common sense."[31] According to the story as he tells it, all members of the group are needed to successfully push a car off of a cliff, so there is little to oppose the obvious conclusion that the act in question is committed by the collective itself, thus supporting the claim that groups can, indeed, commit actions. In addition, it is reasonable to conclude that the action was intentional. We might commonly say "the group decided to push the car off the cliff," not to invoke a meta-group-mind, but to articulate that a decision-making process did take place, and it is not entirely dissimilar to that undertaken by a single individual. Indeed, Peter French argued in *Collective and Corporate Responsibility*[32] that corporations have often very well-established decision-making procedures that allow us to regard their actions as involving a kind of group intentionality, thus providing the foundation for those same corporations to be held responsible for their actions. While the car-pushing group of individuals may not have needed to agree upon vision and mission statements before pushing the car off the cliff, nevertheless there was some implicit decision-making procedure, even if it is only that of *Chad*, the popular white high school athlete, suggesting the group complete the act. The upshot is that if collectives can be thought to be capable of intentional action, then, barring relevant contingencies, they can also be seen as responsible for those same actions, opening up the space for claims of both responsibility and moral blameworthiness.

Just as it takes a group of persons to push the car off the cliff, so is it also the case that there are certain acts of anti-transgender bias that similarly require a collective to accomplish. For instance, when state legislators voted for the notorious North Carolina bathroom bill (HB 2) or when the Texas House voted in favor of SB 17, which allows one to identify "religious convictions" as a justifiable reason to limit or deny professional services without being admonished by relevant licensing, regulating, or professional organizations, these collectives of individuals participated in a collective intentional action. As such, the collective is responsible for the action, and, to some reasonable extent, the consequences thereof.[33] To say "the House passed the bill" is both grammatically and conceptually correct, even if individual members of the collective did not vote for its passing. Indeed, collective responsibility need not "distribute" to all members of the legislative body equally, or at all, depending on circumstances. Thus, any policy, law, or practice agreed to by members of a collective as appropriate, either through formal or informal means, can be similarly regarded.

Perhaps the most difficult type of collective action to analyze with respect to responsibility would be that committed by mobs or groups of individuals who do not seem to employ any kind of group decision-making procedure. Larry May argued in 1989 that even mobs, who tend to commit many actions without prior explicit agreement, are responsible for their actions because the actions are directed and fueled through experiences of identity shared by those in the mob.[34] Accepting this view entails that the so-called "Unite the Right" rallies and related events in Charlottesville, Virginia, in August of 2017, involved agreed-upon actions of an intentional collective, as well as other responses that were dictated by the events as they unfolded over time. What binds the collective to the harm created, according to May, is the shared identity and ideology of the participants, as well as the participants' failure to prevent those actions. So, a mob of individuals united by their cisgender identity and cis-supremacist ideology would be responsible if that identity and ideology combined in a way that resulted in violence against trans or gender non-conforming persons. This is a salient and relevant point in the context of anti-trans violence, since it is the kind of violence that is often perpetrated against trans and gender non-conforming persons who are simply attempting to participate as full members of our shared society. While there are countless examples of such collective violence against trans and gender non-conforming persons, the well-known case of CeCe McDonald comes to mind. Ms. McDonald and friends were simply walking to get a bite to eat at a grocery store when they were met by racist and anti-transgender remarks by a group of white individuals who were outside a bar. One of them, Dean Schmitz, began taunting Ms. McDonald. He jeered, "Look at that boy dressed like a girl."[35] Being identified as a "tranny" escalated the violence which eventually led to Ms. McDonald being hit with a glass of alcohol that badly split open her face and later required stitches.[36] The McDonald case is particularly relevant here since the group of individuals did not *plan* to harass and assault a Black trans woman that evening and had nothing personal against McDonald in particular. To the contrary, fueled by identity and ideology, they simply erupted in hateful racist and cissexist violence at the mere fact that McDonald and friends were walking by the bar. Readers who remember this case might recall that it gained notoriety because McDonald fought back against her attackers. In the end, Dean Schmitz was killed in what many believe were actions entirely of self-defense. Social outcry erupted as McDonald was charged and incarcerated for manslaughter, a deal that was struck as a plea bargain. This case, and many others, illustrate how violence against trans persons is often unplanned, unprovoked, directed by anti-trans animus, and fueled by racism and other oppressions. Even given the realities of sexism, if McDonald were white, cisgender, and wealthy, her efforts to defend herself would have probably been seen as valiant as opposed to blameworthy.

Responsibility: The Individual Case

As described in chapter 2, violence against trans persons, as measured by police statistics, has been on the rise since 2015. Nearly all of the reported homicide cases involve the murder of trans women of color. As was explained earlier in this chapter, backlash can be, and often is, directed toward those who are marginalized due to unjust structural oppressions or who are representative of a perceived change. Violence individually perpetrated against individual transgender persons can be reasonably understood as a kind of directed backlash against the greater acceptance of LGBTQ persons as a collective. Of course, individual cases can be quite different with regard to the motives of the violent perpetrators, but the fact that such rates of violence and harassment are increasing is reason to believe that they are not independent of the national climate, which has nurtured anti-transgender sentiment. Indeed, it is the politicization of trans identities and lives that puts all trans and gender non-conforming persons at increased risk. Nearly unbelievably, however, there are those who would wish to argue that certain violent crimes against transgender persons are not fully intentional and, as such, that the perpetrator is not fully responsible for the act and its consequences.

One way some have thought to justify a mitigation of responsibility for violent crimes is through arguing that the event is a "crime of passion." An unfortunate evolution of the "crime of passion" defense includes those arguments that evoke "gay panic" or "trans panic." It is the so-called "trans panic" defense that is crucial to our study here, but the evolution of this flawed reasoning is instructive. These arguments, in general, attempt to pick away at the *mens rea*, or criminal mental state, of the alleged perpetrator by arguing that they had no criminal intent and that the actions in question were produced by an unbridled emotional state that was beyond the reach of reason. The historically popular example of a crime of passion involves the responses of a man (presumably cisgender and heterosexual) who is surprised to come across his lover (the assumption is that she is a cisgender woman) having sexual intimacies with another (cis/het) man. It has been argued that in such circumstances, the surprised man will not be able to hold himself back from the rage that is assumed to overtake him, and thus he is not responsible for actions while in such a state (usually the murder of the woman or the man she is involved with or both). Those who accept this inappropriate characterization believe that his responsibility is mitigated, and, for the purpose of law, he lacks a criminal mind. This means that the action is not seen as intentional in the sense that it was not premeditated, but more like an automatic response, oddly more similar to a rifle backfiring than intentional human action. In such cases, it is not unusual for the charge to change from one of murder to the lesser offense of manslaughter.

The "gay panic" defense is a subcategory of this kind of "crime of passion" defense, in that it is argued that heterosexual (presumably cisgender) men are thrown into an emotionally unstable and dangerous state upon suspecting that another man is gay and/or is gay and possibly hitting on them. (I am not aware of any legal cases involving "lesbian panic" defenses, which itself is telling and related to the multiple consequences of the collective support of toxic masculinity.) Similar to the case described earlier, the idea is that the man attacking the suspected gay man is not fully liable for his actions since his mental state made him immune to reasonable choice-making. It is argued that the attacker did not plan the attack and, given the circumstances, could not help themselves from the violent response. This form of defense was partially and unsuccessfully used in the trial of Aaron McKinney and Russel Henderson, who were found guilty of brutally murdering Matthew Shepard in 1998, a case that eventually led to federal hate crime bills and a newly inspired attention to and condemnation of violence against the gay and lesbian community. (The Matthew Shepard Act, also called the Hate Crimes Prevention Act, was signed into law during the Obama administration in 2009, over a decade later.)

The "trans panic defense" is an outgrowth of the "gay panic defense" that was first articulated by Edward J. Kempf, a clinical psychiatrist who wished to identify a particular mental disorder related to homosexuality. It is important to note that the characterization of the disorder did not support the idea that "homosexual panic" would lead to and then justify violent behavior, but that is exactly how it has been used in the court of law. Instead, according to Kempf, the panic resulted from the internal struggle of an individual who experienced some same-sex attraction but recognized that society (and perhaps oneself, in the form of internalized homophobia) had an extremely negative attitude toward such attraction. "Homosexuality" itself was included in various versions of the Diagnostic and Statistical Manual of Mental Disorders (DSM) until 1973 and supported the related entry of "homosexual panic disorder" in the 1952 edition. After 1972, the gay panic defense lost even its extremely shaky foundation since both "homosexuality" and "homosexual panic disorder" were deleted from the DSM. Given this history, it is mystifying and unaccountable that it has continued to be used to attempt to mitigate responsibility for violent crimes against gay men as late as 2018.[37]

The "trans panic" defense does not even have the false and confused justification of the "gay panic" defense as employed prior to 1973, since there was never a "trans panic disorder," although it goes without saying that any characterization as a psychological disorder would be flawed. While the "gay panic" defense focuses on the effect of knowing an individual is gay or lesbian, seeing people engage in gay/lesbian sexual activity, or believing that a gay or lesbian person has romantic interest in oneself, the "trans panic" tends to involve the claim that it is the mere fact that a person is transgender that is deemed sufficient for one to not bear responsibility for violence. The film *The Crying Game*, mentioned in a previous chapter, is again instructive here. This film famously memorialized the notion that emotions of disgust and acts of violence are thought to *naturally* follow the recognition of another's trans status when the protagonist Fergus becomes physically ill at the sight of Dil's uncovered body and the recognition that she is transgender. Fergus, after vomiting in the bathroom, violently strikes her, his face contorted both with disgust and anger, and is entirely unable to access the tenderness he had shown her just moments before. This defense was employed in the case of Jennifer Laude, who, in 2014, was choked to death by US Marine Scott Pemberton, who sought to employ her as a sex worker. The high-profile cases of both Gwen Araujo and Angie Zapata also involved the "trans panic defense." In both cases their murderers claimed that seeing the women's genitals, non-consensually revealed, was sufficient to justify a lessening of the criminal charge.

Morgan Tilleman writes persuasively in "(Trans)forming the Provocation Defense" that the trans panic defense is wholly indefensible.[38] Tilleman focuses on dismantling the type of argument that relies on the claim that the perpetrator was provoked into violence by the transgender victim. As explained by the LGBT Bar Association, "The defense of provocation allows a defendant to argue that the victim's proposition, sometimes termed a 'non-violent sexual advance,' was sufficiently 'provocative' to induce the defendant to kill the victim."[39] The defense can also be used to argue that the defendant was made to be temporarily insane or have diminished capacity (due to the identity or body of the transgender person) or that the actions of the defendant should be seen as self-defense, since the individual's identity or body was sufficient reason to think that they were dangerous. It is this kind of claim of provocation that was appealed to by the attorneys of Allen Andrade in the brutal murder of Angie Zapata in 2008. Tilleman explains that the trans panic provocation defense must involve at least one of three different types of provocation, all of which rely on anti-transgender bias and faulty reasoning.

> Trans panic defenses often leave the exact provocation unstated, but the defense seems to break down into three possible "triggers," each of which could constitute the source of adequate provocation: (1) the victim's anatomical sex, (2) the revelation of the victim's anatomical sex, and (3) the victim's alleged act of "sexual deception."[40]

The trans panic defense is entirely indefensible. The first supposed provocation, that is, the victim's body itself, certainly cannot be used to justify the harm of murder or other harm perpetrated against a trans person; indeed, the defense makes the physical body itself sufficient excuse for violence. This form of defense requires no provocative act by the trans person her/him/themselves, but simply being a trans person with a particularly shaped body can reasonably be seen as provoking another into a state of violence or murderous rage. The acceptance of this defense is tantamount to justifying a full-scale attack on trans persons or any other persons whom another may "dislike," find "disgusting," or be "uncomfortable interacting with."[41]

The second possible trigger, the "revelation of the individual's anatomical sex," also fails as a justifiable defense for several reasons. First, in the types of highly publicized cases in which this defense has been used, it is the perpetrators themselves who forcibly reveal the individual's body without consent. Thus, argues Tilleman, there is no *act* of revelation on the part of the trans person. In both the Araujo and Zapata cases, the murderers suspected or already knew of the victim's gender history and thus cannot be said to have been "surprised" and thus provoked by the shape of their bodies. But if it were otherwise?

> Even in the hypothetical situation in which a transgender person affirmatively reveals his or her anatomical sex and thereby contributes to another person's murderous rage, that revelation should not constitute adequate provocation. Instead, it should be read as a speech act—what Nan Hunter calls "expressive identity."[42]

That is, if one were to reveal one's body purposely, and not just, say, in the process of getting dressed or undressed, the act could be understood as conveying a number of different messages, such as "Look how beautiful I am," or "See, I am trans," or, "How about a back rub?" or "I trust you with my body and my identity," or "Let's have sex." Perhaps it is the last two messages that Dil was sending Fergus in that scene of the film. None of these messages are provocation for violence since they do not "incorporate fighting words."[43] One is not sending a threatening message of promised violence or injury, but a message of intimacy and vulnerability.

Lastly, there is the claim that the transgender person deceived the attacker, and that this deception is the provocation for violence and murder. The idea that trans persons are deceivers has a long history and, as such, is a kind of excuse that is readily at hand for those who wish to attempt to justify anti-transgender violence. Recall the double bind of deceivers or make believers from Bettcher's work.[44] She writes,

> I want to be clear that far from "mere stereotype" or "ignorant misconception" this double bind between deception or pretense actually reflects the way in which transpeople can find ourselves literally "constructed" whether we like it or not. That is, if these are somehow "stereotypes," then they are "stereotypes" that we can find ourselves involuntarily animating.[45]

Of course, the claim of *deceiver* requires that there is something that one is being deceived *about*. In most cases, the claim of deception is thought to involve one's gender history or the shape of one's genitals. It is telling that the construction of "deceiver" was also used in arguments against historically early efforts to bring sexual predators to justice: Elizabeth Barnes notes, with regard to reform of sexual assault laws and the ensuing claims of deception, "The backlash against anti-rape measures came quickly, with physicians, judges, and defendants all quick to point to long-established narratives of female duplicity, deception and deceit."[46] The prevailing opinion at the time was that survivors of sexualized violence were either to blame for the attack or were lying about its occurrence. Another double bind.

The assumptions behind the use of the trans panic defense then is that either there is reason to assume that all individuals are cisgender and have predictably typical genitals, or that all who are not cisgender have the duty to constantly announce that fact to individuals they come in contact with to prevent the cisgenderist assumption and the violence that is tied to this assumption. Again, problematically, it is the presumption of being cisgender on the part of the would-be attacker that is, for this claim to work, thought to be a necessary and sufficient condition for the other individual to be seen as actively deceptive. This clearly not only implies impractical and dangerous duties to those who are transgender, but also requires the belief that cisgender status and only typically shaped bodies are appropriate, relegating trans individuals to socially deceiving abnormalities who are attempting to "steal" the privileges of cisgender persons.

Even in the midst of an intimate setting, there is no obligation to discuss one's gender history, and thus no fraud (required for the legal claim of deception) occurs. For a claim of fraud to obtain, argues Tilleman, one's genital shape or gender history must constitute a "material fact" that one is obligated to reveal, but no such material fact is relevant here. Either the shape of one's genitals is immaterial to the sex act (e.g., oral sex doesn't necessarily involve the genitalia of both partners) or there can be no deception or fraud since the shape of one's genitals is obvious to the other party.[47] To claim that one is obligated to discuss the details of one's history and body would mean that it would be necessary to identify if one is or is not a virgin, is or is generally not orgasmic, has or does not have a penis of a certain length or width, etc. Indeed, accepting this view means that nearly all sexual experience related to sexuality, including experiences of sexual assault, would be obligatory revelations. Furthermore, if one were to unreasonably accept such obligations, there would be no reason to believe that this duty to reveal would be specific to trans and not cisgender persons. Writes Tilleman, "One party's preferences do not impose any obligation on others to voluntarily disclose their anatomical sex, any more than a person is obligated to disclose any other relevant genital characteristic."[48]

Most basically, trans panic defense strategies result in condoning and even encouraging violence against LGBTQ individuals, resulting in a failure to protect the most basic rights of those individuals. As such, it is contrary to any stated value of equal rights under the law. Additionally, since the basis of the defense is that one's identity, history, or physical body are so abhorrent as to incite harassment or even fatal violence, these most important aspects of oneself are quite literally used against the individual. When these kinds of defenses are used, it is the wronged individual who comes to be seen as answerable to the violence perpetrated against them. The actual perpetrator is seen not as a thinking, rational agent capable of cool reflection, but as an embodiment of society's thought-to-be predictable negative psychological reaction towards another's sexual orientation or gender history. The trans panic defense is at odds with any semblance of support for the idea that trans persons are as morally valuable as are those who are cisgender, and instead supports the notion that trans individuals are abominations responsible for our own oppression. The American Bar Association, in their Resolution 113A (passed in 2013), are unequivocal in their condemnation of the trans and gay panic defense; such defenses have been banned in eight states and such bans have been introduced in seven more. Neither one's gender identity or history, nor one's sexual orientation, can be seen as a sufficient cause for a potential perpetrator to have diminished capacity to reason, a kind of temporary and triggered insanity. Thus, the crime is fully intentional. As such, those who perpetrate violence against trans persons, whether as part of a backlash response or independent of such, are, barring relevant contingencies, fully responsible for their actions.

CONSIDERATIONS OF SCOPE

The last descriptor of backlash to be considered here is that of scope. Simply put, some backlash responses are more or less expansive, both with respect to the diversity of targets and the severity of the response directed at any given target. Recall from the introduction to this chapter when an example of backlash was characterized as a backlash against analytic philosophy. Given that few individuals understand the discipline of philosophy in general, or that there are different subcategories such as analytic and continental, this means that, to the extent that the term "backlash" applies, it would be a phenomenon of limited scope. This can be compared to the racist backlash that took the form of Jim Crow laws that employed the force of law and other terrorizing tactics to perpetrate grave moral harms against African Americans living in affected areas. It is obvious then, assuming the backlash response is harm-causing, that the greater the scope of the backlash, the greater potential for harm. In the context of anti-transgender backlash and the politicization of trans identity, the backlash response has included proposed and enacted legislation; exclusionary military policies; hate responses targeted at trans persons whose identity is publicized via different media venues; policies in the contexts of medical care and education; increased violence perpetrated against individuals; verbal disavowals by political, social, and religious leaders;

the targeting of trans-advocacy groups (for example, the preeminent transgender rights organization, the National Center for Transgender Equality, received numerous bomb threats in 2019);[49] the use of political and judicial appointments for the purpose of rolling back or limiting civil rights and social participation; and lack of prohibition of discrimination or a denial that discrimination laws apply. The list can also include the targeting of Supreme Court justices who ruled in favor of Obergefell in 2015. The harms of these activities are identifiable physical and psychological harms: increased stress and suicidality, feelings of being terrorized, discrimination, lack of opportunity and any reasonable expectation of safety, social isolation, and others. It is important to note that these harms affect individual trans persons as well as our families, friends, and both personal and national communities. While it can be argued that a response directed at changing the law via the courts is far more acceptable than targeted violence, this claim only involves the *direction* not the *content* of the response. The next two chapters are devoted to analysis and application of the concept of scapegoating. Scapegoating, like dog-whistling, can be seen as a tool of the broader backlash response.

NOTES

1. Jeremy D. Mayer, "Nixon Rides the Backlash to Victory: Racial Politics in the 1968 Presidential Campaign," *Historian* 62, no. 2 (Winter 2002): 351–356.

2. Susan Faludi, *Backlash: The Undeclared War against American Women* (New York: Crown, 1991).

3. Sherry Vint, "The New Backlash: Popular Culture's 'Marriage' with Feminism, or Love Is All You Need," *Journal of Popular Film and Television* 34, no. 4 (Winter 2007).

4. Guiseppina D'Oro, "The Ontological Backlash: Why Did Mainstream Analytic Philosophy Lose Interest in the Philosophy of History?," *Philosophia* 36, no. 4 (December 2008).

5. John R. Wood, "Reservations in Doubt: The Backlash against Affirmative Action in Gujarat, India," *Public Affairs* 60 (Fall 1987): 408–430.

6. See chapter 2 for further details.

7. Don Wildmon, AFA website, 1999 (still posted as of August 2019).

8. Gary Glenn, president of the Michigan chapter of AFA, 2001. From SPLC web page, https://www.splcenter.org/fighting-hate/extremist-files/group/american-family-association.

9. Tim Gilson, "Transgenderism: The Fastest-Growing Insanity the World Has Ever Seen," *Stream Magazine*, https://stream.org/transgenderism-fastest-growing-insanit/.

10. Muri Assunção, "Ohio Lawmaker Blames Trans People, Open Borders, Gay Marriage, Drag Queen Advocates, for Deadly Mass Shootings," *New York Daily News*, August 5, 2019, https://www.nydailynews.com/news/politics/ny-candice

-keller-gop-ohio-blames-gay-marriage-transgender-drag-queen-20190805-rftgwkvvt5ehpgp3daboujo2ry-story.html.

11. Elizabeth Barnes, "Justice, at What Cost?," *History Today* 68 (December 2018).

12. Barnes, 10.

13. King-Kok Cheung, "(Mis)Interpretations and (In)Justice: The 1992 Los Angeles 'Riots' and 'Black-Korean' Conflict," *Melus* 3, no. 30 (Fall 2005): 3–40.

14. Kyung Lah, "The L.A. Riots Were a Rude Awakening for Korean Americans," April 29, 2017, CNN, accessed September 9, 2019, https://www.cnn.com/2017/04/28/us/la-riots-korean-americans/index.html.

15. George M. Fredrickson, *Racism: A Short History* (Princeton, NJ: Princeton University Press, 2003).

16. Not to say that religious based arguments are not still relevant when considering certain subgroups, both within and outside the US.

17. C. Riley Snorton, *Black on Both Sides: A Racial History of Trans Identity* (Minneapolis: University of Minnesota Press, 2017).

18. Snorton, 178.

19. Muska and Olafdottir, *Brandon Teena Story*, quoted in Snorton, 182.

20. Snorton, 185.

21. George Yancy, *Backlash: What Happens When We Talk Honestly about Racism in America* (Lanham, MD: Rowman & Littlefield, 2018).

22. Yancy, 19.

23. Yancy, 21.

24. Yancy, 21.

25. W. E. B. Du Bois, *The Souls of Black Folks* (Chicago: A. C. McClurg, 1931), 2.

26. Fred Dreier, "The Complicated Case of Transgender Cyclist, Dr. Rachel McKinnon," *Velo News*, October 18, 2018, https://www.velonews.com/2018/10/news/commentary-the-complicated-case-of-transgender-cyclist-dr-rachel-mckinnon_480285.

27. Ann E. Cudd, "Analyzing Backlash to Progressive Social Movements" in *Theorizing Backlash: Philosophical Reflections on the Resistance to Feminism* (Lanham, MD: Rowman & Littlefield, 2002).

28. Cudd, 13.

29. Cudd, 5.

30. Gwen Ifill, "Widespread Backlash to Donald Trump's Muslim Ban," *Washington Week*, December 11, 2015, https://www.pbs.org/weta/washingtonweek/episode/widespread-backlash-donald-trumps-proposed-muslim-ban.

31. Steven Sverdlik, "Collective Responsibility," *Philosophical Studies: An International Journal for Philosophy in the Analytic Tradition* 51, no. 1 (January 1987): 61–76, 63.

32. Peter French, *Collective and Corporate Responsibility* (New York: Columbia University Press, 1984).

33. See https://legiscan.com/TX/bill/SB17/2019 and https://www.hrc.org/blog/texas-state-senate-passes-discriminatory-anti-lgbtq-bill.

34. Larry May, "Mobs and Collective Responsibility," *Social PhilosophyToday: Freedom, Equality, and Social Change* 2 (1989): 300–311.

35. Nicole Pasulka, "The Case of CeCe McDonald: Murder—or Self-Defense against a Hate Crime?," *Mother Jones*, May 22, 2012, https://www.motherjones.com/politics/2012/05/cece-mcdonald-transgender-hate-crime-murder/.

36. "Oh, look at the tranny over there, look at that tranny." Andy Mannix, "CeCe McDonald Murder Trial: Behind the Scenes of the Transgender Woman's Case," May 9, 2012, *CityPages*, https://web.archive.org/web/20140114115204/http://www.citypages.com/2012-05-09/news/cece-mcdonald-murder-trial/2/.

37. See case of Daniel Spencer (2015), https://lgbtbar.org/programs/advocacy/gay-trans-panic-defense/.

38. Morgan Tilleman, "(Trans)forming the Provocation Defense," *Journal of Criminal Law and Criminology* 100, no. 4 (2010).

39. See https://lgbtbar.org/programs/advocacy/gay-trans-panic-defense/.

40. Tilleman, 1673.

41. Victoria L. Steinberg, as quoted by Tilleman, 1674.

42. Nan Hunter, "Expressive Identity: Recuperating Dissent for Equality," *Harvard Civil Rights–Civil Liberties Law Review* 35 (2000): 1–55, as quoted by Tilleman, 1676.

43. Tilleman, 1676.

44. Talia Mae Bettcher, "Evil Deceivers and Make Believers: On Transphobic Violence and the Politics of Illusion," *Hypatia* 22, no. 3 (Summer 2007):

45. Bettcher, 50.

46. Barnes, 10.

47. Tilleman, 1678.

48. Tilleman, 1679.

49. Bill Browning, "National Center for Transgender Equality Has Endured Multiple Bomb Threats Over the Past Year," *LGBTQ Nation*, August 29, 2019, Referenced, September 11, 2019, https://www.cnn.com/2017/04/28/us/la-riots-korean-americans/index.html.

Chapter 5

Scapegoating

The Over-Blaming Account

In the previous chapter, the concept of backlash was characterized as a kind of collective response. To claim it is a response is to imply that is a response to *something*, and in this case it is a response to that which is seen as inappropriate, imprudent, wrong-headed, ill-advised, or perhaps immoral. In most cases, it is possible to identify that which catalyzed the response, although in the messy context of human interaction and culture, absolute precision is impossible. Moreover, backlash is a *directed* response. It can be directed *at* individuals or groups of individuals and, as will be discussed in the next few chapters, it can be directed *by* individuals or groups of individuals as well. Backlash can be directed at particular individuals or towards groups through the use of legislation meant to undermine the flourishing of group members, through violence directed at group members, as well as through official and unofficial invisibilizing tactics meant to reduce visibility and thus empathy for group members and eliminate knowledge of their existence and moral value. Because of the variety of ways that collectives and individuals can respond to potentially backlash-inducing events, my characterization of the term is quite broad.

The notion of a "scapegoat" or the act of "scapegoating" is, like that of backlash, a term with which many have familiarity. Most, if queried, could rattle off at least a couple of examples of scapegoating. Perhaps the treatment of Jews by Hitler's Nazi regime might, especially for those of a certain age, be the first example that comes to mind. Scapegoating, as well as its newly characterized cousin, dog-whistling, can be part of a backlash response. We have already discussed backlash responses that include targeting particular populations in various ways. Using scapegoating tactics can be part of a backlash and used to dehumanize and devalue those of particular identities, histories, ethnicities, experiences, or expressions. For example, morally progressive movements that assert the claim "those of community X are valuable and full moral members of our society" can be responded to by claiming that those of community X are responsible for the ills in the broader society, which might include economic struggles, crime rates, child endangerment, or even a dramatic moral decline, thought to lead to the end of the society itself. All too often, such assertions are bolstered by claims that society is weakened by those of community X due to their alleged negative character traits, including such qualities as being dangerous, immoral, lazy, greedy, sick, monstrous, violent, deranged, selfish, etc. In these ways, stereotypes are used, created, and reinforced as a means to justify the claim of blameworthiness that is an important aspect of scapegoating behavior.

In my view, backlash, scapegoating, and dog-whistling can work together toward a common end, and both scapegoating and dog-whistling can be seen as kinds of directed backlash. These three phenomena can work together in various ways, and the recent politicization of trans expressions and identities is related to these three notions. This chapter will offer one way of characterizing scapegoating, one that is analytic in nature and centered around the notion of blameworthiness, or more precisely, an excess of unjustified blame. This view of backlash was first introduced by Gregory Mellema, and I use his general approach but expand his original offering to include four distinct types of scapegoating, still within his general rubric. After an identification of these types, along with clarifying examples meant to support the notion that these kinds of scapegoating strategies are not uncommon, I then offer examples that illustrate how trans persons have been scapegoated in these relevant ways. An alternative characterization of scapegoating is offered in chapter 6.

SCAPEGOATING

An analysis of the notion of scapegoating can be carried out through at least three different conceptual approaches. First, one can focus on the notion of blame as a foundational aspect of the concept. An example of this can be found in the essay "Scapegoats," by Gregory Mellema; this will be the focus of this chapter.[1] Second, particularly since scapegoating is historically so ubiquitous, one can focus on a sociological or even linguistic explanation and analysis of scapegoating episodes. Few theorists have written more on scapegoating than René Girard. Girard's work blurs the boundaries between anthropology, philosophy, hermeneutics, literary critique, and religious studies in his thorough treatment of scapegoating as a regular phenomenon of human society. A Girardian approach will be featured in the next chapter. Lastly, scapegoating can be analyzed by focusing on an investigation of power dynamics between groups. In order to be successful, scapegoating others requires a difference in power dynamic between those scapegoated and those characterizing the scapegoat as blameworthy or undesirable. Such a power imbalance allows this narrative to be popularized in the community, especially the dominant subcommunity from which the stigmatizing narratives originate. This kind of power dynamic is relevant to scapegoating in general and also to the practice of dog-whistling in particular, the topic of chapter 7.

FOCUS ON BLAMEWORTHINESS: S-B SCAPEGOATING

Mellema's characterization of a scapegoat is "a person . . . being blamed for something more than he or she deserves and that some blame could or should in all fairness be directed at others."[2] For ease of later reference, this characterization of scapegoating will be referred to as S-B (scapegoating through claims of blameworthiness). Mellema presents the following schema:

X makes Y a scapegoat only if:

1. S is a state of affairs which has occurred or is widely believed to have occurred.
2. X forms a judgment (or otherwise imputes guilt or blame) that Y is blameworthy for S's occurrence.
3. X's judgment exaggerates the degree to which Y is blameworthy for S's occurrence.
4. X's judgment understates the extent to which X knows (or truly believes) that others contributed to S's (actual or alleged) occurrence.[3]

Most obviously, the S-B account rests on an incorrect belief or report of blameworthiness, however the question of intentionality can vary with context. For example, statement two implies that X has come to a particular judgment, a belief of blameworthiness. Accepting that one does not believe something they know to be untrue (even though they might dishonestly tell others they believe it is true), there is the assumption here that this initial belief is in "good faith." It is a belief that X can be mistaken about, but X is not actively attempting to distort what they know to be the truth. The second stipulation of these schema allows the exaggeration of blameworthiness to be intentional. That is, X intentionally scapegoats Y through this exaggeration and also through the understatement that others are also responsible for the event in question. Those that intentionally scapegoat another are not making merely an intellectual mistake of misunderstanding the situation, but are actively targeting another for blameworthiness and harm and intentionally misleading others to also accept the belief. Assuming that the agent in some way benefits from their scapegoating scheme, they are, contra Kant, using another as a mere means to an end. This kind of action is closely tied to the concept of dog-whistling, as characterized by Ian Haney-López, which will be the focus of chapter 7. Intentionally leading certain others into scapegoating or using dog whistles means that one is responsible not only for misleading others, but for the predictable harm to the individuals being scapegoated.

On the other hand, one can unintentionally scapegoat another individual or group of individuals. Mellema clarifies that this can happen through a case of mistaken identity—one thought they were scapegoating Y but it was Z that instead was being unnecessarily blamed. It is also very possible that one goes along with the claims of X or others and simply believes that they are not scapegoating Y, but that Y is blameworthy in the way suggested by X. In such a case the individual that goes along may not have adequately investigated their own biases with regard to Y. They failed to ask themselves why it was so easy to believe that Y was blameworthy as claimed? Is sexism, racism, classism, transphobia, or transmisogyny at play here? Are all of these biased systems being employed at once? Additionally, the person going along with the scapegoater may simply be intellectually lazy and unconcerned that they believe claims on insufficient evidence, or too distracted to actually look into the veracity of the claim. As will be clearly explained in the next chapter, those that are scapegoated are generally those that certain others already have biases against, and the scapegoater is weaponizing those biases for personal gain.

One can see by Mellema's schema, particularly statement four, that his account of scapegoating is primarily focused on events collectively authored and the contexts in which only a subset of that collective, maybe a single individual, is found disproportionately blameworthy for the event. I believe it is quite reasonable to broaden this view to include events that are not collectively authored. Indeed, such cases seem relatively common when thinking of when leaders attempt to place the blame on their subordinates for their own personal foils. Being found responsible for a harm or untoward event generally, or being blamed for that event, is most often something folks prefer to avoid. Those with enough power often try to find ways to get out of such disagreeable contexts by scapegoating others, even when, contrary to Mellema's schema, the act is by an individual. Numerous examples come to mind, when those in power intentionally scapegoat a subordinate, with the hope of avoiding answering to their own individually authored actions.

S-B Scapegoating: Four Types

If we generally follow Mellema's lead in a kind of S-B analysis, it seems clear that there are at least four ways that an individual or a group can be scapegoated. All involve inappropriate blame and, often tied with that, inappropriate and unjust response or punishment. First, an individual or a group can be blamed for something in excess of what is just, even when they do bear at least some limited responsibility for the untoward event. Consider cases in which a collective is responsible for an act, yet only one individual of the collective is blamed (again, Mellema seems to be thinking primarily of these types of cases). For example, consider a group of graffiti artists who all scatter when they see the oncoming police car, except for one artist, *Skyler*, who is too focused on their design to notice the arrival of the police. In this kind of instance, Skyler is a kind of scapegoat for the collectively authored crime when they are blamed disproportionately to their shared contribution to the act. Of course, there are contextual considerations that are relevant in all cases of scapegoating. In cases such as this, scapegoating may be more likely to occur if there has been a great deal of pressure from the local community to apprehend the graffiti artists and the police are thought to be inadequately handling what is seen as property damage. Skyler may receive disproportional blame and punishment as a way of "setting an example" for those who in the future might consider engagement in similar public expressions or, as we will consider in more detail later, if Skyler is representative of a marginalized collective. We can call this type of S-B scapegoating *type 1*.

The second kind of S-B scapegoating involves an individual or a group being inappropriately blamed for something for which they share no responsibility. If we slightly change the example above, assume it is not the case that *Skyler* simply was too focused on their work to flee as did their friends, but that they were simply innocently walking by the scene when the police cruiser arrived. Real-life examples of this kind of scapegoating unfortunately abound. The most famous case to come to mind is that of the "Exonerated Five," the five men previously known as the "Central Park Five," who were unjustly found guilty for the assault and rape of a white woman jogger, Trisha Meili, in New York's Central Park in 1989. Antron McCray, Kevin Richardson, Yosef Salaam, Raymond Santana, and Kory Wise, aged fourteen to sixteen, were exonerated after the real rapist came forward in 2003. Matias Reyes confessed to the crime and his DNA matched that which was found at the scene, which was sufficient to set the individuals, by that time men, free. Context is important here as well. As is obvious by a consideration of the facts of the case, structural and individual racism, of the police department, the judicial system, and the press, further inflamed by racist public outcry, resulted in the innocent youth being blamed, convicted, and imprisoned.

The historic trope of the innocent white woman being attacked by men of color that was directed as a weapon against the Exonerated Five has been used to unjustly punish men of color for hundreds of years. At times it has even been used when the accuser is actually the blameworthy party, as in the case of Susan Smith in 1994. Smith reported that a Black man car-jacked her Mazda with her two children in the back seat. She pleaded for the fictionalized abductor to return her children, when it was actually Smith herself who had drowned them by submerging her car into a local lake. Undoubtedly, this is not the only example of such a ruse; perhaps such cases should be called "attempted intentional scapegoating."

The previous two types of S-B scapegoating cases involve an actual harm or untoward event for which a group or an individual is inappropriately blamed. Either they are blamed in excess of what is otherwise fair based on their personal contribution, or they are blamed even though they bear no responsibility for the event in question. While these cases are undoubtedly morally reprehensible, it is even more disturbing to recognize that there have been numerous cases of scapegoating *without any* antecedent untoward event, and it is these types of S-B scapegoating that comprise our third type. Here, the event used to justify the scapegoating may be consciously fabricated or simply a function of wholly biased and irrational thinking. In these cases, individuals may believe that such an event has occurred based on scanty evidence, bias, prejudice, or a belief in harmful stereotypes. This, coupled with an incautious desire to see someone answer for the fictional harm, leads one to erroneously placing unjustified blame on those already marginalized. Unfortunately, a list of examples is again easy to produce. The previous two examples involved anti-Black racism and the employment of the false and racist narrative that Black men and boys are dangerous and likely to be sexual predators. The Scottsboro Boys trials in 1931 and the tragic death of Emmett Till in 1955 are two examples of innocent individuals being blamed and punished for fictionalized offenses. In the case of Emmett Till, the fictionalized "offense" was an account of him making advances toward a white woman. Till made no such advances, but, of course, such should not be considered an offense in the first place. Similarly, nine young men, "The Scottsboro Boys," were accused of raping two white women, an event that never actually occurred and for which at least one accuser eventually recanted. The unjust treatment of Charlie Weems, Ozie Powell, Clarence Norris, Andrew and Leroy Wright, Olen Montgomery, Willie Roberson, Haywood Patterson, and Eugene Williams was simply reprehensible. That fact that their immoral and biased treatment eventually resulted in the Supreme Court ruling that all accused have the right to adequate counsel and that juries need to be racially diverse does little to justify the harms experienced.

While anti-Black racism and the demonization of Black and Brown men is the context for many of these types of scapegoating episodes, as in the previous type just considered, other contexts exist as well. From the blaming of the Jews for "torturing" the communion host in the Middle Ages, to the Salem Witch Trials in 1692, to the internment of Japanese Americans during WWII, unjust treatment is built upon the belief in the guilt of the scapegoat as a dangerous outsider, and it is this outsider status that is seen as related to being morally or criminally responsible for the act in question. In most cases, common stereotypes about marginalized persons are sufficient to deliver such plausible belief to the privileged and epistemologically reckless majority in power.

The fourth and last kind of case of S-B scapegoating occurs when an individual or a group is blamed for an event for which they did somehow participate, but that the event or participation in question is not at all blameworthy in nature. Consider the cruel legacy of US and Canadian schools that contributed to a cultural genocide of Indigenous people by making it against the rules for Indigenous children to participate in their traditional cultural practices or even speak their own language. Clearly, contrary to such practices, it is not blameworthy to participate in one's heritage and culture, speak one's own language, and resist colonization. Rather, it is laudable, heroic, and valuable to do so. It is both a basic human right and even much more than that, since this infringement of an individual right has ramifications for the rights of the collective, past, present, and future. Infringements of cultural rights represent serious multilayered harms. All S-B type 4 cases involve individuals being blamed for certain events that did take place but that participation in these events is not blameworthy, and is at times even praiseworthy. Thus, scapegoating can occur when others accept a narrative that an action is blameworthy, but in reality, the event itself is valuable, meaningful, or simply morally neutral. Prohibitions against cross-dressing, infringements of gender norms, or looking "too gay" involve persecution of others and collectives for actions that are not just morally neutral but laudable.

S-B SCAPEGOATING AND TRANS AND GENDER NON-CONFORMING PERSONS

Assuming that the above taxonomy is useful, how does this apply to transgender and gender non-conforming persons in the US? Evidence suggests that individual trans, gender non-conforming, and gender non-binary persons of different positionalities have been scapegoated in ways relevantly similar to the examples and schema just offered. First, consider the harms perpetrated on incarcerated trans persons that are over and above their court-ordered sentences. Assuming that those judicial sentences are morally justified in the first place (big assumption), in addition to "serving their time," incarcerated trans individuals are forced to endure a litany of institution-supported injustices. Trans persons who are incarcerated are subject to assault and sexualized violence from other prisoners and prison staff, medical care is often withheld, and solitary confinement is often employed—not for reasons related to the individual's misdeeds in the prison environment, but as a result of prison officials being unwilling to do what is necessary to keep the individuals safe and an apathy towards these harms. This apathy and even animus is evidence not just of bias but deep dehumanization. Solitary confinement is well known to be one of the most harmful types of punishments ever perpetrated against a fellow human being, one that can produce long-term, serious, unjustified harm.

Having one's actual experienced punishment be far and above one's sentence is also evident in the juvenile justice system. Wesley Ware, in "Rounding up the Homosexuals: The Impact of Juvenile Court on Queer and Trans/Gender-Non-Conforming Youth," brings evidence to exactly this conclusion.[4] As with their adult counterparts, queer, trans, gender non-conforming, or non-binary youth fall victim to institutionally instantiated policies and entrenched practices that result in an enhancement, intensification, and prolonging of punishment. With regard to the latter, Ware reports that sufficient rehabilitation is thought to include rehabilitation of *character* thought to be measured by one's conformity to traditional gender norms. "Guised under the 'best interest of the child,' the goal often becomes to 'protect' the child—or perhaps society—from gender-variant or non-heterosexual behavior."[5] Ware explains,

> Even more troubling, unlike the adult criminal justice system where individuals either "ride out their time" or work toward "good time" or parole, youth's privileges in prison and eventual release dates are often determined by their successful completion of their rehabilitative programming, including relationships with peers and staff. Thus, youth who are seen as "deviant" or "mentally ill," or who otherwise do not conform to the rules are denied their opportunity for early release. In fact, in the last four years of advocacy on behalf of queer and trans youth in prison in Louisiana at the Juvenile Justice Project of Louisiana, not one openly queer or trans youth has been recommended for an early release by the Office of Juvenile Justice.[6]

Many have written about the school-to-prison pipeline, giving evidence that children of color and/or disabled children are funneled into the prison system by the policies and practices of their K–12 educational institutions. Such practices curtail learning, life chances, and the flourishing of individuals and communities. Related to scapegoating as described here, the use of the term "pipeline" is meant to convey the inappropriate targeting of some youth for more serious punishment than is just and the failure to attend to their lived experiences in ways that are supportive rather than dismissive of serious challenges and barriers to learning and thriving. There has been less written about a school-to-prison pipeline for queer, trans, gender non-conforming, and non-binary youth of various positionalities, but some work in this area is beginning to be published, such as Snapp et al.'s "Messy, Butch, and Queer: LGBTQ Youth and the School-to-Prison Pipeline."[7] This study supports Ware's assertion that LGBTQ youth are overrepresented in the juvenile justice population. Specifically, they make up 5–7 percent of the general population but 13–15 percent of the incarcerated juvenile population.[8] Additionally, there is evidence that LGBTQ students are more likely to be detained for nonviolent infractions like running away, being late for school, or prostitution at levels twice that of their cisgender and heterosexual peers.[9]

According to Snapp et al., there are various pathways by which LGBTQ students are pushed out of school and, as a result, more likely find themselves under the control of the juvenile justice system. Two of these pathways include being punished for violating traditional gender norms and being punished for attempting to defend themselves against bullies, both of which fit into the third type of scapegoating identified earlier. Homelessness is the all-too-common experience of queer and trans youth experiencing rejection by their birth family. One of the ramifications of homelessness is that students are over-blamed for infractions or fictionalized infractions of school policy or civil law.[10]

Violating gender norms can not only make one a target of harmful bullying but can also mark one as a general troublemaker who is likely to be non-conforming to school policy. Participants in the study remarked that merely being gender non-conforming can lead to over-blaming and over-punishing of students above what is reasonable. One participant reported,

> I've seen a great deal of students who have been pushed out [of school] because they are perceived to be LGBT or are. I've noticed that [for] the gender non-conforming females who may want to dress in more male gender-based clothing. The level of punishment may be much more severe than a gender conforming student who can have just as much of a strong temperament. But this [gender non-conforming] person makes other people uncomfortable, and level of suspension may come at a faster and higher rate.[11]

The asymmetry of gender norms that, depending on context, generally cisgender girls and women can more often bend such norms without social disapproval, means that gender infractions affect gendernon-conforming youth very differently.¹² For example, students assigned male at birth are more likely to be punished for being gender non-conforming because of exceedingly narrow expectations of what is considered suitably masculine. Snapp et al. describe the story of one student, Nathaniel, who was suspended for merely wearing hair extensions, thus employing a double standard since many students who were assigned female at birth were allowed to wear them.¹³ Alternatively, students assigned female at birth may come under added scrutiny if they bend gender norms and may be more likely to be seen as a troublemaker who is guilty of other rule infractions. Consider the following testimony:

> The teachers . . . they thought we were selling weed in school, they thought that me and her were both selling weed 'cause like, the way we were dressing, 'cause we were the only girls at that middle school that dressed like boys. So, it was like "now we're bad."¹⁴

Being already labeled as a troublemaker makes it much more likely that one will be blamed in excess of one's responsibility. Thus, a pipeline is created that begins with over-blame in the school, then ostracism and further "acting out," and may lead to eventual interaction with the juvenile court system.

Experiencing bullying is another context in which there are multiple reports of school personnel over-blaming and punishing children who are simply attempting to keep themselves safe in an often-toxic environment. Zero-tolerance policies can result in not just the abuser but the abused being suspended or expelled even when there is only defensive action being exhibited, even just that of putting one's hands over one's head.¹⁵ Multiple studies support the claim that gender non-conforming and trans students experience bullying at worrisome levels. The always helpful school climate reports of the organization GLSEN report that trans and gender non-conforming students receive even more harassment than those who are LGBQ but not trans, gender non-conforming, or gender non-binary. According to their 2019 report, harassment of gender non-conforming and transgender students spiked in the year 2017, corresponding to a spike in proposed anti-transgender legislation and the accompanying politicization of trans identities.¹⁶ In the event that the youth has evidence that they are not going to be protected by school personnel, they may realize that it is up to themselves to put up a fight or risk being hurt even worse. There is a possible chain of events, described by one participant in Snapp's study:

> It's pushing them to this point where "you're not protecting me," "you're not listening to me," and so "I have to fight back on my own." And when they fight back, "boom, now you did something so we can kick you out."¹⁷

Rejection by family, an all-too-common experience for LGBTQ youth, is often an antecedent condition for unjust punishment. Youth who have become homeless due to family rejection are picked up due to simply being homeless, on suspicion of participating in survival sex work or infractions of drug laws, and thus enter the juvenile justice system with sometimes few means of a speedy exit. As Snapp et al. describe it,

> They were on the streets because they'd been kicked out of their homes. . . . They were getting picked up for hustling, but more often than not they were just getting picked up because they were homeless youth on the street.[18]

The first two types of S-B scapegoating identified can occur when the claims of blameworthiness are out of proportion to the agent's responsibility; when the punishment, in practice, constitutes an exaggeration of blameworthiness; or when one is blamed for something for which they are not responsible at all. There is numerous evidence that all three types exist with regard to both trans and gender non-conforming youth, as well as adults. From being held in penal institutions contrary to one's identity and safety, to unjust treatment while incarcerated, to cases in which trans persons are given sentences in excess to their blameworthiness (recall the CeCe McDonald case, in which her attempts at self-defense were punished by a forty-one-month prison sentence), to transgender and gender non-conforming students who are more apt to be blamed and are sometimes eventually pushed out of school due to their identity and expression, there are numerous cases to indicate that trans and gender non-conforming individuals are over-blamed, thus exemplifying S-B scapegoating of the first and second type.

The third and fourth types of S-B scapegoating—which occur either when an individual or a group is blamed for a fabricated event, or when the event in question actually occurred but is not a reason for an ascription of blame to those responsible—are also experienced by trans and gender non-conforming persons. While "pure" cases of this third and fourth type exist, more often we see examples in which a kind of intersection of these two types obtain. That is, an event does occur, but the event is mischaracterized as something that is blameworthy. Unfortunately, and tellingly, sometimes the alleged blameworthiness of the event is related to the fact that a trans or gender non-conforming person plays a role in the event. Consider the harassment and abuse that philosopher and world-champion cyclist Veronica Ivy was subject to as a result of her winning her division in the UCI Masters World Track Cycling Championship. Professor Ivy is responsible for her win, but her achievement has been distorted by some into a case of "cheating" even though she diligently followed all rules and requirements of USA Cycling. This case gained prominence in October 2019 when the president's son, Donald Trump Jr., tweeted that he was "Sorry to all the female athletes who spent their lives mastering their games."[19] Ivy is not being suitably praised for her athletic accomplishments, but instead has been blamed for a distorted mischaracterization of the event, an event of cheating that never in fact occurred. The fact that the president's son used what should be celebrated as an impressive win as an opportunity to support transphobia and trans scapegoating is just one piece of evidence of how the politicization of trans identities affect blameless individuals.

Fairly winning cycling championships is not the only kind of action that can be mischaracterized and used as justification to blame trans persons for otherwise non-blameworthy events. Consider the experience of trans women who are unjustly targeted by the police as prostitutes based on the contents of their purse. These kinds of policies and practices were investigated in four US cities—New York, Washington, DC, Los Angeles, and San Francisco—and the results were published in the *Journal for the International Aids Society*.

> Our research indicated that in all four cities, police stopped, searched, and arrested people involved, or believed to be involved, in sex work using possession of condoms as evidence of intent to engage in prostitution-related offenses. Though few prostitution or loitering cases proceed to trial, prosecutors in New York, Los Angeles, and San Francisco have introduced condoms as evidence of prostitution-related offenses in criminal court.[20]

Carrying condoms in one's purse is not a blameworthy activity, but this action becomes distorted and is falsely believed to imply thought-to-be criminal activity. As one New Orleans trans woman describes her experience, "In the French Quarter I was at [a bar] with a man and the cops asked only the trans women to go outside and they searched us. If we had condoms we got arrested for attempted solicitation."[21]

The investigation was conducted in 2013, when such reports of guilt being inferred from condom possession was just beginning to get some attention. Despite the publicity and investigation given to this matter then, there is evidence that it has continued to be a problem. New York City, in an effort to crack down on sex trafficking, increased its police presence and also its arrest rate of suspected sex workers. As can be unfortunately predicted, trans women are being unduly targeted, whether or not they are engaged in the profession. Indeed, the crime of "walking while trans" means that trans women are harassed, unjustly arrested, and often then victims of abuse from NYPD personnel. According to investigative reporter Emma Whitford, certain areas of town that tend to have a relatively large population of women who are trans are regularly "swept" by NYPD's vice squad, making foot travel or even socializing in public putting oneself at risk of being picked up. Whitford reports,

> Trans women are often assumed to be sex workers, yet police officers don't see them as victims worthy of protection; the stigma surrounding sex work is compounded by the stigma surrounding their gender identity. Efforts to protect and bolster trans rights have yet to affect the NYPD in any meaningful way.[22]

I am persuaded by the arguments in favor of the decriminalization of sex work across the board. Criminalizing such work sets the conditions for police to harass and target workers who are poor, are persons of color, are Indigenous, and are LGBTQ. Targeting, harassing, and sometimes prosecuting women who are trans or cisgender due to the presence of condoms is not only unjust but also discourages safe sex practices that can quite literally keep people alive and healthy. Still, my focus here is narrower. Targeting, blaming, and sometimes punishing trans women for the mere act of carrying condoms, or simply being read as trans, is yet another example of trans persons being unjustifiably blamed and punished, a key element of S-B scapegoating. These cases involve S-B scapegoating of the fourth type, being blamed and/or punished for something that is not actually blameworthy.[23] (It should be noted that the "Walking While Trans" law in New York was repealed in February 2021. This is surely a step towards justice for New York State trans persons. I hope that the practice of harassing trans persons on the street has been "repealed" as well as the law.)

As I was attempting to ready this manuscript for the publishers, another case of trans scapegoating, that of type three, was the topic of numerous news stories. Even though this even occurred in 2021, it is so relevant to the discussion here and the extent of trans scapegoating it bears mention. Recall that type 3 scapegoating involves one being blamed for something that did not, in fact, occur. In July of 2021, a woman (cisgender) and another who assisted her, produced a video in which they complained to spa employees that "a man with a penis" was seen in the women's facilities.[24] This particular spa is welcoming to gender transgressive persons. The video did go viral, with many anti-trans persons across the area becoming enraged at the occurrence. The woman being accused of offending others with her physical body was never featured on the video, nor were the children that were claimed to be in danger due to the presence of the woman. In the end, it was found that the story was entirely fabricated, perhaps for the reason of easy internet notoriety or demonization of trans persons generally. Given the politicization of trans persons, however, enough of a fervor was manufactured by the deceiving video that demonstrations and anti-demonstrations were held outside the spa. Violence broke out, sending one woman to the hospital. I retell this story here since it illustrates an extreme level of trans demonization. Even claiming to have seen a thought-to-be-offensive trans body is a catalyst to a kind of witch hunt in which neither trans persons nor our supporters are safe.

S-B SCAPEGOATING THE COLLECTIVE OF TRANSGENDER AND GENDER NON-CONFORMING PERSONS

The examples identified as falling into one of the four types of S-B scapegoating generally involve individuals who are over-blamed and over-punished, and whose blame and punishment can be linked to their being trans or gender non-conforming. In addition to the kinds of examples already presented, it is not uncommon for certain individuals, some with extensive social and political followings, to explicitly blame trans individuals as a group for societal ills, or simply denigrate our characters, lives, and existence. This kind of disrespect is obviously related to claims of blameworthiness, for to say that a population of individuals is "sick," "confused," or "morally abhorrent" is to implicitly claim that society would be better off without such persons, that such persons should not be supported by society, that they should be blamed for their condition, or that such persons should be advised, prayed, incarcerated, punished, or counseled out of their/our abnormality. Such attacks generally come from one of three different sources: leaders and or spokespersons of evangelical Christian organizations or communities, self-identified radical feminists who wish to exclude trans persons (especially women) from meaningful societal participation (or worse), and politicians and social leaders who use anti-trans rhetoric and tend to support policy against trans inclusion and trans flourishing. To be clear, it is not the case that all Christian or evangelical Christian leaders or congregations, radical feminists, or politicians oppose just treatment of trans persons, but it is primarily from these three groups that such public scapegoating originates.

In our present information age, nearly anyone with access to an internet search engine can uncover plenty of examples of anti-trans rhetoric falling within these three categories just identified. While it is not helpful to present a full and complete account of the explicit anti-trans rhetoric now in the news, it may be useful to identify at least a couple of paradigmatic examples of such. Firstly, some Christian leaders have attempted to lead the charge to exclude trans persons from social participation and moral respect—much in the same way that these same individuals have historically targeted lesbian and gay persons. Gay men and lesbian women have been blamed for a variety of events ranging from the fall of the Roman Empire to natural disasters (earthquakes, hurricanes, floods, infestations of animals considered pests), terrorist attacks, and even economic downturns. Most of these arguments rely on the claim that LGBTQ persons are living in direct contradiction to god's will and the natural order, and that god, based on this infraction, will turn their back on humanity, thus ushering in a wide host of ills. While LGBQ individuals are sometimes still targeted in these ways, the continued social acceptance of this community and the greater visibility of the trans and gender non-conforming community means that these attacks have been redirected or at least expanded to include transgender persons. For example, well-known evangelist Billy Graham's daughter, Ann Graham Lotz, claimed that the criticism over North Carolina's bathroom bill, HB 2, was evidence that god had decided to abandon the US and leave it vulnerable to numerous negative consequences. She stated, "The one in North Carolina on HB 2, which is to protect our children in bathrooms and locker rooms, has become something where the Justice Department is suing us for something that's just common sense. . . . To me it's evidence that God has backed away." She claimed that the Obama administration's support of transgender persons was "craziness" and that it was due to this craziness that god had left the US vulnerable. She stated, "What happens then is God abandons us and backs away, He takes His favor and blessing away from us. I think that's why God allows bad things to happen. I think that's why He would allow 9/11 to happen, or the dreadful attack in San Bernardino. To show us we need Him."[25]

The Grahams are not the only religious figures who have taken up anti-trans rhetoric of late. The (in)famous "Activist Mommy," Elizabeth Johnston, whose video blog of 8.63K subscribers has catapulted her to prominence, is vehemently anti-trans. Like Graham, she regards respecting trans persons and supporting our social participation as "gender insanity." Johnston believes that trans persons (she predictably targets Caitlyn Jenner for abuse) are "fighting their true biological identity" and that efforts at trans inclusion are "one of the most embarrassing moments in our nation's history." Johnston states unequivocally, "When you allow for anything other than biological male and biological female it's Banana-land!" and while her rhetoric can seem humorous to some, her constant characterization of trans and gender non-conforming persons as mentally ill is not only a mischaracterization apt to marginalize but ableist.[26] Individuals like Graham and Johnston are supported in their rhetoric by some churches and national organizations, some of which are identified as hate groups by the Southern Poverty Law Center (SPLC), including the powerful Focus on the Family, the Family Research Council, the Alliance Defending Freedom, and the American Family Organization. The SPLC identifies over forty more such hate groups, some of which have broad followings. Their common focus on anti-trans rhetoric is not only harmful in the short term but presents a dangerous precedent which others may follow, leading to yet more potential harm and scapegoating.

Self-identified radical feminists who are not inclusive of trans persons (especially trans women) have been around since the late 1970s. Janice Raymond's book of radically invalid arguments, *The Transsexual Empire: The Making of the She-Male* (first published in 1979), and Sandy Stone's apt response, *The Empire Strikes Back: A Posttranssexual Manifesto* (1983), were the first to set the boundaries of this debate. The quantity of this kind of public rhetoric is too great to recount here in full detail, but it is noteworthy to view a number of examples. Among the list of doomsday predictors include feminist social critic and writer Camile Paglia, who believes that androgyny, the blurring of strict gender norms of presentation, is indication that the end of society is near. Paglia claims that this is evidence of a "culture that no longer believes in itself" and that gender-bending cultures are likely to be overtaken by those that still "believe in themselves," that is, still believe in a kind of "heroic masculinity" that can overtake the gender-bending societies that "feel that they are very sophisticated."[27]

Most generally, those who self-identify or are identified by others as Trans-Exclusionary Radical Feminists (TERFs) are those who object to trans persons' full participation in society (especially trans women). They believe that trans masculine persons are confused by patriarchal devaluing of womanhood, that trans feminine persons are merely wielding the power of the patriarchy to have access to women's safe spaces, and that all of this "gender insanity" is due to a lack of recognition of patriarchal power and a lack of womyn-born-womyn feminist empowerment. Notably, philosopher Sheila Jeffreys suggests that trans men transition primarily as a way to procure male privilege: "Instead of working collectively to create social change, they can choose to change only themselves, though with considerable consequences for others, and can seek to escape one by one."[28] Feminists such as Germaine Greer, Meghan Murphy (author of the blog *Feminist Current*), Sheila Jeffreys, and many others give voice to such sentiments, including the claim that, even in the face of cisgender privilege, cis women are regularly invisibilized or put at risk due to trans-inclusive policies, and even that such policies should be understood as a new form of misogyny.[29] Julia Beck, a self-identified lesbian feminist who has received notoriety after being asked to leave Baltimore's LGBTQ Commission, is quite explicit that the acronym of LGBT represents an "unfair" association and that, in essence, the T should be dropped given the nefarious social goals of trans persons. Beck believes that trans-inclusive policies, especially with regard to gender spaces, result in "every woman and girl at risk for male violence."[30]

Additionally, more than a few politicians and other social leaders have relatively recently been vocal in their derision of the trans community as a whole. For example, former Minnesota Republican congresswoman Michele Bachmann was quoted as saying, "These are transgender

Marxists—transgender Black Marxists—who are seeking the overthrow of the United States and the dissolution of the traditional family."[31] Consistent with the fear-mongering that is so prevalent in anti-trans rhetoric, Ben Carson, the former US secretary of housing and urban development, stated that "big hairy men" were identifying as women in an attempt to gain access to women's homeless shelters and that such shelters were justified in denying all services to women who are trans, thus employing the same scare tactics used by many to exclude trans persons from needed services.[32] At the same time Secretary Carson was making these comments, the governor's race in Kentucky was being dominated by anti-trans rhetoric in the hopes of convincing constituents that one candidate's support of LGBTQ persons in general was evidence that he, Andy Beshear, wished to "destroy girls' sports," and that his "extreme" views were sufficient reason to vote for incumbent governor Matt Bevin. The attack ad produced by the anti-choice PAC Campaign for American Principles (CAP) was based on Beshear's general support of LGBTQ equality.[33]

Fox News personality and thought-influencer Laura Ingraham has repeatedly joined this fray. In one show, she interviews Dr. Paul Nathanson, professor and co-author of a new book called *Spreading Misandry: The Teaching of Contempt for Men in Popular Culture*.[34] The podcast episode itself is titled "Transhumanism and the Assault on Traditional Gender and Masculinity," and gives Nathanson the pulpit to argue that trans and gender non-binary persons are the terrible result of feminists challenging traditional gender norms.[35] Ingraham seems to agree, as she states, "Their goal ultimately is the destruction or elimination of the traditional family, though, is it not? That's what we really want to get at here. That's really what's going on."[36] While it is somewhat unclear whether the "their" in the above quote is to refer to trans, gender non-conforming persons, gender non-binary persons, or feminists who question gender norms and critique masculinity, it is clear that in this view, the existence of trans and gender non-conforming people serves to decimate the family and eventually society. Nathanson ends on a particularly radical note,

> I think that the trans people have taken it one step further because by abandoning gender altogether, not simply re-writing it, they're basically trying to use social engineering to create a new species. Which is what, in fact, the transhumanists have been doing for the past half century. Using medical and other technologies to develop a new species.[37]

The above examples are not even close to exhaustive with regard to the quantity of anti-transgender rhetoric that was common between 2015 and 2020. These examples are merely representative. It is noteworthy that Trump himself said little directly against transgender and gender non-conforming people, even while his administration initiated policies that rejected the advances of the Obama administration and degraded LGBTQ rights in general and the rights of transgender persons in particular. Still, his own silence on this issue does not mean that his administration and his supporters were not hearing a message loud and clear. Timothy Snyder's small volume entitled *On Tyranny: Twenty Lessons from the Twentieth Century*, though published in 2017, became popular in the period running up to the 2020 election, and within it explains the idea of "anticipatory obedience."[38] The first of Snyder's twenty lessons is "Do Not Obey in Advance." In the short chapter he writes, "Anticipatory obedience is a political tragedy. Perhaps rulers did not initially know that citizens were willing to compromise this value or that principle."[39] When they do, in fact, sacrifice their principles and do what they imagine the ruler would want them to do, then the ruler recognizes just how influential they really are. Anticipatory obedience is seen by Snyder as coming into play when Austrian Nazis were more oppressive against the Jews than even Hitler would have guessed. Anticipatory obedience also comes into play in the corporate world, where those who wish to impress the boss go beyond their expectations, sometimes leading to moral atrocities. In such cases, the leader or boss can claim they are free of moral criticism, since they did not explicitly direct the individuals involved to complete those specific acts. What might be called anticipatory obedience occurred in July of 2020, when an anti-Trump rally was met with a counter-rally whose original message was "Blue Lives Matter." At this rally, unprovoked and undirected, members of the pro-Trump, "All Lives Matter" crowd began to chant "kill transgenders."[40] The political climate had eroded to the degree that such a dangerous and reprehensible sentiment was assumed to be consistent with Trump's policies and values, or at the very least, a sentiment one would not feel ashamed to chant in public. This may have been the first time in our country's history that such words were chanted—an indication of just how dangerous things had become. Anticipatory obedience may have been again on display on January 6, 2021, when insurrectionists stormed the US Capitol. The lesson to take from the "kill transgenders" rally is not that the government was directly suggesting that US citizens accept this kind of sentiment, but that the social climate had already been degraded to such an extent, at least partly by unjustly blaming trans and gender diverse persons for a variety of societal ills, that it was deemed suitable by some individuals in that context. Hurtful and dangerous anti-transgender rhetoric of our society's leaders, whether they be political, religious, feminist, or otherwise, makes a difference. Leaders across the nation have openly used hateful language against individual persons and have derided the community as a whole. This type of scapegoating leads to real consequences and can no longer be dismissed as the rants of the uninformed.

The above identification of anti-transgender rhetoric from contemporary politicians, media figures, religious leaders, and radical feminists is only the tip of a large iceberg of what has occurred between 2015 and 2020, and beyond. I am not going to argue against ridiculous claims that trans persons are attempting to become a new species, that our inclusion in society will result in natural or economic disasters, that all trans women are violent towards cisgender women, or that trans men are simply confused pawns of the patriarchy or, perhaps worse, simply out to garner male privilege. I have engaged in more rationally made claims already in this book. Instead, the point here is to recognize that to the extent that our lives become politicized in these ways, the required structures necessary for flourishing—including health care, employment, access to homeless shelters, education, the right to live free of harassment and imprisonment—all become threatened and progressively out of reach. Demonization by church leaders, radical feminists, conservative media personalities, and politicians affects the policing activities of armed police officers, as well as the gender policing of teachers, juvenile corrections facility staff, and cisgender women in bathrooms who have been misled to believe that their restroom facilities are under a kind of violent siege. While these realms are not independent of each other, neither are the already fully instantiated systems that result in structural racism, sexism, ableism, classism, ageism, and other oppressions. Indeed, the kinds of anti-trans rhetoric just identified will probably not result in a middle-aged, middle-class, white trans man such as myself being stopped and searched for condoms upon suspicion of solicitation. Anti-trans rhetoric, policy, and other scapegoating techniques will always result in the gravest injustices being perpetrated on those already burdened by structural and historic injustice. For this reason, anti-racists and anti-sexists also need to be supportive of trans inclusion and flourishing. Similarly, those who are supportive of trans inclusion and flourishing need to be anti-racist and anti-sexist, for without such an orientation, only the most privileged of trans persons will benefit.

CONCLUSION

This chapter began with an introduction of one characterization of scapegoating, one that focuses on unjustified blame. Mellema's original scheme was used as a basis to articulate that there are four different ways that this kind of scapegoating may occur, and examples of such scapegoating of trans, gender non-binary, and gender non-conforming persons were offered toward the conclusion that trans and gender non-conforming persons are indeed scapegoated in these ways. Secondly, examples of anti-trans rhetoric used by some politicians, thought leaders, media personalities, religiously affiliated leaders, and self-proclaimed radical feminists who argue for the exclusion of trans persons (TERFs) have been cited toward the conclusion that trans persons as a collective, and not just as individuals, are claimed to be responsible for various ills including the end of girls' sports, violence against cisgender girls and women, a kind of post-humanist eugenics program, general social unrest and "insanity," and even the eventual end of civilization itself. To the extent that transgender and gender non-conforming persons are not responsible for these ills, that we are over-blamed simply due to our gender expression or identity, or to the extent that what is considered inappropriate (e.g., trans girls and women participating in sports, or persons living authentic lives that deny gender binary assumptions) is actually *not* inappropriate, these claims too can be understood as S-B scapegoating. As mentioned, the examples identified herein are not at all exhaustive of the immense amount of anti-trans rhetoric that has existed in the years between 2015 and 2020. To those who might argue that such rhetoric is relegated to the political fringe and thus has little real social effect, I would remind my objector that the individuals mentioned have followings that encompass literally tens of thousands of persons, if not many more. In fact, I have left the YouTube and blogging culture warriors that exist at the rhetorical fringe off of this list. Claiming trans and gender non-conforming persons are blameworthy in the ways identified here is unethical not only because these claims of blameworthiness are, at best, unjustified, but because the construction of trans and gender non-conforming persons as sick, mentally ill, dangerous, or religious abominations is obviously marginalizing in its own right. Being the target of scapegoating and being socially marginalized are not disparate phenomena; rather, the more one is marginalized the more one may become scapegoated and vice versa. Lastly, while much of the anti-transgender rhetoric has originated in conservative and evangelical spaces, it has found a home even in Democratic circles. Award-winning memoirist Jennifer Finney Boylan wrote her usual column in the *New York Times* after the 2016 defeat of Hillary Clinton by Donald Trump. The title of her piece is "Really, You Are Blaming Transgender People for Trump?"[41] In this column, she responds to those who blamed the Clinton loss on the Democratic Party's support of so-called "boutique" issues that include transgender rights and well-being. Writes Boylan, "The phrase echoed unpleasantly in my mind. A boutique issue? Is this what my fellow Americans had thought of my fight for dignity all along?" Referencing Bill Maher's position that his own "boutique issue" of legalizing cannabis be set aside as a way to help ensure a Democratic win, Boylan writes, "Apparently providing a person like me with health care and protecting me from violence and discrimination in the workplace were on the same order of magnitude as the right to roll a doober." Indeed, increased politicization of any population means that actively advocating for the well-being of those individuals becomes overly politically charged. In various ways, I have seen such advocacy suddenly ceased or sometimes simply kept secret to avoid being a source of political weakness. An alternative view of scapegoating, one that *starts* with marginality as opposed to claims of blame-worthiness, is the subject of the next chapter. Employing a more Girardian analysis to this topic makes clear, as if it isn't already obvious, that scapegoating is not just about an over-preponderance of blame, but that some are more likely to be scapegoated due to existing marginalizing structural systems.

NOTES

1. Gregory Mellema, "Scapegoats," *Criminal Justice Ethics* 19, no. 1 (Winter/Spring 2000).
2. Ibid., 1.
3. Ibid., 3.
4. Wesley Ware, "Rounding Up the Homosexuals: The Impact of Juvenile Court on Queer and Trans/Gender-Non-Conforming Youth," in C*aptive Genders: Trans Embodiment and the Prison Industrial Complex*, ed. Eric A. Stanley and Nat Smith (Edinburgh: AK Press, 2011).
5. Ware, 80.
6. Ware, 81.
7. Shannon D. Snapp, Jennifer M. Hoenig, Amanda Fields, and Stephen T. Russell, "Messy, Butch, and Queer: LGBTQ Youth and the School-to-Prison Pipeline," *Journal of Adolescent Research* 30, no. 1 (2014): 57–82.
8. Snapp et al., 76.
9. Snapp et al., 58.
10. Brandon Andrew Robinson, "The Lavender Scare in Homonormative Times: Policing, Hyper-Incarceration, and LGBTQ Homelessness," *Gender & Society* 34, no. 2 (2020).
11. Snapp et al., 67.
12. The claim that girls and women can bend gender norms with fewer negative repercussions in relation to boys and men is indeed relative to context. Tiny, cute, white tomboys, as I was myself, seem to be given more gender freedom than, say, a larger-than-typical Black girl who also expresses herself somewhat masculinely. Any and all such claims are dependent on context which includes economic class, ability status, ethnicity, etc.
13. Snapp et al., 68.
14. Snapp et al., 67.
15. Snapp et al., 70
16. GLSEN School Climate Survey, 2019 https://www.glsen.org/sites/default/files/2020-10/NSCS-2019-Executive-Summary-English_1.pdf.

17. Snapp et al., 70.
18. Snapp et al., 74.
19. Marisa Shultz, "Trump Jr. Derides Transgender Cyclist Who Won Championship," *New York Post*, October 21, 2019.
20. Margaret H. Wurth, Rebecca Schleifer, Megan McLemore, Katherine W. Todrys, and Joseph J. Amon, "Condoms as Evidence of Prostitution in the United States and the Criminalization of Sex Work," *Journal of the International AIDS Society* 16, no. 1 (2013), 10.7448/IAS.16.1.18626.https://www.ncbi.nlm.nih.gov/pmc/articles/PMC3664300/.
21. Human Rights Watch, "In Harm's Way: State Reponses to Sex Workers, Drug Users, and HIV in New Orleans," 2013, https://www.hrw.org/sites/default/files/reports/usnola1213_ForUpload_3.pdf.
22. Whitford, Emma, "When Walking as Trans Is a Crime: The NYPD Says It Is Taking a More Sensitive Approach to Sex Work, but Not Everyone Benefits," *NY Magazine*, *The Cut*, January 31, 2018, https://www.thecut.com/2018/01/when-walking-while-trans-is-a-crime.html.
23. Just as I am finishing up this manuscript, the "Walking While Trans" law has been repealed in NYC. Yo Jurcaba, "New York Repeals 'Walking While Trans' Law after Years of Activism," NBC News, February 2021, https://www.nbcnews.com/feature/nbc-out/new-york-repeals-walking-while-trans-law-after-years-activism-n1256736.
24. Evan Urquhart, "Violence Over a Transphobic Hoax Shows the Danger of Underestimating Anti-Trans Hate," *Slate*, July 9, 2021, https://slate.com/human-interest/2021/07/wi-spa-la-transphobic-protest.html?via=rss_socialflow_facebook&fbclid=IwAR1Ql-agAwhDJC7GAK1Z5Lw6YHq5HXq9zaH12DjetKv8ncAfCpj3baLUe5c.
25. Harriet Alexander, "God Let 9-11 Happen in Anger at Transgender Silliness, Says American Evangelical," *The Telegraph*, May 14, 2016, https://www.telegraph.co.uk/news/2016/05/13/god-let-911-happen-in-anger-at-transgender-silliness-says-americ/.
26. Elizabeth Johnston, "Activist Mommy," June 14, 2017, https://www.youtube.com/watch?v=L0MGOVKxvW0.
27. Ron Dreher, "Paglia: Transgender and Civilization's Decline," *American Conservative*, March 8, 2017, https://www.theamericanconservative.com/dreher/paglia-transgender-civilizations-decline/.
28. Sheila Jeffreys, *Gender Hurts: A Feminist Analysis of the Politics of Transgenderism* (New York: Routledge, 2014), 122.
29. This moniker the "New Misogyny" is taken from a talk sponsored by the Seattle Library on February 1, 2020, featuring Meghan Murphy, Saba Malik, and Kara Dansky. The title of the talk is "Fighting the New Misogyny" and is advertised to offer a "critical analysis of gender identity" and argue for "sex based women's rights." https://www.eventbrite.com/e/fighting-the-new-misogyny-a-feminist-critique-of-gender-identity-tickets-85012638089.
30. Julia Beck interviewed by Tucker Carlson, *Tucker Carlson Tonight*
31. Sakshi Venkatraman and Brooke Sopelsa, "'Transgender Black Marxists' Seek to Overthrow the U.S., Trump Backer, Bachmann Says," NBC News, September 9

2020, https://www.nbcnews.com/feature/nbc-out/transgender-black-marxists-seek-overthrow-u-s-trump-backer-michele-n1239683.

32. Alexa Diaz, "HUD Chief Ben Carson Reportedly Made Dismissive Comments about Transgender People during a California Trip," *LA Times*, September 2019, https://www.latimes.com/politics/story/2019-09-20/housing-secretary-ben-carson-transgender-comments-san-francisco.

33. Juwan J. Holmes, "Trans People Have Become Pawns in the Kentucky Governor Race," *LGBTQ Nation*, September 16, 2019, https://www.lgbtqnation.com/2019/09/rightwing-pac-scare-mongering-trans-rights-kentucky-governors-election/?fbclid=IwAR0H8qbHtfs-5oyPQPHk2kgZ1PGuj5qwe-j84m_AQY6UiOu_P9qwRC9s11g.

34. Paul Nathanson and Katherine K. Young, *Spreading Misandry: The Teaching of Contempt for Men in Popular Culture* (Montreal: McGill-Queen's University Press, 2001).

35. Paul Nathanson interviewed by Laura Ingraham, "Transhumanism and the Assault on Traditional Gender and Masculinity," *The Laura Ingram Podcast*, https://podcastone.com/episode/Transhumanism-and-the-assault-on-traditional-gender-and-masculinity-.

36. Ibid.

37. Ibid.

38. Timothy Snyder, *On Tyranny: Twenty Lessons from the Twentieth Century* (New York: Tim Duggan Books, 2017).

39. Ibid., 18.

40. Bill Browning, "Trump Supporter Starts 'Kill Transgenders' Chant at Rally," *LGBTQ Nation*, July 27, 2020, https://www.lgbtqnation.com/2020/07/trump-supporter-starts-kill-transgenders-chant-rally/?fbclid=IwAR1WKbyhnDHyQjSndtYMDOPqjLRfYPgu1N5ClSXx-Z_fWB3qGwp6pL2CTmk#.Xx8wirQHdDU.facebook.

41. Jennifer Finney Boylan, "Really, You Are Blaming Transgender People for Trump?," *New York Times*, December 2, 2016, https://www.nytimes.com/2016/12/02/opinion/really-youre-blaming-transgender-people-for-trump.html.

Chapter 6

Scapegoating

The Girardian Account

The examples used in the last chapter to illustrate different forms of S-B scapegoating (i.e., scapegoating characterized as a focus on unjustified blame) are only a very small sample chosen to illustrate the many ways that trans, gender non-binary, and gender non-conforming persons have been over-blamed and/or demonized in ways that can be tied to their/our gender expression or identity. These examples, which include the targeting of individuals or persons as a group, are offered as evidence that trans, gender non-binary, and gender non-conforming people have been victims of S-B scapegoating. Still, one may wish to argue that there is something insufficient about centering a conceptual analysis of scapegoating as the over-blaming of individuals or collectives. Recall that Mellema's original schema is focused on unjustified blame but that characteristics of the scapegoated individual or collective were not mentioned. As may be obvious by the examples offered in the last chapter and common experience, individuals who are S-B scapegoated are generally those who were *already* marginalized in society through racism, ableism, classism, ageism, sexism, homophobia, xenophobia, transphobia, or a combination thereof. Certainly, it seems uncontroversial to note that some individuals are more likely to be scapegoated (over-blamed) than are others. Picture again an innocent individual strolling by the scene that graffiti artists had just fled as the police cruiser approached. In the last chapter this example featured *Skyler*, but now imagine the person is *Becky*, a white, gender normative, professionally dressed woman in her thirties. It is difficult to imagine her being accused of the vandalism that is the source of concern for the police. It is theoretically possible that she could be blamed for the graffiti, but it is much more likely that *Becky* will be allowed to continue on her way, unimpeded and unaccused. On the other hand, a young man who appears to have brown or black skin will be more likely to be stopped and questioned, or worse; he may lose his life due to merely "looking suspicious" or reaching for his cell phone.

As a result of this concern that there is more to scapegoating than over-blaming, we might attempt to bolster the S-B account by simply noting that marginalized persons are more likely to be over-blamed (and thus scapegoated) than are those who are not so marginalized. However, this seems to be related to the construction of being in the "wrong place at the wrong time" that we discussed but dismissed as problematic in the case of the killing of Phillip DeVine. As Snorton so aptly explains, to narrate the event that DeVine was simply in the *wrong place at the wrong time* when he was murdered seems to normalize and even condone the actions of his killers. It seems to suggest that statements like "*Of course, being a Black, disabled young man in a living room which needs to be crossed to perpetrate a crime will result in death*" should be accepted. One might argue and say that to claim DeVine was in the *wrong place at the wrong time* may simply mean that he was not the planned target of the killers, but then, why was he shot? Alternatively, and more appropriately, one can understand that it is the blameworthy racism of the angry white men (John Lotter and Tom Nissen) that needs to be of focus, not DeVine's "bad luck." Similarly, *Skyler* (from our earlier example), imagine them as an Indigenous young man with long black hair, being blamed for graffiti that he didn't produce shouldn't be seen as simply having "bad luck" when he was strolling by the scene when the police arrived, nor should *Becky* be seen as having "good luck" because she wasn't similarly blamed. Instead, it is more likely that *Skyler* would be blamed and scapegoated because he is Indigenous, just as DeVine was murdered due to a combination of the racist and ablest murderous attitudes of Lotter and Nissen. To take this analysis one step further, one can argue that scapegoating is directed at the marginalized *because* they are marginalized, and that blame, justified or not, is simply a vehicle of marginalization wielded by the relatively powerful and privileged. Blame as a vehicle or tool of marginalization is a handy one that is often unjustly wielded. Of the social realities that undergird scapegoating, C. Allen Carter, noted for his work with Edwin Burke's sociolinguistic theory of scapegoating, reflects, "In short, no individual, group, gender, generation, nation, or ideology is immune from the tendency to seek someone to blame for its own troubles."[1] Certainly, Carter is correct here, and when one who is over-privileged searches for another to unjustly blame, those otherwise marginalized become targets. Understood more broadly, over-blaming and scapegoating others not only can mean the relatively privileged are found faultless, but that a certain power is unleashed against the marginalized that can be used in various ways with predictable results. Different forms of marginalization present opportunities for over-blaming, made plausible in this context of injustice. Especially since 2015, being trans or otherwise gender transgressive has come to present a more likely opportunity.

SCAPEGOATING: A GIRARDIAN ACCOUNT

The above comments motivate a study in a different, perhaps a more sociological, view of scapegoating. The S-B account's focus is on an unjustified belief in the blameworthiness of an individual or collective. But, given how common scapegoating has been to the human condition, why is this particular practice so terribly common? True, scapegoating involves blame, but it also involves a kind of societal dismissal or casting out, and this act of ostracism has been as much, if not more, basic to the practice of scapegoating as has been the factor of unjustified blame. Biblically, the scapegoat was literally cast out of society, and it was thought that to the scapegoat were transferred the sins of the society as a whole. In Leviticus we find, "But the goat chosen by lot as the scapegoat shall be presented alive before the Lord to be used for making atonement by sending it into the wilderness as a scapegoat."[2] Traditionally, there was thought to be a kind of uncleanliness or contagion to the scapegoat: "The man who releases the goat as a scapegoat must wash his clothes and bathe himself with water; afterward he may come into the camp."[3] Are these accounts of the Old Testament, and other ancient works that characterize and narrate the nearly ubiquitous stories of scapegoats, related to contemporary practices and especially the relation of trans and other gender-variant individuals to the dominant culture?

To answer these kinds of questions we can look to the work of René Girard. Few have written more on the idea of scapegoating than he. Girard's work is expansive and defies easy categorization; while it is often regarded as anthropological philosophy, it has long tentacles into the fields of psychology, sociology, literary criticism, hermeneutics, theology, and religion. In the hermeneutical tradition, his theory is built upon a study of texts, including great works of literature, Greek myths, the Bible, and ancient folklore. Through this study, Girard believed that he found a common pattern, one too prevalent and assertive to ignore. For Girard, scapegoating is a recurring phenomenon in human communities and is key to understanding society-formation, unity, and even the nature of human desire. In this chapter I will briefly outline Girard's position, especially as it is related to our study here. As will be made clear, his view seems especially fruitful when inquiring about the politicization of trans individuals.

134   Chapter 6

THE MIRACLE OF APOLLONIUS OF TYANA

In *I See Satan Fall Like Lightning*, Girard uses the story of the "Miracle of Apollonius of Tyana" to illustrate the scapegoating process.[4] Apollonius of Tyana was a first-century Neo-Pythagorean who was known as a teacher and miracle worker. In contrast to the original audience of this story, contemporary intellects probably find the narrative less miraculous and instead more gruesome, but even this is relevant to Girard's understanding of scapegoating. The context involves a community in the midst of a plague, which, as Girard explains, is a setting of many other scapegoating episodes.[5] As Girard explains, the scapegoat is a person or a group to whom blame can be ascribed, persecution met upon, and whose casting out results in the consolidation, cleansing, and reunification of the rest of the community. The following account is attributed to Flavius Philostratus, the Greek author of the *Life of Apollonius of Tyana*:

> "Take courage, for I will today put a stop to the course of the disease." And with these words he led the population entire to the theatre, where the image of the Averting god has been set up. [The Averting god in this case is Hercules, as will become clear later.] And there he saw what seemed an old mendicant artfully blinking his eyes as if blind, and he carried a wallet and a crust of bread in it; and he was clad in rags and was very squalid of countenance. Apollonius therefore ranged the Ephesians around him and said: "Pick up as many stones as you can and hurl them at this enemy of the gods." Now the Ephesians wondered what he meant and were shocked at the idea of murdering a stranger so manifestly miserable; for he was begging and praying them to take mercy upon him. Nevertheless, Apollonius insisted and egged on the Ephesians to launch themselves on him and not let him go. And as soon as they began to take shots and hit him with their stones, the beggar who had seemed to blink and be blind, gave them all a sudden glance and showed that his eyes were full of fire. Then the Ephesians recognized that he was a demon, and they stoned him so thoroughly that their stones were heaped into a great cairn around him. After a little pause Apollonius bade them remove the stones and acquaint themselves with the wild animal which they had slain. When therefore they had exposed the object which they thought they had thrown their missiles at, they found that he had disappeared and instead of him there was a hound who resembled in form and look a Molosian dog but was in size the equal of the largest lion; there he lay before their eyes, pounded to a pulp by their stones and vomiting foam as mad dogs do. Accordingly, the statue of the Averting god, namely Hercules, has been set up over the spot where the ghost was slain.[6]

I recount this story at some length to illustrate common features of a Girardian view of scapegoating. Recall that the name of this ancient story is "Miracle of Apollonius of Tyana." At the time, Apollonius was being cast as a miracle worker, one to rival the Jesus of the early Christians, yet solidly within the Greek Pagan tradition. The *miracle*, at least as originally told, was that Apollonius was able to see the true nature of the individual who otherwise appeared to be an innocent, disabled, and homeless older man. It is Apollonius who reveals the man to be a dangerous demon, the demon responsible for the death, illness, anxiety, and destruction of the plague itself, and it is he who not only punishes the demon for the harm of the plague but also prevents him from causing more havoc. According to Girard, a shared sense of community is found as a result of this transformation and of participating in the collective act of unjustified violence: "Apollonius knows what he is doing when he chooses a victim no one will mourn, for in this way he doesn't risk aggravating the disorder he is trying to pacify. It is good strategy."[7] Once told, the Ephesians together, led by their miracle worker, vanquished the source of evil in their community. In this scapegoat story, as in most such stories, at least temporary solidarity, safety, and security are won at the expense of the scapegoat.

A twenty-first-century reader of the story, more apt to believe in dangerous power dynamics than demons, would understand that the old man is more *socially transformed* into a beast rather than revealed as one. Transformed, that is, in the eyes of the Ephesians. Scapegoating involves demon *creation* in the eyes of the powerful majority, not demon *identification*. As explained by Girard, "Such things can happen, especially in our time, but they cannot happen, even today, without the availability of an eminently manipulatable mass to be used by the manipulators for their evil purposes, people who will allow themselves to be trapped in the persecutors' representation of persecution, people capable of belief where the scapegoat is concerned."[8] However we imagine these events in the first century to have taken place—how the persuasive oratory of Apollonius and the grief and desperation of the Ephesians combined to weaponize the Ephesians as executors of what was undoubtedly an innocent man—the structure of the story is familiar. There is ample evidence that the masses remain vulnerable to this kind of manipulation and even to a greater degree in our social media–soaked age.

GIRARDIAN SCAPEGOAT CHARACTERISTICS

Like our story of the graffiti artists, it is easy to imagine that the old man in the "Miracle of Apollonius of Tyana" just happened to be strolling along when he caught the attention of Apollonius. Claims of miracle-working aside, why did Apollonius target this man as a scapegoat? Why was he regarded not as *Becky* discussed earlier and allowed to simply continue on his way? Girard asks this question, both for this story and the dozens of others that inform his view. Most generally speaking, those likely to be persecuted as scapegoats are in some sense outsiders or have an attribute that is seen as placing them apart from the majority in a way that can come to be characterized as significant. In the case of the "Miracle of Apollonius of Tyana," the old man exhibited three such characteristics: being poor, being a foreigner, and being disabled (recall, he originally seemed to have a visual impairment).

In *The Scapegoat*, Girard presents a comprehensive study of characteristics whose presence makes it more likely that one will be scapegoated. Three of these characteristics are particularly relevant to our purposes of applying Girard's ideas to the politicization of trans and gender non-conforming persons. The first of these is the attribute of being thought to be a person or group that is transgressive of accepted sexual norms.[9] Such claims of sexual social deviance may be basically true or made plausible through fictitious charges of norm infraction or even false accusations of sexual crimes including rape, incest, or bestiality. According to Girard, these norms and related taboos are central to a society's structure and so rejection of such norms comes at a high social cost. Quite obviously, LGBTQ individuals qua LGBTQ individuals are identified and stigmatized through a rejection of cisgender heterosexual norms. Those who reject LGBTQ equality or harbor animus against LGBQ or trans persons often do so because they find these norms to be vitally important and believe that rejecting them to differing degrees is not just bad for the individual (and possibly reflective of an immoral character) but is a danger to the community as a whole. Janice Raymond infamously argued that trans women were essentially rapists in their legitimate desire to be seen as women, and there is a long history of marginalized persons (LGBTQ or otherwise) being regarded as sexual predators.[10] Indeed, claims of sexual predation have historically been used as a tool to ostracize and marginalize individuals and collectives. From the stories that Christians have told of Jewish men, to the demonization of men and boys of color, to the assumed pedophilia of gay men, to the Trump administration so casually referring to immigrants and asylum seekers as "criminals, drug dealers, and rapists," to the QAnon conspiracy that powerful Democrats are active in an international pedophilia ring, such tropes are repeatedly used. In the same vein, the ads used to gain support for "bathroom bills" invariably feature ominous music, a stereotypically attractive young cisgender woman, and the strong message that she is being put at risk for sexual assault due to the possibility of a trans woman using the restroom. In this way that is comparable to the story of Apollonius of Tyana, the notion of a *trans woman in a bathroom* is transformed into that of a *dangerous and violent intruder in a bathroom*. The connection between being a trans woman and being a sexual predator can hardly get more explicit. Additionally, the claims mentioned in the previous chapter by Dr. Paul Nathanson, that trans persons are attempting to conjure our own species, are yet a different and particularly dramatic kind of othering that can be seen as related to unfounded claims of bestiality. If we are no longer of the human species, are we then non-human beasts with all that generally implies in our anthropocentric culture that regards humans to have a special moral value over and above all other species. Indeed, for those who see our bodies as mutilations and our histories as distortions of the good and natural, even having relations with trans persons can be seen as morally inappropriate and results in even our lovers tainted or polluted through contagion. It is a heart-breaking reality that there are reports that partners of trans persons are sometimes subject to harassment and even violence themselves, or that they turn on their partners—seemingly as testament that they are not so contaminated by the scapegoated person as some might predict.[11]

The unfortunately familiar second type of scapegoat marker is being part of a religious or ethnic minority.[12] In Girard's view, being part of such a community can serve to implicitly challenge the social norms of the majority and in so doing show them as potentially arbitrary or contingent. Having different religious practices or beliefs illustrates that those beliefs and practices that vary from the majority are not just possible but can lead to thriving individual lives and nurturing communities. Unfortunately, examples present themselves with little mental effort, including the Nazi-organized genocide against Jews and others, the recent crimes against the Rohingya Muslims in Myanmar, the ongoing and historic marginalization of the Roma people in central Europe, the Armenian Genocide of 1915, and the genocide against Indigenous persons in North America and worldwide.

Being seen as an outsider as far as being physically different or disabled is another attribute that may lead to an individual or group being scapegoated.[13] Girard explains that disability can make a person an easy target, and claims of disability can be used to further marginalize an individual, disabled or not: "If a group of people is used to choosing its victims from a certain social, ethnic, or religious category, it tends to attribute to them disabilities or deformities that would reinforce the polarization against the victim, were they real. This tendency is clearly observable in racist cartoons."[14] Here, bias and ignorance about disability is weaponized against those who are atypical, whether presently disabled or not. In this way, the difference is constructed not just as a form of value neutral diversity, but a dangerous characteristic to all others in society and society itself. Physical difference is storied as *monstrous* or *mutilated* and different life choices are characterized as *dangerously deviant*, *sick*, or *deranged*.

APPLICATION OF GIRARDIAN SCAPEGOAT CHARACTERISTICS

As is probably obvious by the previous discussion, Girard's work on scapegoat characteristics folds easily into the present analysis. In the previous chapters, evidence has been presented toward the claim that transgender persons, especially those who are also people of color, Indigenous, poor, homeless, disabled, etc., are more likely to be targeted for discrimination, violence, and scapegoating. Transgender persons, as well as those who are or are also lesbian, gay, queer, gender variant, poly, asexual, pansexual, BDSM practitioners, etc., are often seen as blameworthily defying and denying sexual norms, which do in fact seem a foundational structure in society, at least presently. As already mentioned, what is perceived as rejection of cisgender and heterosexual norms can be storied as a small step away from bestiality, incest, and sexual assault, thus bringing to bear predictable collective abhorrence. Furthermore, trans persons are often regarded as embodying a rejection of "god's plan," as if our mere *existence* is evidence of our explicit renunciation of religious norms, religious norms that, at least in the case of Christianity, are considered by some to be under threat. Some perceive a threat of this kind imminent and quite serious. Quite surprisingly, there is recent evidence that the majority of evangelical Christians believe that Christians are being discriminated against, even discriminated against at a rate higher than that of Muslims in US.[15] Some believe that such beliefs of discrimination or threats of persecution are due to a kind of "information bubble" that has been affected by what is generally called the "political polarization" of society, an ongoing descriptor of our times, especially during the Trump presidency. Indeed, it is this same information bubble and feelings of persecution that fuels the perceived need for the "religious freedom" bills that were discussed in chapter 2. Such thinking would have us believe that merely being in the presence of, or engaging in business with, someone with alternative beliefs and norms is threatening to one's own. With regard to trans and gender nonconforming persons, if one's own body, expression, and pronoun use are thought to be an obvious and willful rejection of religious norms, then even being in our presence can be regarded as a threat to such norms. The offense and the person become inseparable to such an extent that the scapegoat "need only be himself," and demonization follows.[16] It is relevant that those who are the most likely to see themselves as discriminated against and their values as under assault are also the group more likely to be non-supportive of LGBTQ equality and trans justice.

Girard's contention that one kind of difference can often lead to claims of another kind of difference also has both historical and contemporary relevance. Not only have homosexuality and, later, transgender expression and identity been officially regarded as mental illnesses or "disorders," but even after homosexuality was no longer included in the DSM in 1973, and the article on transgenderism and gender dysphoria was slightly revised in 2013, the claims that trans and non-heterosexual persons are "sick" or "mentally ill" or "confused" persist, as do claims that trans persons are monstrous and that affirming surgeries are "mutilations." Indeed, trans persons who are also marginalized due to being Indigenous, being a person of color, being poor, or being disabled have every "marker" that makes them likely to be scapegoated when conditions obtain, and more likely to "attract disaster."[17] For those of us who blend in with the cisgender majority, it is our insider-outsider status that at once makes us at times temporarily invisible (and thus safe) and also makes our histories reason for unfounded charges of deceitfulness.[18]

DIFFERENCE IN THE CONTEXT OF SIMILARITY

It is nearly a truism that individuals or groups are picked out and marginalized due to being different in some way, but to reduce Girard's claims to this truism is to do a disservice to his more nuanced analysis. The *difference* that is the most important here is not the visible, perceived, or fictionalized difference itself but differences as they relate to the system of societal norms. Such difference exposes these norms and their attending prioritization as often arbitrary, certainly contingent, criticizable, and changeable.[19] As Girard explains, "Religious, ethnic, or national minorities are never actually reproached for their difference, but for not being as different as expected, and in the end for not differing at all. . . . In all the vocabulary of tribal or national prejudices hatred is expressed, not for difference, but for its absence."[20]

How can we make sense of Girard's claim that the scapegoat mechanism is fueled not by difference but for its opposite, or more carefully put, that scapegoating persists in contexts of sameness in which difference is identified and constructed to be significant beyond justification? This makes sense when we recognize that criticism of social norms is only seen as a true challenge from one who is similar enough to accept those social norms or champion others. There needs to be sufficient similarity, otherwise the challenge can be met with "Well, of course you'd do it differently." As expressed by Herman Hesse, "If you hate a person, you hate something in him that is part of yourself. What isn't part of ourselves doesn't disturb us." This idea can be the basis of a generalization that does not apply in all contexts, but there is something about it that rings true. It is those that reflect one's own culture, character traits, humanity, desires, faults, and frailties, but do so in a way that the same one would reject, that often are targeted with the least amount of tolerance or acceptance.

Somewhat paradoxically, similarity can breed an expectation of sameness in other areas, whereas difference can provide a context for accepted distinctions. Consider the *Phallostethus cuulong*, a kind of fish found in Vietnam, which sports its genitalia on its head, just below the mouth. Predictably, this creature has atypical copulation techniques, and while humans are the only species who seem to think that genitalia need to be nearly constantly covered, at least most other species do not display them as a kind of headwear. Nevertheless, no one seems troubled by the fish and its life of constant and explicit genital exposure; it is so different from us that its different lifestyle, if we may call it that, does not challenge our own social norms in the least. Similarly, consider the lesbian seagulls that became the topic of conversation in early arguments for the "naturalness" of homosexuality. Unlike human lesbians, the seagull's sexual preferences have been the topic of curiosity, not animus or hostility. The same might be said of sex-changing lizards and so-called hermaphroditic banana slugs. The above examples also attest that the easiest way to gain mention on the "strangest of animals" list is to be able to boast of a difference from humans that involves sexuality or genitalia. It remains a favorite of fetishized difference even when there is little value judgment. Indeed, ask any trans person who has had to field the nearly constant, inane, and reductionist questions about personal genitalia, questions asked typically without offering any description of the questioner's genital package.

A more nuanced understanding of Girard's view of scapegoating is that it is not simply being different or being an outsider that can lead to being a scapegoat; instead, the point here is that it is difference in the context of sameness that can be seen as a challenge to social norms and value judgments. The *Phallostethus cuulong* and even the lesbian seagulls are too different from humans, or seen as such due to the firmly instantiated anthropocentrism of the dominant culture, to threaten the norms of the majority. If Girard is correct, it is distinction within a sea of similarity that can partially explain, but not justify, why cisgender parents reject their trans children and send them out into the streets to fend for themselves, to become vulnerable to harms that are then stacked upon that of the original and devastating parental rejection. It seems to be the sentiment, "You are so much like me, raised by me, how could you possibly reject this norm that so structures my world?" While it seems popular to suggest that children are rejected due to their difference (e.g., being trans), Girard would argue more specifically that it is their similarity that gives them the status to implicitly or explicitly challenge the differences held sacrosanct by the rejecting parents. Trans and gender non-conforming persons challenge the gender binary, the thought-to-be differences between men and women, understandings of masculinity, femininity, identity, gender itself, and even parenthood. Such lives illustrate a dismissal of the value of gender differences that much of the rest of the society holds foundational to the point of being sacred.

For those who oppose LGBTQ equality and justice for trans and other gender expansive individuals, the disarming fact of the matter is our marriages (even those considered a same-sex marriage), our relationships (even if to more than one person at a time), our days which consist in waking up (hopefully in a safe place) and brushing our teeth (assuming this is an option), our moments filled with aspirations of living the good life that is connected to those we care about, our desire for financial security and equal participation in society are all very similar to those of our cisgender and heterosexual societal siblings. Even the most radical among us, and I am not including myself in this group, lead lives that generally resemble non-LGBTQ persons in many ways. It is not my intention to broach the contentious topic of whether trans or LGBTQ folks have assimilated more than we/they should have, or whether there is a moral responsibility to be anti-assimilationist or, on the other hand, to live a life that minimizes feather-ruffling of the dominant cisgender heterosexual culture, even if for prudential reasons. Instead, my claim, consistent with that of Girard, is that as humans, we bear striking similarities and the mundaneness of these similarities does not reduce their significance. We need nourishment of a certain sort; our bodies and psyches are vulnerable to harm of many different kinds; we express emotions in observable ways (even when one's positionality disallows others from understanding the emotional response, or it needs to be constantly hidden); we tend to care for others and wish to be cared for in return; we generally wish to be treated justly, even if we may disagree on how exactly justice is characterized. Despite the ridiculous claim of Dr. Paul Nathanson, we indeed are humans, with all that entails.

THE MONSTROUS AS REJECTION OF DIFFERENTIATION

In a way reminiscent of "the Miracle of Apollonius of Tyana," the US dominant culture, and many others, have had a long history of demonizing individuals and groups and using various tools to do so. One such method is to construct the individuals as being subhuman or monstrous. Individuals who are foreigners, thought to be enemies of the state, people of color, Indigenous persons, those who are disabled, and those thought to be "sexually deviant" have been represented as monstrous, abominable, heinous, disgusting, etc. Doing so is an attempt to justify immoral and unjust treatment, with the assumption that monsters or animals (to which Black, Indigenous, people of color, the poor, LGBTQ, and disabled persons have historically been compared) are less morally valuable and in many ways are either masses to manipulate and use to one's own end, or represent a kind of dangerous force to be vanquished. It was just in the summer of 2019 when scholars and others took note of how many times President Trump used the term "infestation" when describing refugees on the southern border of the US. The word "infestation" is used to describe the unwanted presence of insects, those that can cause harm to humans, such as an infestation of "killer" bees, or termites that can silently undermine the structure of one's home. Dehumanizing humans involves efforts to fetishize and obsess over real and fictionalized difference; scapegoating and oppression in general require such fetishizing, for otherwise the enormous evidence of sameness would result in empathy rather than stigma and animus.

Monsters, according to Girard, are indicative of the kind of rejection of differentiation that he believes is the heart of the scapegoating mechanism. Monsters embody a transcendence of typical differentiation; their very existence, even if fictional, is a rejection of typical differences of species (some seem to be combinations of several different species), a defiance of norms (some seem to regularly eat children alongside other shocking norm-denying activities), and of typical abilities (some breathe fire, are able to fly, or have acid for saliva, etc.). Tellingly, Mircea Eliade's study on monsters in Greek mythology identifies monsters that are androgynous, can "change their sex" or dress, and purport themselves to be the "opposite" sex.[21] While being androgynous or having the power to change one's gender characterizes one with a special spiritual insight in some cultures, it leads to rejection and oppression in the globally dominant cultures of Europe and their colonial progeny.

LGBTQ individuals, and here the focus is on trans and gender non-conforming and gender non-binary persons, have a long history of being seen as monstrous to those who oppose our full social participation and reject our moral value. First and most basically, our bodies have been seen as monstrous when they do not, or it is assumed that they do not, conform to cisgender standards. Our bodies, lives, and identities may have what are considered by others to be mismatched pieces, thus rejecting the dichotomy of sexual and gender differentiation and the gender norms that are based on this unjustified expectation. Allen Andrade, who was found guilty for the murder of Angie Zapata in 2008, reportedly used the "it" pronoun when referring to Zapata, when describing the brutal beating. "I thought I had killed it," he is reported as saying.[22] Here, the "it" pronoun designates a monstrous status—a genderless and thus valueless existence. Whether the term "it" refers to the monstrous, a non-human animal, or an inanimate object, "it" designates a kind of moral relationship, or more precisely, a *lack* of moral relationship since it assumes that the entity referred to as "it" is not capable of such a relationship. Particularly in the dominant anthropocentric culture, a relationship to an *it* is one of carefree, often cruel, and thoughtless dominance. It is carefree and thoughtless since, literally, no thought, care, empathy, sympathy, or concern is relevant when dealing with an *it*. One can throw *it* away, waste *it*, destroy *it*, or display *it*; such choices are entirely up to the "non-it" who controls *it*. It can be even used to display one's good taste, or even one's stylish-in-some-circles progressive politics. At least, that is the belief of the dominant particularly anthropocentric culture that continually relegates so many and so much to the categories of either profitable or useless.[23] Theorist Mel Y. Chen has experimented with claiming the "it" pronoun as its own, thus further blurring the lines not only between gender categories, but also between the morally valuable and what is seen as the merely prudentially useful or otherwise expendable.[24] I applaud Chen's challenge to both anthropocentrism and cisgender heterosexual dominance. This challenge leads us to question why referring to a person as an "it" is so disconcerting while at the same time recognizing it as a word used as a weapon to harass and devalue trans and gender non-conforming persons worldwide. Speaking personally, I remember quite well being called an "it" late at night outside a Phoenix, Arizona bar. This experience did not lead me to feel camaraderie and respect for the nonhuman world in that moment, even though I am apt to have such camaraderie. Instead, I was concerned how I was going to get to my truck and away without being beaten up.

C. Riley Snorton, in his influential work *Black on Both Sides: A Racial History of Trans Identity*, tells the story of Peter Sewally/Mary Jones, whose lithographed image in 1836 of a smartly attired young Black woman, with the words "Man Monster" under the image, made money for the lithograph producers even as it demonized the individual.[25] Again we see the interplay between the familiar, a woman, representing the social and gender norms of the day, along with the moniker "monster" and the implicit message to "not be fooled" by this individual who is storied to be using middle-class respectability only to deceive the unwary; the unaware are destined to be conned both by the image of respectability and that of womanhood. Indeed, the fact that Sewally/Jones is Black is even more cause for caution to the whites viewing the image. A Black woman in respectable and fashionable dress ("Ain't I A Woman?")? A lower-class person trying to look upper-crust? A criminal trying to look respectable? Or perhaps (gasp), a man attempting to pass himself off as a woman? Norms of class, race, and gender are rejected at once, as are the norms of legal behavior if it is true, as testified, that Sewally/Jones was not only skilled at providing fine company for gentlemen of New York, but of relieving them of their wallets by evening's end. Independent of the actual crime committed (or not committed) by Sewally/Jones, it is undeniable that racism played a role in their demonization and unjustified social admonishment. To ask why they were characterized as monstrous, on top of it all, is to ask why Michael Brown was similarly characterized in 2014 by the police officer who fatally shot the unarmed youth, or to ask why anyone would be characterized so. Again, the miracle of Apollonius is not that Apollonius was able to discern and reveal the demon posing as an old supplicant, but that he was able to make the Ephesians *believe* the elderly man was the demonic source of the plague. This "miracle" is a function of power and the power of narrative to transform the marginalized, including trans, gender non-binary, and gender non-conforming persons, into threatening monsters, those of dangerously distorted bodies and minds, those who are constructed to be scapegoats.

GIRARDIAN MIMETIC DESIRE

Any application of Girardian scapegoating would be incomplete without a consideration of one last foundational aspect of his theory. Girard's analysis begins with a claim about human nature, more specifically, the nature of human desire. Girard and many others would reject the view that one's desires are entirely individual and unique to the character and personality of that person. I, for instance, might claim that my preference for vanilla ice cream is entirely my own and is based simply on what *tastes good* . . . to me. We can call this the Individualistic Account. Some might disagree with this very individualistic view and mention that my preference for vanilla ice cream over other varieties is, at the very least, partly a function of the fact that I live and was raised in a society in which ice cream is eaten on occasion and that vanilla ice cream is thought to be a kind of treat, and that vanilla ice cream is regularly available. This view would see personal preference as permeable to social conditions and not only a result of an individual living in an isolated, atomistic way. I call this the Permeability to Culture Account.

In relation to the two views of human desire sketched out above, Girard goes further, but in the same vein as the Permeability to Culture Account. Girard argues that desire is fundamentally mimetic, that what is desired is not desired because we each have a bundle of individual preferences that are, to one degree or another, influenced by culture, but that we desire that which we see others desiring. That is, individual A desires X because individual B desires X. Mimetic desire is a desire that is copied or mimicked from another. Famously, Girard argues that society itself would not be possible unless we exhibited a mimetic nature. Simply put, we are, in a fundamental way, mimickers. Language, culture, and generally learning to fit into a society in a way that supports individual and collective thriving are dependent on how well we learn to mimic others in the production and execution of social norms. Even for one not completely in agreement with Girard's view, there is much that rings true here. What is language but a mimicking of noises and symbols? What is culture but a mimicking of activities and attitudes and preferences? How does one learn to use the quadratic equation but by mimicking the teacher or tutor who has mastered the activity by mimicking someone else? Personally, I reflect that for many years my professed "favorite movie" was also the favorite movie of my elder sister. I notice that many of my "personal" preferences are also those of my elder siblings, whom I undoubtedly mimicked as the youngest born. Learning at least starts with mimicry, even if later that learning is the basis for a creative evolution. Mimetic desire goes a long way toward explaining fashion or consumeristic trends, favorite music groups or TV shows, and, if we accept Girard's account, scapegoating.

According to Girard, mimetic desire does more than just fuel consumeristic choices, it also fuels character traits, attitudes, and actions that are much less morally neutral. Envy, jealousy, bitterness, acts of theft and embezzlement, and an endless competition for goods and attention also follow from mimetic desire left unchecked. There is nothing especially worrisome about me having the same favorite movie as my elder sister, but there may be when the mimicking desire is not about asserting a favorite movie, but rather asserting a biased view of who is to be valued and who is to be hated. Girard argues that mimetic desire is so foundational to human nature, and also to human conflict, that the tenth of the famous Ten Commandments in many ways encompasses the content of many of the others. One translation of this commandment is: "You must not be envious of your neighbor's goods. You shall not be envious of his house nor his wife, nor anything that belongs to your neighbor."[26] Indeed, if no one coveted their neighbor's goods then there would be little motivation to commit murder, adultery, or to steal. Girard explains, "We assume that desire is objective or subjective, but in reality, it rests on a third party who gives value to the objects. This third party is usually the one who is closest, the neighbor. To maintain peace between human beings, it is essential to define prohibitions in light of this extremely significant fact: our neighbor is the model for our desires."[27] Without such prohibitions, the world would soon resemble a Hobbesian nightmare, or "mimetic crisis." It is the scapegoat process, theorizes Girard, that turns the Hobbesian mob into a directed weapon. From a war of all against all, it becomes an attack of "all against one."[28]

Going back to the story of Apollonius, recall that the Ephesians were first aghast at the thought of stoning the stranger. No one wanted to "throw the first stone." This last phrase may bring to mind the Biblical story of Jesus, whose injunction, "Let any one of you who is without sin be the first to throw a stone at her," came when an alleged adulteress was presented to the crowd to suffer death by stoning.[29] No one wants to throw the first stone, for in doing so, one is not mimicking another, not falling into step with what is seen as culturally *normal*, but putting oneself in the place of obvious social criticism if one's action is not followed up with other's similar action. It is much easier to throw a stone or perpetrate an injustice if one is the hundredth, or thousandth, one to do so, if one has been acculturated that such behavior is acceptable, if one is part of the mob, department, platoon, or corporation that is full of those who desire to throw stones and commit other injustices, full of those who support disrespectful and dehumanizing actions and attitudes. For Girard, scapegoating is a ubiquitous part of human society since we are primed to be vulnerable to mimicry and the force of social pressure to not color too far outside the lines. According to this view, it is as hard to throw the first stone as it is to keep from throwing the last.

Again, our social media–drenched lives seem to make mimicking hateful language and attitudes exceptionally easier than in the past. The organization Ditch the Label recently reported their findings regarding anti-trans bullying online. Assisted by the analytics of the research organization Brandwatch, their findings led them to describe this kind of online abuse to BBC reporter Ben Hunte as "inhumane."[30] Among the worst social media sites were sites like YouTube and others that feature video content. On these types of sites, roughly 80 percent of the content was abusive. YouTube comments were found to be 78 percent abusive and the category of "other," which includes other video sites or those which post reviews, was found to be 82 percent abusive.[31] Jay Hulme, a twenty-two-year-old children's poet and transgender man, describes his own experience: "It can be a full-scale hate storm with thousands of people attacking me relentlessly for days, or individual accounts sending general hate. I've been called an abuser, a sexual harasser, a sexist. I think the worst ones would have to be the times people call me a pedophile, just because I'm trans and write books for children."[32] The experience of Mr. Hulme is in no way unique to trans, gender non-binary, and gender non-conforming persons today. For most, this form of abuse is a newly learned behavior that starts with recognizing the frequency of the abuse and that it is generally accepted, learning the language of abuse, and then mimicking the hateful rhetoric of others. It is more than troubling to realize that, to revive our previously mentioned example, it is not the case that folks are holding stones but being too hesitant to throw the first one. To the contrary (recall the previous chapter's content regarding the frequency of anti-transgender rhetoric) first stones have been repeatedly thrown by those with cultural influence and power, and with the help of contemporary technology these "stones" can be shared countless times.

CONCLUSION

I have used a Girardian view of scapegoating as a basis of this chapter not because I am a full-throated proponent of his theory in all its respects. In this chapter I have identified aspects of his far-reaching view that seem justifiable and relevant to the politicization of transgender and gender transgressive persons and have not focused on the aspects of his theory that seem less applicable or helpful. For those who are more familiar with his scapegoat theory in total, I offer just a few particulars. First, like many, I am sympathetic to characterization of desire as mimetic, but am cautious to assert that all instances of human desire are essentially and purely mimetic in nature. Certainly, we mimic each other, but learning and creating is often more than simply mimicry, even though it may start that way. In concert with Girard, I tentatively can accept the claim that some form of societal unification has historically occurred after scapegoats were identified and vanquished. This is consistent with the broader idea that collectives gain solidarity through the identification of common enemies. I am skeptical that any solidarity from this source is anything but temporary and superficial. Scapegoating is morally reprehensible behavior and cannot serve as the basis for societal cohesion. In the end, the truth of atrocities becomes known, and this ushers in a time of societal reckoning for past harms. This reckoning is often divisive and painful to those subject to historical and generational injustice as well as those who realize the truth of their own dominant group's oppression. I am skeptical, however, that in societies in which mimetic contagion has achieved a fevered Hobbesian pitch, that the scapegoat process will organically funnel all that collective anxiety and hatefulness into a weapon against a single scapegoated person or collective. Contrary to Girard's assertion that "the initial proliferation of scandals leads sooner or later into an acute crisis at the climax of which unanimous violence is set off against the single victim, the victim finally selected by the entire community,"[33] there is evidence to suggest that more than one group can be scapegoated and a consolidated focus on just one person or group need not occur. Hitler's Nazi regime is a case in point. While the genocidal campaign against Jews in Germany and occupied countries is most cited as evidence of a single scapegoat, it was not only those of the Jewish community who were sentenced to the hell of the Nazi concentration camps, but also LGBTQ persons, ethnic Roma, and others. Additionally, intersectional analysis provides the means necessary to recognize that targeted biases always are carried out and experienced intersectionally.

Still, a Girardian view can still be instructive, especially in our times. The growth and use of the internet, and how it has established social media and has made available immense stores of information, has not only allowed many trans, gender non-conforming, and other marginalized groups a way to understand ourselves in new ways through immense opportunities for connection; it has also taught many others just how to use language in ways that are demeaning and derogatory against trans and gender transgressive persons. Many have come to learn of the appropriateness of "they" as a singular gender-neutral pronoun and learned its respectful use, while others have learned the white power symbol and different occasions to flash it in one's outstretched hand when one's face is out of view. To some extent, both of these expressions initially involve mimicry. A Girardian analysis is, however, broadly applicable to the recent politicization and scapegoating of trans and other gender transgressive persons. He not only aptly describes and explains a collective behavior that is unfortunately familiar to many, but in doing so gives us the tools to understand and attempt to push back on a process that can gain momentum all too quickly. Again, recall the S-B scapegoating of the previous chapter. The Girardian position is a crucial addition to this view since scapegoating is not an equal opportunity endeavor. Meaning, those from marginalized and minoritized social groups will be more likely scapegoating because of their marginalized and minoritized status, regardless of their actions or inactions for which they are over-blamed.

In understanding the relationship of our present social context to our internal nature of mimetic desire, some might wish to add more outwardly originated forms of social control such as a Foucauldian conception of discipline, which metes out belonging or strict punishment for abiding by or rejecting the institutional norms in place that benefit the powerful. Obviously, this view complements our understanding of our common social context. Gender transgressive individuals of various backgrounds have experienced strict social discipline when their/our expressions are unintelligible or devalued by the binary believing majority. In our present era, people are learning to be anti-trans through the animus expressed not only by other individuals, but also by the current social climate. This climate, especially in the years 2015–2020, was dominated by Trumpian dehumanizing personal sarcasm and trans oppressive national policies, meaning that there are fewer limits to these actions and attitudes for the general population. Individuals learned to mimic Trump and this, in turn, helped to consolidate his power. Weaponizing public opinion, fear, and frustration has long been an often-used tool for politicians in both major political parties. The next chapter focuses on the topic of dog-whistling and the related notion of virtue signaling, and the extent to which these tactics have been used to further politicize transgender and other gender transgressive persons.

NOTES

1. C. Allen Carter, *Kenneth Burke and the Scapegoat Process* (Norman: University of Oklahoma Press, 1996), 20.
2. Leviticus 16:10.
3. Leviticus 16:26.
4. René Girard, *I See Satan Fall Like Lightning*, translated with a foreword by James G. Williams (Maryknoll, NY: Orbis Books, 2001).
5. A well-known example of scapegoating in the context of plague is that from this history of fourteenth-century Europe when the Jews were scapegoated for the Black Plague. Guillaume de Machaut's account of the persecution of the Jews for the Black Death between 1349 and 1350 is instructive reading.
6. Flavius Philostratus, *The Life of Apollonius of Tyana, the Epistles of Apollonius and the Treatise of Eusebius*, trans. F. C. Conybeare, Loeb Classical Library, 2 vols. (Cambridge, MA: Harvard University Press, 1912), 1: 363–367, quoted in Girard, *I See Satan Fall Like Lightning*, 49–50.
7. Girard, *I See Satan Fall Like Lightning*, 76.
8. René Girard, *The Scapegoat* (Baltimore: Johns Hopkins University Press, 1986), 40.
9. Girard, *The Scapegoat*, 15.
10. Janice Raymond, *The Transsexual Empire and the Making of the She-Male* (New York: Teachers College Press, 1979).
11. Consider the merciless killing of Mercedes Williamson in 2015. Her boyfriend, Joshua Vallum, was convicted of this crime and it was designated a hate crime. The defense employed the "trans panic" defense and that Vallum didn't know of his girlfriend's history, but there is evidence against this as well. Tracy Williams (Tracy Single) was also killed by her boyfriend, Joshua Dominic Bourgeois, in August of 2019. Bourgeois was not charged with a hate crime.
12. Girard, *The Scapegoat*, 17.
13. Girard, *The Scapegoat*, 18.
14. Girard, *The Scapegoat*, 18.
15. Emma Green, "White Evangelicals Believe They Face More Discrimination than Muslims," *Atlantic*, March 10, 2017 (based on PRRI Survey, 2017), https://www.theatlantic.com/politics/archive/2017/03/perceptions-discrimination-muslims-christians/519135/.
16. Girard, *The Scapegoat*, 36.
17. Girard, *The Scapegoat*, 26.
18. Talia Mae Bettcher, "Evil Deceivers and Make Believers: On Transphobic Violence and the Politics of Illusion," *Hypatia* 22, no. 3 (Summer 2007): 43–65.
19. Girard, *The Scapegoat*, 21.
20. Girard, *The Scapegoat*, 22.
21. Girard, *The Scapegoat*, 34.
22. Monte Whaley, "Smile Called Provoking Act in Transgender Case," *Denver Post*, May 7, 2016 (updated from September 18, 2008), https://www.denverpost.com/2008/09/18/smile-called-provoking-act-in-transgender-case/.

23. Vandana Shiva. Interviewed in *The Call of the Mountain: Deep Ecology and Arnie Naess*, directed by Jan van Boeckel, produced by Karin van der Molen/Pat van Boeckel, 1997. Paraphrase.

24. Thinking Trans, Trans Thinking Conference, 2018, Washington, DC.

25. C. Riley Snorton, *Black on Both Sides: A Racial History of Trans Identity* (Minneapolis: University of Minnesota Press, 2017).

26. The Ten Commandments, https://www.topmarks.co.uk/judaism/the-ten-commandments.

27. Girard, *I See Satan Fall Like Lightning*, 9–10.

28. Girard, *I See Satan Fall Like Lightning*, 24.

29. John 8:7 NIV.

30. Ben Hunte, "Transgender People Treated 'Inhumanly' Online," BBC News, October 25, 2019, https://www.bbc.com/news/technology-50166900?SThisFB&fbclid=IwAR0qpV2Ifs5iNWwq3qiaG8XGFxhJZXUcfvFWmwDbZaeJi4QRV30OlbN23PI.

31. Brandwatch, Ditch the Label, "Exposed: The Extent of Transphobia Online," https://www.brandwatch.com/reports/transphobia/.

32. Ibid.

33. Girard, *I See Satan Fall Like Lightning*, 30.

Chapter 7

Dog Whistles and Virtue Signaling

The power to influence public opinion, whether it be in the form of favorable praise or animosity and anger, is one of the most powerful tools that one can wield. Leaders can inspire soldiers to put their lives on the line for king, country, or ideals that may seem threatened. Politicians and social leaders from Apollonius, to the Reverend Martin Luther King Jr., to David Duke, Dolores Huerta, Donald Trump, and Greta Thunberg all recognize that such a power can multiply one's own influence a hundred- or a thousandfold. Influencing the masses to believe something and then act in accordance with that belief can pave the way toward social change, substantial wealth, political power, a personal legacy, or combinations of such. Whether one has a natural gift for such influence or is a person who intentionally studies to produce the rhetoric and performance that affords maximum control, the power brokers of any society recognize that influencing the masses and targeting and directing that power can yield dramatic results. As was discussed in the previous chapter, scapegoating others certainly can result in the amassing of power by over-blaming others, perhaps to keep oneself seemingly blameless or for other political reasons, or to unify certain groups of a society against others, again to gain political influence and power.

Dog-whistling is related to scapegoating in that it generally uses, in a way reignites, certain unjustified negative stereotypes and false narratives and uses the reignited biases to help insure political power. What is less discussed is the practice of "virtue signaling," here relevant as the flip side of the dog-whistling practice. Dog-whistling appeals to conscious and unconscious bias through fearmongering and well-worn marginalizing tropes. But, without the implicit promise of attending to the fear that results, such a strategy may simply result in widespread agitation, and not the sought-after political victory. The feelings of distress, fear, and being unsettled need to be comforted by a character that can calm the fear and vanquish the thought-to-be-danger. To accomplish this, one must signal to others that one has the strength of character, political savvy, commitment, and virtue to attend to the manufactured distress. This is the role played by "virtue signaling." In this chapter, both dog-whistling and virtue signaling will be evaluated in the context of the politicization of trans identity and expression. Challenges to their application will be discussed, with support for the conclusion that both terms are relevant to our recent political context.

HANEY LÓPEZ'S DOG-WHISTLING

Ian Haney López's influential work, *Dog Whistle Politics: How Coded Racial Appeals Have Reinvented Racism and Wrecked the Middle Class*, first available in 2014 and revised in 2016, provided a new tool to explain and analyze one kind of dynamic between politics and public opinion.[1] While not focused on anti-trans or anti-LGBTQ policy or sentiment, López's work serves to deepen the present analysis in a variety of ways. We have discussed that backlash can be understood as a kind of collective response and that scapegoating can be seen as a strategy of backlash. In this section, dog-whistling, a close cousin of scapegoating, is shown to be yet another kind or aspect of a directed backlash response. As I will explain, trans-focused dog-whistling has become more common since 2015 and has been used in attempts to win political campaigns as well as serve as a kind of virtue signaling to those who want others to believe that they regard "transgenderist ideologies" as dangerous to themselves, their children, and the health of society.

López's coined term "dog whistle politics" and the picture of the large erect-eared Doberman on the cover of his book brings to mind a common understanding of the term. Literally, a "dog whistle" is a whistle that, due to its particularly high frequency, is one that only a dog can hear. Since the sound of a dog whistle is generally undetectable to the human ear, calling a dog with such a whistle can be a kind of secret communication between the caller and the pet. In terms of political analysis, the analogy is that certain constituencies have a kind of receptivity to particular messages sent by politicians to gain their attention and support. Those groups and individuals outside the constituency being enticed may not hear the "whistle," and thus these appeals, that are often racist in nature, can go unnoticed and uncriticized.

According to López, a dog whistle is somewhat like a secret handshake and occurs when "a politician is speaking in code and he knows that the intended audience will understand, but he hopes it will be unintelligible to most of the general audience."[2] Dog whistles can be effective because conscious or unconscious bias results in an individual responding in predictable ways and this response can be so directed to win elections or achieve other political goals. While there has been an increase of publicly expressed hateful language (here thinking of the white nationalists' "Unite the Right" rally in Charlottesville, Virginia, in 2017, and other similar events), it is still the case that most racists and anti-Semites do not explicitly espouse such beliefs publicly. Anthony Appiah was right in 1990 when he commented on the strange phenomenon that there was "a good deal of racism about," but then, as now, it is difficult to find any self-proclaimed racists—at least outside the few contexts in which the ideology is proclaimed explicitly and openly.[3] Given that few individuals publicly espouse their racist beliefs openly, it is not surprising to learn that coded language is used in public spaces, since it allows politicians and others mostly unnoticed access to the power of individuals' collective biases. López explains how politicians have intentionally targeted such individuals for their own political ends. Like the erect-eared Doberman on the book cover, those harboring racist beliefs or sympathies are primed to *hear* the dog whistles and act in ways directed by the dog-whistling politician. For example, the innocent sounding concern of "property rights" can influence and activate those whites who are worried that they may someday have people of color residing in their neighborhoods. Identifying oneself as a politician who is "tough on crime" can similarly activate and enthuse individuals who are worried that Indigenous persons, Black, Latinx, and all people of color, recent immigrants, or those without houses will be adequately restrained and "suitably dealt with" by certain politicians and not by others. Tellingly, to "get serious" about crime or homelessness doesn't typically involve looking into the factors that cause individuals to engage or be unjustly regarded as engaging in criminal behavior. Instead, to "get serious" more often means to use the power of the state to incarcerate individuals and thus make the privileged believe that their lifestyle and property is "safe" from the threat of thought-to-be dangerous *Others*.

López's analysis is focused specifically on the use of racist dog whistles that became an important part of the "Southern Strategy" adopted by Richard Nixon and by subsequent GOP politicians since that time. Understanding the use and effectiveness of dog-whistle politics allows one to look through official party lines decrying the ills and ideology of racism, and instead decipher the coded messages that serve to motivate many white voters who can be taught to obediently *heel* through their fears of "inner city crime," "welfare queens," dangerous "illegal aliens," "those who want free stuff," "free loaders," those whose presence is seen as a threat to "property values," "the safety of our community," or even "family values." None of these ideas sound *prima facia* racist, but the image that is conjured is not one of *Leave It to Beaver* white middle-class cisgender heteropatriarchy. Instead they are coded messages that are racist in implication and intention, more than explicit reference. Dog-whistling, as it has been conceived by López, became a strategy of the

Republican Party, when they gave up on acquiring any significant support from Black voters and decided instead to exploit the country's racist divisions to maximize white loyalty. As López explains,

> In 2005, he [Ken Mehlman, Republican National Committee head from 2005 to 2007] used a speech before the NAACP to admit that his party had exploited racial divisions, and had been wrong to do so. "By the seventies and into the eighties and nineties," Mehlman said from a prepared text, "Republicans gave up on winning the African American vote, looking the other way or trying to benefit politically from racial polarization. I am here today as the Republican chairman to tell you we were wrong." These apologies at once confess to racial pandering and also implicitly promise to sin no more. This is a promise that the GOP will struggle to fulfill, for this party is now essentially defined by race: it is almost exclusively supported by and composed of whites.[4]

Now, to be clear, it is not López's intent to claim that dog-whistling is a strategy used only by those in the GOP. Especially when Democratic candidates need to shift to the center of the political spectrum to pull votes from independents and moderate Republican voters, the same tactics have been used by Democrats. If being seen as "soft on crime" will mean that an election is likely lost, Democrats, too, have used the same scheme. A well-known case in point involves Bill Clinton's characterization of the "super-predator," an obvious monsterization of the Black and Brown men living in the inner city. Clinton was created to be a "New Democrat," one that is "resistant to black concerns, tough on crime, and hostile to welfare."[5] This strategy found less publicized criticism in 1990 than it would today—as illustrated by how the "super-predator" statement and attending policies represented an old yet still festering sore to which Hillary Clinton had to respond in her own presidential run when she was critiqued by members of the Black Lives Matter movement and sympathetic others.

TRANSPHOBIC DOG-WHISTLING

While López's work focuses on racist dog-whistling, it stands to reason that dog-whistling can be used to benefit the whistler when other biases are also activated with coded language. Dog-whistling can be used as a tool to take advantage of the politicization of a group and the conscious and unconscious biases that many have come to hold against members of that group. One of the major theses of this project is that in the last decade, and especially in the years 2015 to 2020, the lives and identities of trans persons have become part of the national political conversation. How one feels about our existence and our lives is now an issue that is discussed in state legislatures, Supreme

Courts, religious pulpits, and even award shows. The intersection of the evangelical Christian right and the conservative wing of the Republican Party foster spaces that nurture and disseminate anti-trans sentiment (adding to this mix self-described radical feminists who are trans-exclusionary makes for odd bedfellows, indeed). In fact, a major factor that motivated me to write this book is my concern that being anti-trans seems to be well on its way to being a kind of litmus test for politicians to have true "conservative credentials." Will being anti-trans, and its thought-to-be-justifying rhetoric, serve a similar purpose as being pro-life or pro-NRA? In at least some contexts, having the right kind of "conservative chops" requires that repealing *Roe v. Wade* be at least on one's political bucket list if not one's life work. Will having a stance on the legitimacy of my and others' gender identity be similar, or will it fade into history as a kind of temporary anti-trans frenzy?

History will be the judge of the extent to which trans identity remains politicized into the future, but signaling one's anti-trans stance to potential voters for the purpose of garnering votes and gaining political power is clearly evident in some recent political contests. Already mentioned is the political attack ad in the state of Kentucky used by incumbent Matt Bevin against Democratic challenger Andy Beshear. Bevin's assessment that Beshear was too radical for Kentucky was at least partly based on Beshear's generally pro-LGBTQ stance which, according to the ad, was sufficient information to claim that Beshear is in favor of the cessation of all girls' sports (since, the argument goes, they would be taken over by girls who are trans). While Bevin's tactics did not win the race, the fact that trans issues were even part of the conversation is noteworthy. Ralph Abraham, Republican gubernatorial candidate in Louisiana, explicitly displayed his anti-trans credentials in his 2019 ad, in which he faces the camera and verbalizes a number of statements he takes to be eight facts, including "Life Begins at Conception," "Government Is Too Big," "President Trump Is Doing a Great Job," "Facts Matter More than Feelings," and, with a chuckle, he adds, "and as a doctor, I can assure you, there are only two genders."[6] The last statement, complete with the chuckle, can be considered an anti-trans dog whistle. Note that the word "transgender" is not mentioned, nor is there any kind of explicit reference to anti-transgender legislation. The comment that "there are only two genders" is meant to convey that the speaker believes that trans and gender non-binary persons are confused and incorrect in our articulation of our identities. Taken most explicitly, the jab seems to be against gender non-binary people most centrally, but I believe that sympathetic hearers will understand the statement to refer to transgender persons more generally, even those of us who are binary identifying and/or appearing. I expect that the speaker's intent is to imply the assertion of the more complete idea, "There are only two genders and one's gender identity and expression necessarily corresponds to one's sex assignment at birth." Abraham's reference to his training as a medical doctor assures the viewer that he has the authority to recognize the current *gender insanity* for what it is, and that he can be counted on to make sure that such *insanity* does not adversely affect Louisiana's cisgender heterosexual citizens or institutions. Lastly, it is well known that President Trump's administration has reversed the gains made by the Obama administration that served to protect transgender and gender non-conforming adults and school children. When asked about his efforts to make the "official" designation of gender to be male or female, as assigned at birth and later unchangeable, the former president replied that such a proposal is important due to his commitment to protecting the country: "I am protecting everybody. I want to protect our country."[7] Here, Trump was not only offering himself as the protector of the country, but also implicitly asserting that the country requires protection from transgender persons and our attempts to live authentic lives.

Dog-whistling is effective in that the racist or other marginalizing content of the whistle is not explicit but meant to be heard by those receptive to the message. With regard to anti-trans dog-whistling, rather than explicitly saying that "trans persons are not deserving of equal social participation or medical care" one might instead discuss ways in which one can support measures that "keep our girls safe," or those that are from organizations that "value men and women as created by God." One need not demonize trans persons directly, but expressing a valuing of "biological realities" or "girls' sports" is evidence that the speaker is sending an anti-transgender message to those who can hear and, presumably, join them in countering dangerous "transgenderist ideology." The political ads and rhetoric of anti-trans politics, like the dog-whistling of López's articulation, nurture fear on the part of the message receiver. Fearmongering distortions equate the idea of supporting trans persons in using the gendered facility that is consistent both with their identity and important safety concerns with putting young cisgender girls at risk of sexual assault; supporting trans girls and women in the human right of fair athletic competition with the end of girls' sports programs; backing policies that set the foundation for flourishing lives for trans, gender non-binary, and gender non-conforming persons with bringing about god's abandonment and risking Sodom and Gomorrah type consequences.

This kind of appeal to fear, anxiety, unrest, and dread is certainly consistent with López's characterized dog-whistling, especially when it results in an increase in the political power of the whistler. Racist dog-whistling *works* since many white individuals, few of whom have investigated the racism inherent in the white-dominated culture, are primed to have these biases activated and are unconcerned that they might thoughtlessly respond in ways directed by the dog-whistling politician. They are not aware that they have biases or that the biases they have might be used for another's benefit.

Whether or not one thinks that anti-trans dog-whistling obtains in a way similar to the dog-whistling of López's chief concern depends partly on the extent to which one can claim that individuals are similarly *primed* to respond to anti-transgender dog whistles. As will be discussed later in this chapter, being "similarly primed" means not only that those primed individuals will respond en masse to political dog whistles, but that the mimetic nature of assertion or denial is relevant to gaining sufficient power for scapegoating agendas.

REACTIVATION OR CREATION OF BIASES? A DEBATE

The question of whether listeners are "primed" with conscious or unconscious biases against a given population is relevant to whether the dog-whistling is effective. To the question of whether individuals are so primed with regard to anti-transgender rhetoric, there seems to be at least two different ways to respond. Firstly, some might argue that the concept of dog-whistling is not applicable in the context of anti-trans related politicization because the antecedent conditions of López's focus, regarding internalized bias, do not obtain in the case of anti-trans attitudes, or at least it is significantly different than the racial bias that exists in so many, especially white persons, in the US. After all, goes this argument, it seems plausible that just a generation ago few cisgender persons, if queried, would have espoused anti-transgender sentiment if asked directly. Asked if one was worried about transgender persons in bathrooms, most would likely misunderstand the context of the question. Fifty or sixty years ago, one might think of a personality like Christine Jorgenson if the word "transgender," or more precisely "transsexual," were to come up in conversation. But one's sentiments towards Jorgenson or even Renée Richards and her mid-1970s tennis career, were less dependent on political association. It is interesting to compare the story of Richards, who sued the United States Tennis Association when they attempted to require chromosome tests for players in 1976, to the claims of the ruin of girls' sports now. Since Richards was assigned male at birth, the results of the test would have barred her from playing. Even though she ended up winning her case at the Supreme Court level and was able to play, her case was not politicized as are issues of trans inclusion today. Meaning, at the very least, this was not something that was a partisan issue and not something to entice readers to the polls. In the end, one might argue, the history of racism (and other oppressive systems) in this country is simply longer, more entrenched, and thus has had more of a morally distorting effect on the attitudes and values of the racially and otherwise privileged than one could expect from the only relatively recent visibility of trans, gender non-binary, and gender non-conforming persons' expressions and identities. The US has a long history of structural racism, and it has played such a foundational role in the making and continuance of the US that unconscious racial bias has become the rule and not the exception for white Americans, which, according to this position, is quite different from anti-trans bias. The heart of this argument is that, given the relative newness of issues related to transgender flourishing and civil rights, there is simply no great store of internalized bias to reignite by dog-whistling attempts. Given that it is this reignition or reactivation of conscious or unconscious biases that are key to López's account, then the notion of dog-whistling would not appropriately fit this context.

I admit, there was a time when I was more sympathetic to the argument just recounted. I am less so presently. The argument fails to recognize the degree to which the gender and sex binary has been firmly in place in the dominant culture and has negatively constrained the lives of countless individuals for centuries. Such "constraints" include compulsory heterosexuality and compulsory expression of gender identity thought consistent with assigned sex at birth, compulsory binary gender expressions and social roles. Attempting to exist outside the lines of the sex-gender binary has resulted in social disciplining tactics ranging from schoolyard taunts to harassment, discrimination, and extreme violence. And again, this has been the case for *centuries*. More is known now about historical figures whose lives were unique (at times both burdened and blessed) due to their gender identity or expression than ever before. Histories, such as Susan Stryker's *Transgender History: The Roots of Today's Revolution*,[8] C. Riley Snorton's *Black on Both Sides: A Racial History of Trans Identity*,[9] and Leslie Feinberg's ground-breaking work, *Transgender Warriors: Making History from Joan of Arc to Dennis Rodman*,[10] and books on figures such as physician Michael Dillon, *The First Man-Made Man* by Pagan Kennedy, as well as Dillon's own autobiography and story of his self-conceived and directed medical transition, *Out of the Ordinary: A Life of Gender and Spiritual Transitions*, and many others make it obvious that social ostracism and oppression are not new for those attempting to live authentic lives outside of binary expectations.[11] The trans tradition of memoir-writing gives us even more perspective on the lived experiences of trans and gender transgressive persons, as do the plethora of studies in the social sciences and by transgender advocacy groups that continue to verify that on nearly every measure (employment, housing, health care, harassment, income level, etc.) transgender persons are hurting when compared to our cisgender siblings. This information taken together is more than sufficient to claim that anti-transgender bias has existed for the entire history of the United States, and even before this time when looking to the cultures of the colonizing European nations. This nation has been home to families that have been raising their children to be tacitly or vehemently against the inclusion of trans and gender non-binary persons for centuries. Upon this thick foundation of bias and misunderstanding, the basis for anti-transgender dog-whistling is clearly set.

For these multiple reasons identified, including that identified at the beginning of this chapter, I believe that the notion of dog-whistling is generally descriptive of one aspect of the anti-trans backlash of recent years. Specifically, this dog-whistling has contributed to the backlash for as the fears were continually stoked, individuals were more likely to respond negatively to calls for justice for all genders. The statements by politicians used in the last section represent examples of anti-trans dog-whistling. Fear is stoked and directed in ways that allow some politicians to be seen as the protector of "family values," "Christian culture," and vulnerable (cisgender) children that are seen to be at risk from "transgenderists." This *can* lead to getting voted into office, regardless of whether any anti-transgender proposals become adopted. It is true that transgender rights have only relatively recently been in the national debate, but this is not so much evidence of a lack of bias against transgender and gender non-conforming persons as it is a testament that beliefs, attitudes, and actions consistent with the traditional gender binary have been so overwhelmingly socially compulsory that this aspect of the dominant culture has not been challenged in this way before. Societal discipline against those who attempt to live outside the lines of traditional notions of gender has been so severe that attempting to live as a trans or gender non-binary or non-conforming person has been nearly unthinkable for most of our nation's history.

While dog-whistling can be theoretically used against any marginalized class, the history of racism and politically armed trans animus are significantly dissimilar and this is important to note. As two distinct vectors of oppression, they have different histories and different strategies, and this is true even though both vectors are often used against one individual. To explain, consider the two dog-centered analogies that have been offered in this chapter. First, the analogy that certain coded language is a kind of "dog whistle" was first made by López. As described earlier, dogs don't need to be trained to hear a dog whistle; instead, they hear it as a result of their hearing mechanisms that allow them to typically hear frequencies that are undetectable to the human ear. Basically, a dog whistle can easily get the attention of the dog, and thus can be used as a training technique along with verbal cues and treats. Secondly, earlier in this chapter I mentioned how dog whistles can be used to make certain constituencies "heel" on call. The word "heel" in this sense generally means that the dog stays close to the side of the human, walks with them in step, sits when the human pauses walking, pivots appropriately when the directing human changes directions, and in competition heeling, closely watches the dog handler's face to be ready to carry out any command. In relation to hearing dog whistles, heeling is a *trained* behavior. Teaching a dog to heel appropriately typically takes many hours of careful instruction; it is not an innate ability.

In using the analogies of dog whistles and dog training offered above, it should not be inferred that López believes racism is innate; rather, the use of this term underscores how centuries of accepted and supported practices of structural racism have primed some folks to respond to dog whistles *almost as if* it were a kind of innate response. The fearmongering content of racist and anti-trans dog whistles are similar, as is the intended result of political influence, but the mechanisms between the content and the desired outcome are distinct. It has been within the last decade that there has been a concerted effort to teach the public just why they should be afraid of trans persons, why our existence is thought to be threatening to cherished institutions, why measures to ensure our flourishing represent "dangerous ideologies." Anti-trans dog-whistling is attempting to both create, reignite, and direct conscious and unconscious bias. Given the popularity of gender binarist ideology, it is fairly easy to arouse suspicion and fear against those who express and identify themselves outside these narrow confines, yet directing this bias towards recent targets such as school children who would like to use the bathroom or play sports requires a more concerted effort.

VIRTUE SIGNALING AND DOG-WHISTLING: TWO SIDES OF THE SAME COIN

Impotent Legislative Proposals

One of the many interesting aspects of the recent anti-trans legislative wave since 2015 is just how many bills are proposed but fail to eventually be adopted or even voted on. Seeing the extensive lists of failed proposals might be reason for one to think that these bills actually have very little support and that they are futile acts in the face of growing acceptance of social justice for trans persons. While this may be partly true, there is another understanding of these impotent proposals which supports the claim that there is a different kind of political game going on, one that some call "virtue signaling." Looking closely at the anti-trans and anti-LGBTQ bills proposed between 2015 and 2020, it is obvious that very few bills actually were passed and signed into law. For example, lawmakers in Colorado in 2018 proposed three different bills (SB 361, HB 922, HB 1206) but the session ended before much could be done. This was also seen in Georgia, Iowa, and other states. Some of these bills died in committee, were vetoed by their governor, or simply failed. This is the story of literally hundreds of such potential laws; it almost seems as if they were proposed to die before ever being actualized. If it is the case that some lawmakers are proposing legislation with little hope of shepherding the bill to fruition, then it may be the *performance* of the act that is its true end. Given the costs of the economic boycott of North Carolina after the passing of their HB 2, politicians may have been less inclined to support explicitly anti-trans policies as law and more interested in simply going on the record as sponsoring such legislation. It is the *act* of sponsoring or proposing these measures that is seen to provide evidence of one's so-called family values, one's religious character, or even one's moral piety. It is a performance that is meant to illuminate the politician's character and commitment to certain ideals, and that even in the face of tough opposition, they will continue to fight for those values that are both directly opposed to justice for all and whose support is likely to get them elected again next term.

While dog-whistling can activate biases against the marginalized through fear, virtue signaling serves to comfort the fearful that they have a champion to right these fabricated wrongs and protect those storied to be vulnerable to the harms brought on by the marginalized. Indeed, merely sowing fear may not result in political power, but only foment social unease, suspicion, and even panic. To make that fear work in a political context, one also needs to present oneself as the individual who has the strength and character to face the fictionalized impending danger and vanquish it, to be ready, even against all odds and against a formidable ideological enemy, to pursue safety for the dog-whistle responders. Like dog-whistling, this kind of virtue signaling can be somewhat undercover and involve coded language that some constituencies are primed to hear. Dog-whistling can increase levels of fear and anxiety about a particular group of marginalized persons, whereas its attendant virtue signaling can serve as an answer and salve to that fear and anxiety. To those whites who became fearful of "super-predators" ready to sell their children drugs, thought-to-be-virtuous "tough on crime" politicians were there to readily apply to the job of keeping their (white) children safe. To those parents concerned for the safety of their cisgender daughters, thought-to-be-virtuous "no nonsense" gender binary traditionalists are there to make sure that those (cis)daughters are safe from would-be "men in dresses" who are storied to pose them harm. Indeed, stoking fear through dog-whistling or more explicit measures would be ineffective if those fears could not be relieved and confidence restored.

Political virtue signaling and dog-whistling exist as two sides of the same coin. Together they allow one to first foment fear, then offer oneself as the virtuous defender. Alternatively, one can virtue signal that one is ready to fight what is thought to be the righteous fight, when and if certain dog-whistling becomes politically prudent. Proposing bills, even when there is little chance of having them pass, may involve this kind of virtue signaling. As fodder for both resumes and future campaign advertisements, they message not only that there is reason to be fearful, but that one is ready to be the champion for those relatively privileged and whose fears have been fanned. Proposing anti-trans legislation signals to others that they are ready to champion such bills presently and that they will be willing to sponsor such bills in the future when such support is more forthcoming. They have the thought-to-be strength of character to do so—this is the message of the signal.

Where dog-whistling is focused on distortions of the *Other* and tends to use fear related to that *Other* as a kind of political lever to hoist and direct public opinion, virtue signaling is much more about oneself and uses not fear but comfort and trust as its levering emotions. There is, of course, a dialectic in place in that saying "I am your kind of politician because we both believe the *Other* is [dangerous, wrong, confused . . . etc.]" does imply a negative judgment on the *Other* in question while at the same time conferring a positive judgment on the virtue signaling. The content of the initial phrase involves inclusion (I am one of you) not exclusion (they are not us). To be "one of us" is to be predictably on the side of the collective courted, to be against the "agendas" of the *Other*.

ORIGINS OF VIRTUE SIGNALING

I did not coin the term "virtue signaling." It was popularized in 2015 by James Bartholomew, writing for the *Spectator*.[12] According to Bartholomew's original characterization of the idea, to virtue signal is to communicate, via voice or social media, that one is virtuous by expressing approval or, more often, disapproval of certain ideas or practices. Bartholomew believes that often the virtue signaling expresses a strong negative reaction to something as a performance to illustrate their own admirable character. He uses the example of the phrase "I hate 4x4s!" which can be used to express the virtue of caring about the environment. Social media is well suited for such expressions, as Bartholomew states, "Twitter lends itself very well to virtue signaling, since it is much easier to express anger and scorn in 140 characters than to make a reasoned argument."[13] In the current contexts it is relatively easy and popular to express such anger or faux anger. "Biological sex is a scientific fact, Get Over It!" could be used as a signal to those who believe that the assumptions and beliefs of gender binarism and gender essentialism are true and thus that trans and gender non-binary persons are either fooling ourselves, perhaps by way of patriarchal myths, or actively attempting to deceive others.[14]

PRO-TRANS VIRTUE SIGNALING

Just as dog-whistling is used by those of all political stripes, virtue signaling is as well. Democrats or progressives can signal to those who are concerned that the party is trending too far to the left and may wish to signal to constituencies that they reside in the thought-to-be-virtuous middle. Alternatively, the politicization of trans identity means that our concerns are not just a flash point for some conservative politics, but that we have become a kind of darling of the far left. At different points in this volume, Talia Mae Bettcher's essay that describes the double bind of trans persons, who are seen as either a "make believer" or a "deceiver," has been referenced. I generally agree with Bettcher and believe that her work on this issue has been vital towards gaining a philosophical understanding of the social context in which many trans persons reside. However, I have argued that there is at least a common third kind of characterization that I believe is an important part of the trans and gender non-binary experience. Yes, we are often negatively viewed as deceivers or make believers, but the third option is something far more positive. For those wishing to display their *progressive* credentials we become a vehicle with which to do so. We are like the new exotic animal whose acquisition is boasted about by the zoo managers, the one Black friend of the white person who has been surrounded by only white people their entire lives, the non-Jew who has experienced a Seder supper with a close Jewish family. Certainly, one cannot be anti-Semitic if one has gone to the Seder and been welcomed with open arms; one can't be racist if one has a friend who is Black; or be anti-Arab if one has visited a mosque. In the same vein, there is a narrative that one is suitably and undeniably progressive whose life is committed to social justice . . . as demonstrated by the fact that they know trans or gender non-binary persons.

To be politicized in a politically polarized environment such as the contemporary US means that the trans and gender non-conforming communities are regularly damned or made darlings depending on who is thought to be the receiver of the virtue signaling. This was evident in the recent series of Democratic candidate presidential debates taking place in the summer and fall of 2019. Two interesting kinds of signals were fairly obvious. In the first debate, held in Miami, Beto O'Rourke, Cory Booker, and Julián Castro spoke Spanish at the debate. Speaking Spanish was undoubtedly a strategic move to demonstrate to the Miami audience that the concerns of Latinx Americans were ready to be championed by the speaker. While the accents of the non-Latinx candidates were somewhat jarring, for the most part the signal seemed to have been mostly favorably received. Secondly and more related to our topic here, one candidate, Julián Castro, spoke of trans issues when discussing the issue of abortion rights. Castro, formerly the housing and urban development secretary, wanted to convey that abortion rights were important to those who are transgender. His remarks were, "I believe in reproductive justice, and what that means is just because a woman—or, let's not forget someone in the trans community, a trans female—is poor doesn't mean they shouldn't have the right to exercise the right to choose."[15] As part of the viewing public, upon hearing Castro's comments I was first somewhat happily surprised that one of the candidates would publicly note that abortion issues are relevant to transgender persons. But this positive response was quickly replaced with disappointment since Castro seemed to be confused whether it is trans women or trans men who might come to need abortion services. Trans men typically have spent at least some time of their lives with uteruses, unlike trans women, and so some of these men can get pregnant. The positive response related to being seen and recognized in this political atmosphere was tempered with "Wait, does he even know about the trans community?" or perhaps the thought that this was a kind of vacuous virtue signaling meant to, yes, get the attention of the very small portion of the population that is trans but, perhaps more importantly, signal to others his robust progressive credentials. Of course, Castro might have simply confused himself when he spoke on this matter, due to his own nervousness and only recent familiarity with these issues. The notion is not to roast Castro by any means, but to present an example that may be more virtue signaling than policy identification. Tellingly, trans issues were not mentioned by any of the candidates participating in a different Democratic candidate debate held on the National Transgender Day of Remembrance, November 20, a fact noticed by many. Perhaps due to this slight, in the following debate (on December 19) Elizabeth Warren implied that if she were to be elected that she would hold a Transgender Day or Remembrance Vigil on the White House lawn. In Warren's defense, she did also have a plan for LGBTQ+ justice that is outlined on her web page, but the comment itself was far more superficial and out of place.

OBJECTIONS TO THE IDEA OF VIRTUE SIGNALING

In this chapter I have presented three main ideas: First, I have demonstrated that anti-transgender dog-whistling has occurred and has been used in hopes of garnering votes and political influence. Secondly, I have introduced the notion of virtue signaling and how this is an important aspect of dog-whistling that has been used to signal either one's virtue as being against what is thought of as the "transgenderist ideology" or that one is firmly progressive, as demonstrated by one's support of the flourishing of trans and gender non-conforming persons. Lastly, I have argued that the employment of both dog-whistling and virtue signaling is evidence of the politicization of trans and gender non-conforming lives. These tactics both demonstrate and further this politicization. I recognize that there may be objections to these ideas and so will spend the rest of this chapter identifying and responding to such objections.

The most obvious objection to the material in this chapter may be regarding virtue signaling. One might argue that virtue signaling is inherently a part of politics. Successful campaigns often are about the virtues, or in some case vices, of the candidates or their rivals. Politicians have a relatively short time to signal to their prospective constituencies, and it is not unethical for them to attempt to give the public a glimpse into what they value, what they stand for, what they will fight for. Perhaps campaigning necessarily requires virtue signaling. "Photo ops" of kissing babies, and having beers with the "regular guys," may be chosen to show how down-to-earth or approachable one is. Campaign photos in outdoor scenery may be chosen to display the candidate's "toughness" or their connection with the land and working-class values. Politicians can be confident that their actions are going to be dissected for signs of both virtue or vice, so it only makes sense that they pay close attention to how their character is being viewed and make decisions to reflect their more positive attributes. Relatedly, regarding pro-trans virtue signaling, one might question why this would be a problem, especially to those who are advocates for trans rights and flourishing. Isn't any mention of support of transgender and gender non-binary persons a good thing?

I agree that politicking necessarily involves some forms of virtue signaling and generally for the reasons identified. However, there are two basic reasons that some forms of virtue signaling are problematic. First, it is an important part of dog-whistling. Dog-whistling, the weaponization of conscious and unconscious bias against a marginalized group for the reason of securing political power, is wrong. It leads to further marginalization of the targeted group, more scapegoating, and more targeting, all which decrease the flourishing of those members of the marginalized group and those related to them in significant ways. Dog-whistling, and its helper virtue signaling, use the politicization of a marginalized group as a mere means to the end of gaining political, and often economic, influence. Using marginalized others as mere tools to political success is morally worrisome, even for non-Kantians. A combination of dog-whistling and virtue signaling support oppressive structures and political climates that are unjust. Secondly, while politics is fraught with virtue signaling, some of which may be morally neutral, to the extent that it is purely performative and prudential, it can lack true commitment and concern. In the end, it is manipulative of both the marginalized group being used as a means and the audience who is expected to decode the signals. Authenticity matters, and there is a difference between being authentic about a particular matter and merely trying to appear so. To the extent that pro-transgender virtue signaling is used to demonstrate one's progressive chops but is done without having a clear and respectful understanding of the important issues involved, it too is simply using an oppressed group as a mere means to an end of political influence. Undoubtedly, I am in favor of political measures that support flourishing for everyone, but, too often, efforts come in the form of sound bites, not real action that can make a difference in people's lives.

A second objection might be that, in the information and ego-heavy age of social media, virtue signaling rules the day; it is the new currency of communication. Again, my response has to acknowledge that virtue signaling, which I expect has many forms, is rampant, especially in social media settings. Facebook, Twitter, Instagram, and other platforms in many ways are geared to lead users to the most favorable image of themselves, whether one wants to focus on real or conjured virtue, one's thirst for adventure, a take-no-prisoners bitchiness, a heart of a social-justice warrior, or perhaps the image of a harried but loving parent. Social media is indeed social—meaning that it is a public performance of one's ideas, activities, challenges faced and won. But as with politicians, authenticity matters. Distortions of oneself or others involve deviations from honest and open communication and, to differing degrees, can come to resemble manipulation just as it does in the more political realm. As has been made clear in the years since the election of 2016, social media is by no means wholly a social good. It can serve as the conveyer of bullying and hate that is then transmitted and reproduced in seconds; it can influence others mimetically, shaping desires and biases in ways that we as a collective are just coming to understand. Certainly, one can agree that ego performance is at an all-time high, and not agree that this is something to accept without criticism.

Lastly, one might object that it is simply too difficult to identify instances of either dog-whistling or its companion virtue signaling. Returning to López's examples, might it not be the case that some politicians really were (are?) worried about property values and are not attempting to ignite biases against communities of color? Perhaps some individuals actually believe it is the case that there is widespread welfare fraud, and that being prudent with taxpayer's money means to disallow such fraud as part of being a good steward of public monies? Might not some individuals actually believe that cisgender women need to be protected from trans women while using the restroom and that being ready to fight these kinds of fights is virtuous?

Again, like the objections already considered, this objection may sound acceptable at first glance. This is especially true if one is of the group of persons to whom such signals are directed. Indeed, *this is why they work.* It is true that one of the aspects most damning about dog-whistling and virtue signaling is that they represent an *intentional* performance that, when coupled together, can be rightly identified as manipulative and damaging. Intentionality, however, is notoriously difficult to ascertain since it is undetectable to all except the agents themselves. Opportunities for deceit mean that simply asking about one's intention may not provide a reliable remedy to this problem since the performance in question can simply be maintained. Given that responding to the performance is also a performance, there is little chance that the performer will suddenly "fess up." Still, there are many morally untoward actions for which intentionality is a key feature, but this has never been reason to find the identification and analysis of such acts time wasted. Alternatively, it is possible that one may, genuinely, not be wishing to employ a "dog whistle" and is not aware that their views are those that feed into historic biases and risk harm. We might call this "unintentional dog-whistling." In such cases, the politician has failed to exercise suitable levels of responsibility. If the alleged dog whistles are not meant to be so but are simply policy positions, then they need to be thoroughly investigated in ways that include historic and current perpetration of injustice. Policies that are based on claims that further marginalize the already marginalized, that are based on negative stereotypes, are epistemologically and morally irresponsible. I do not suppose politicians will suddenly become saints, but I do believe that a world in which integrity is no longer valued is a world in which none of us would wish to live.

It cannot be denied that dog-whistling and its attendant virtue signaling can be both politically prudential and harmful. Dog whistles employ well-worn stereotypes, some of which are consistent with the scapegoat markers identified by Girard and discussed in the previous chapter. Dog whistles bank on making distortions of other persons believable, and political virtue signaling comforts those whose biases are ignited and directs them toward certain political ends. In the context of the politicization of trans persons in the US, to the extent that a politician's views on our lives and identities are salient to their election or reelection, virtue signaling can involve a distortion of who we are as a group and can create and reignite unjustified biases against trans and all gender-expansive persons, all for the political aspirations of the politician. Even if politicians are using their familiarity with the issues important to trans and gender non-conforming persons to bolster their "lefty" credentials, the act can be superficial and merely performative, thus encouraging the politicization of our lives without remedy of the serious issues facing this population, setting the stage for ongoing politicization and harm.

NOTES

1. Ian Haney López, *Dog Whistle Politics: How Coded Racial Appeals Have Reinvented Racism and Wrecked the Middle Class* (Oxford: Oxford University Press, 2013).

2. Ian Haney López, "Dog Whistle Politics," Duke University Sanford School of Public Policy, video, March 8, 2017, https://www.youtube.com/watch?v=00FNvIC5N7g.

3. Kwame Anthony Appiah, "Racisms," in *An Anatomy of Racism*, ed. David Theo Goldberg (Minneapolis: University of Minnesota Press, 1990).

4. Haney López, 1.

5. Haney López, 108.

6. Ralph Abraham, "Abraham for Governor," Abraham Campaign, August 22, 2019, video: https://www.youtube.com/watch?v=0YkAm6NY8oU.

7. Kevin Lamargue, for Reuters, "Trump Says Transgender Policy Is Meant to 'Protect the Country,'" NBC News, Oct. 23, 2018, https://www.nbcnews.com/feature/nbc-out/trump-says-transgender-policy-seeks-protect-country-n923266.

8. Susan Stryker, *Transgender History: The Roots of Today's Revolution*, 2nd ed. (New York: Seal Press, 2017).

9. C. Riley Snorton, *Black on Both Sides: A Racial History of Trans Identity* (Minneapolis: University of Minnesota Press, 2017).

10. Leslie Feinberg, *Transgender Warriors: Making History from Joan of Arc to Dennis Rodman* (Boston: Beacon Press, 1996).

11. Pagan Kennedy, *The First Man-Made Man* (New York: Bloomsbury, distributed to the trade by Holtzbrinck, 2007).

12. James Bartholomew, "The Awful Rise of Virtue Signalling," *Spectator*, April 18, 2015, https://www.spectator.co.uk/2015/04/hating-the-daily-mail-is-a-substitute-for-doing-good/.

13. Ibid.

14. Talia Mae Bettcher, "Evil Deceivers and Make Believers: On Transphobic Violence and the Politics of Illusion," *Hypatia* 22, no. 3 (Summer 2007).

15. Antonia Blumberg, "Julián Castro Gives Nod to Trans Community While Sharing His Abortion Views," *HuffPost*, June 26, 2019, https://www.huffpost.com/entry/julian-castro-democratic-debate-reproductive-justice_n_5d141d98e4b0e455603742aa.

Chapter 8

"But for" and the Bostock Decision

Discussion of the Obergefell decision was the focus of chapter 1. It also serves as a marker of a new era. This new era included the right to a same-sex marriage (again, for those that qualify, otherwise often excluding some in the disability community) and also a time of unprecedented targeting of the transgender population. The chapters on backlash, scapegoating, dog-whistling and virtue signaling are offered as a way to conceptualize the ramifications of the politicization of trans persons in the years between 2015 and 2020. Now, chapter 8 focuses on an analysis of the Bostock decision that was announced July 15, 2020. The Bostock case serves as the temporal endpoint of this study, but this does not mean that the anti-transgender backlash will necessarily dissipate as a function of the court's decision. It does mean, however, that the court was finally required to think deeply about anti-transgender discrimination and the fact that, in the end, such discrimination was recognized is historically significant.

The cases of Gerald Bostock, Donald Zarda, and Aimee Stephens were presented to the US Supreme Court on October 8, 2019. The question put to the court was whether discrimination on the basis of sexual orientation and gender identity amounted to discrimination on the basis of sex, thus making such forms of discrimination prohibited by Title VII. The Obergefell ruling of 2015 provided the legal guarantee that individuals of the same legal sex could marry, and while this result was celebrated as a significant victory for the status and civil rights of LBGTQ persons, it did not prohibit individuals from being fired by their employers for exercising this right to marriage or for even having, or being seen as having, the identity of an LGBTQ person. Recall that chapter 2 included the arguments by those who were skeptical of the prioritization of same-sex marriage. Anecdotally, it seemed that the anti-trans backlash increased such skepticism especially among those who were most affected by it. In October 2019, what I call the "Bostock cases" together were presented to the US Supreme Court, presented a kind of correction or at least an important successor to the Obergefell ruling, and increased LGBTQ equality. Whether the Bostock decision was a kind of correction from Obergefell or Obergefell was a catalyst that positively set the stage for the Bostock ruling, these two cases are of utmost importance to the legal and social status of LGBTQ Americans.

The time between the presentation of the Bostock cases and the announcement of the ruling nine months later was one of the most unusual and difficult periods of American history. After years of living with the Trump administration's harmful policies and sexist, racist, ableist, and xenophobic rhetoric; fighting against hundreds of anti-trans legislative proposals; condemning the erasure of trans identity and humanity from federal web pages; and participating in marches and other events meant to affirm the value of Black lives and protest against police brutality that erupted after the May 25 murder of George Floyd horrified the country, many in the country were already exhausted by the continual stream of terrible news. When Bostock was argued, no one in the country could have guessed that the decision would be delivered to a country decimated by the COVID-19 virus, leaving over one hundred thousand people dead by the time the decision was announced and an economy that was transformed from being a driver of financial security to being an invitation to deadly infection.[1] Given these incredible collective challenges, and the ensuing "COVID-brain" that distorted any realistic sense of time, many except a few avid Supreme Court watchers and politically minded LGBTQ folks probably remembered that the decision of this historic case was pending. On June 15, 2020, the decision was made public that affirmed that employment discrimination on the basis of sexual orientation and gender identity was, indeed, discrimination because of sex. As such, employment discrimination because of sexual orientation or gender identity is prohibited as a matter of law. While the reception of the decision was celebrated, it did not rise to the level of collective enthusiasm as did the Obergefell decision five years earlier. Whether it was related to the COVID requirements for social distancing, the political context of the Trump administration, or simply exhaustion by those who were in favor of the court's decision, the celebrations across the country seemed fairly subdued when compared to Obergefell five years earlier. The size and scope of the celebrations notwithstanding, this was one of the most historic court rulings in American LGBTQ history.

This chapter presents an explanation, analysis, and critique of the Bostock decision. The Bostock decision actually includes ruling on three separate cases. Two of these cases, brought by Gerald Lynn Bostock and Donald Zarda, involve the plaintiffs being fired after it became known to their employer that they were gay. The third case involves that of Aimee Stephens, a transgender woman, who was fired after she announced to her employer that she was going to begin living full-time as a woman. Her supervisors responded that "this is not going to work out" and fired her shortly thereafter.[2] There is no dispute that it was sexual orientation (in the cases of Bostock and Zarda) and gender identity (in the case of Stephens) that were seen by the employers as significantly and justifiably relevant to decisions involving ongoing employment. The question these cases posed to the court was not whether discrimination on the basis of sexual orientation or gender identity is fair or otherwise morally justified, but whether such discrimination falls under the umbrella of actions that can be rightly characterized as discrimination "because of sex."

I present two levels of analysis. The first is within the textualist framework of the current Supreme Court; the second is a critique of the textualist framework itself. With regard to the former, both the court's opinion, written by Justice Gorsuch, affirming that the treatment experienced by Bostock, Zarda, and Stephens was unlawful discrimination under Title VII, and the dissenting opinions, written separately by Justices Alito and Kavanaugh denying the same, all identify textualism as the most acceptable justification scheme within which to argue their conclusions. Textualism, steadfastly championed by late Supreme Court Justice Antonin Scalia, is seen by some as a remedy against what is perceived as the dangers of an ideologically driven Supreme Court that "legislates from the bench." Textualism is a theory of legal interpretation that regards the only appropriate reading of the law to require a *common sense* understanding and application of the language used. Upon close analysis, it is clear that, even within the framework of textualism, Alito's dissent strays from an analysis of the *meaning* of Title VII and into the realm of the 1964-era *imagined application* of the statute. In a paradoxically contorted move, Alito argues that regardless of the relationship between sex, sexual orientation, and gender identity, the fact that individuals are *likely* to discriminate against LGBTQ people as a class justifies such discrimination. I will explain this claim shortly. Disturbingly, Alito's listing of potentially bad consequences of the court's ruling makes clear that he and others of the minority opinion regard trans, gender fluid, and non-conforming persons as not worthy of civil rights protection and that such inclusion not only imposes an undue burden on society and the courts but threatens other fundamental rights crucial to a just society. While the court's application of Gorsuch's version of textualism has provided a historically significant win in the context of civil rights legislation and dominated over Alito and Kavanaugh's misapplication of the same general theory, the justifiability of textualism is still in question. This contemporary application of Title VII repudiates any idea that we should limit our understanding of the applications of civil rights legislation to the imaginations of those who may have had a severely limited sense of justice that serves to privilege only a few. Given rapidly changing understandings and terminology, what Alito and Kavanaugh regard as the *common sense* rendering of a statute's language would reproduce past injustices.

THE CASE—THE BASICS

As mentioned, the Bostock decision combines three different cases, those involving Gerald Lynn Bostock, Donald Zarda, and Aimee Stephens, which judgments together serve as a legal clarification on the employment rights of LGBTQ persons. The fact that they were combined in this way illustrates the court's, and possibly the country's, recognition that discrimination on the basis of real or perceived sexual orientation and gender identity are historically and conceptually linked. It is not unfathomable that Stephens's claims of unlawful discrimination on the basis of gender identity could have been seen as significantly dissimilar from those of Bostock and Zarda to require a contrary ruling, or that Stephens's case could have even been rejected by the court in the first place. The fact that it was not so rejected, that it was combined with the Bostock/Zarda cases, and that the three cases were seen together as either meeting or not meeting the requirements to be under the protective umbrella of Title VII is noteworthy. It means that, despite the anti-trans legislative attempts and the politicization of trans identity in the years between 2015 and 2020, the employment rights of transgender and gender non-conforming individuals were, at the very least, understood as a significant legal question worthy of consideration by the Supreme Court. Of course, bringing cases of these sorts to the Supreme Court had an element of risk, for a negative decision that affirmed an employee's decision to discriminate on the basis of sexual orientation and gender identity would have had far-reaching and catastrophic consequences.

TEXTUALISM: AN OVERVIEW

As mentioned above, textualism is a theory of legal interpretation made particularly popular by Justice Antonin Scalia. Those who prefer a textualist interpretation of law believe that the law should be interpreted and applied in a way that is determined by the meanings of the terms used in the statute. While textualism focuses on the meaning of the written law, there is a recognition that language changes over time in both nuanced and drastic ways. This being the case, some textualists wish to "stick a pin in" the meaning of the statute when it was written and designate this meaning as that which is to be employed in future cases. In essence, some textualists wish to "time stamp" a statute's meaning as a way they believe shows appropriate fidelity to the law and results in consistency and clarity in its application. Textualism can be understood as a response to what some consider "legislating from the bench," a claim often used as a criticism of court decisions that seem to go beyond the written text and begin to intrude into the realm of what some believe as appropriate for only legislative action. As a theory of legal interpretation, textualists contrast their approach to that of the Warren Court (1953 to 1969) that was seen by some as too liberal. Judges, so goes the argument for textualism, are not legislators who are elected to make law. Instead, they are (*simply*) to apply the law consistently in a way that is given by the meaning of the law itself. In this view, if the meaning of the law is insufficient to justify a particular ruling, then elected congressional lawmakers, if there is a will and a way forward, need to change or "update" the law, rather than having this "update" occur through judicial decision. Recall that textualism was also referred to in chapter 1 of this work, the chapter dedicated to a consideration of the Obergefell decision and marriage equality in general. Those who dissented the Obergefell decision, thinking especially here of Chief Justice Roberts, used the tenets of textualism as their justification. To put it in the simplest terms, because neither the Constitution (specifically the Due Process Clause) nor any federal legislation provide an explicit civil right to same-sex marriage, the dissenters argued that they could not rule in favor of Obergefell and the other plaintiffs. As will be obvious, the opinion of the court for the Bostock cases is written in an explicitly textualist way, perhaps hoping to avoid the criticism of not sufficiently adhering to this particular and currently popular theory of legal interpretation.

Even for those not familiar with the extensive literature on textualism, it is not difficult to imagine that a focus on the meaning of the statute can involve a variety of subtleties. For example, one must determine whether the language used in the text of the statute meant the same thing to the authors of the statute as it does to readers today. If we do attempt to "time stamp" the meaning of the language used, do we then prohibit applications of the law if the original meanings turn out to be criticizably narrow or if new information becomes known? If the meaning of the law is unclear, do we simply take the literal meaning of the words separately or in phrases?[3] Especially if language has changed, some argue that we must go to great lengths to investigate what the language used meant to those authors. Questions of meaning or original meaning are related to questions of intentionality. One might ask, "What did the authors *intend to mean* by the language used?" This last concern can be distinguished from the authors' intention or prediction of the scope of the statute. "What did the authors of the statute intend to result from the application of the statute, and within what contexts did they predict such application?" For instance, if the authors of Title VII intended that women be able to live their lives free of workplace discrimination because of their sex, then is the consequence that men also have protection against workplace sexual harassment somehow inappropriate? Gorsuch uses the case of *Oncale v. Sundowner Offshore Services* as a precedent-setting example since the case involved a man, Oncale, claiming sexual harassment from other men. Even though this use of Title VII was perhaps not in the minds of the lawmakers who passed the legislation in 1964, it was seen as a violation of Title VII by the court in 1998. As will be explained later, Alito's dissent responds to the Oncale case, arguing that it is not precedent-setting, especially in the case of Stephens, since considering harassment or unfair discrimination against transgender persons was not merely slightly out of the intended scope of the law but, according to Alito, entirely unfathomable by the lawmakers in 1964. Responding to Gorsuch's claims that while sex discrimination experienced by men was not the "primary evil" that the crafters in 1964 intended, but that this form of discrimination is still within the scope of the law, he writes,

> it would be a wild understanding to say that discrimination because of sexual orientation and transgender status was not the "principle evil" on Congress's mind in 1964. Whether we like to admit it now or not, in the thinking of Congress and the public at that time, such discrimination would not have been evil at all.[4]

Even if we accept Alito's claim regarding the predicted scope of the statute's application by its ratifiers and writers in 1964, there is still the question as to whether this concern is relevant to determining the scope of the law in 2020. This is just one way that those who all profess to ground their rulings in the text of the law can be proponents of very different decisions.

Of course, intentionality, whether one is attempting to decipher what the authors of the law *intended* to convey through the language or what they *intended* to be the effect of the law, is notoriously difficult to determine. This is true, in part, because the originators of the law could have a multitude of intentions, not all directly concerning the effect of the law on society. As well described by Duncan Kennedy in "Freedom and Constraint in Adjudication: A Critical Phenomenology,"[5] judges (and I'd argue that the same could be said for lawmakers) are not above considering other factors that might bias their decision-making in a multitude of ways. Realistically speaking, when writing or passing legislation various concerns may present themselves—many of which have little to do with the content of the law itself. One might consider the ramifications to one's reputation, the successes or failure of subsequent political campaigns, one's legacy, one's conscious or unconscious allegiance to a particular worldview, or even one's relationship with important loved ones. To appropriately identify the application of the law, the intention of the lawmakers may be relevant in some respects but can also lead us into dangerous and unhelpful rabbit holes. This is especially true when considering attitudes towards transgender persons, which have changed considerably in the last fifty years.

Putting the above complexities aside for the moment, nearly all textualists believe that when the meaning of the law is quite clear and when the meanings of the terms have not changed over time, the role of the judiciary is to straightforwardly apply the law as written. It is arguable that such straightforward application is rarely *all* that is required at the Supreme Court level, for it is those cases that are in need of Supreme Court review due to inconsistencies in the lower courts. On the other hand, it may be the case that a straightforward understanding and application of the law is only difficult due to the biases of the influential majority (for example, when the law seems to clearly protect a marginalized group, but those in power cannot accept such only due to their own biases). To boil down the basic differences expressed in the majority and minority opinions in this case to their most basic level: the majority of the court believes that an application of the terms used in Title VII supports a ruling that discrimination on the basis of sexual orientation and gender identity *do* constitute discrimination on the basis of sex, whereas those who disagree with this view believe that this interpretation of the law distorts the meaning of the text and that a fuller consideration of the meaning of the statute that was held in 1964 by its authors supports the conclusion that sexual orientation and gender identity *do not* constitute discrimination on the basis of sex. In the next sections, both sides of the decision will be explained. While both are within the textualist tradition, their conclusions radically diverge.

THE COURT'S RULING: GORSUCH AND THE MAJORITY

Given that both the majority and dissenting arguments claim textualism as their justificatory scheme, what is at issue most relevant to this particular court is the *meaning* of the text of Title VII, which was originally drafted as part of the Civil Rights Act of 1964 and then amended in 1991. The text of Title VII most at issue here is that which prohibits employment discrimination on the basis of sex. The language of this part of the statute is as follows:

(a) Employer practices
It shall be an unlawful employment practice for an employer—

1. to fail or refuse to hire or to discharge any individual, or otherwise to discriminate against any individual with respect to his compensation, terms, conditions, or privileges of employment, because of such individual's race, color, religion, sex, or national origin; or
2. to limit, segregate, or classify his employees or applicants for employment in any way which would deprive or tend to deprive any individual of employment opportunities or otherwise adversely affect his status as an employee, because of such individual's race, color, religion, sex, or national origin.[6]

There is no question that Bostock, Zarda, and Stephens were discriminated against, as each of them was fired by their employers for being gay (in the first two cases) or being transgender (in the case of Stephens). It is important to realize, however, that "discrimination" by itself can be a neutral act and legally permitted in many circumstances. As Alito explains in his dissent, an employer can lawfully discriminate on the basis of an employee being born under the astrological sign of Scorpio. An employer's notion that Scorpios are inherently bad employees may be misguided, for sure, but since astrological signs (in general) or Scorpios (in particular) are not listed as being included in the protected categories, then discrimination against them, while unfair and unjustified, it is not unlawful. So, the question is whether or not discrimination against LBGTQ persons is more like discrimination against Scorpios (legally permitted but unjustified), discrimination against those who are not adequately qualified (legally permitted and justified), or a form of unlawful discrimination since it is a form of sexual discrimination. In each of the three cases, the employers thought that the plaintiff's sexual orientation or gender identity was relevant to their employment and made decisions based upon what they took to be a justified discrimination on that basis.

Since the meaning of the term "discrimination" as descriptive of the action of the employers is not at issue, what basically needs to be considered is whether this kind of discrimination can be understood as being "on the basis of sex" or "because of sex." Thus, the terms "sex" and "because of" or "on the basis of" are the most at issue. As is consistent with the textualist position, Gorsuch, writing for the court, looks to the 1964 definition of "sex," which is reported as the "status as either male of female [as] determined by reproductive biology."[7] The majority of the court accepts this, albeit very binary, meaning as that which was being referenced in the statute. (The court does concede that these binary categories may include expectations of gender and sexual orientation, but doesn't believe this concession is particularly relevant to their main argument.⁸) While transgender and non-binary affirming individuals have long argued that this meaning of "biological sex" is exceedingly binary and thus non-inclusive of both gender and sexual variance, the court is correct in claiming that this binary understanding of the term was what was assumed in 1964.⁹

After clarifying the meaning of the term "sex" as it is used in the statute, the meaning of "because of" as in "discrimination 'because of' sex" needs to be evaluated. The court agrees that the meaning of "because of" is understood here as the ordinary meaning used in common language and is synonymous with the notions of "by reason of" or "on account of." None of this seems particularly controversial, but it is noteworthy that the next step in Gorsuch's argument creates a cleavage in the understanding of the notion of "because of" that is being employed by the majority of the court, as opposed to that which is being favored by Alito and Thomas. Specifically, Gorsuch and the majority, unlike Alito, prioritize the meaning of "because of" through the "but-for" construction:

> In the language of law, this means that Title VII's "because of" test incorporates the "simple" and "traditional" standard of but-for causation. That form of causation is established whenever a particular outcome would not have happened "but for" the purported cause. See *Gross*, 557 US at 176. In other words, a but-for test directs us to change one thing at a time and see if the outcome changes. If it does, we have found the but-for cause.¹⁰

The employment of the but-for causation standard by Gorsuch is key to understanding a significant difference of reasoning employed by the two sides of the court on this issue. Tellingly, neither Alito nor Kavanaugh's dissent ever mentions the "but-for" standard for causation—not once in over a combined eighty plus pages of analysis which harshly criticizes the majority opinion. As mentioned earlier, textualists would agree that if the meaning of the statute is unambiguous and can be straightforwardly applied, little further analysis is needed. While the majority does not support their justification of the ruling with only the "but-for" based argument, it does endorse the conclusion that a straightforward application of the statute is really all that is needed here. Alito disagrees with this and argues that further investigation of what the authors/ratifiers of Title VII meant with their chosen language is required.

So, what is the "simple test" that employs the "but-for" standard and is used to determine whether an act of discrimination is "because of sex"? The test involves identifying the relevant actions in question, in this case being fired from one's employment, changing just one variable in the scenario, and then determining if the outcome would change. In Title VII sex discrimination cases, the relevant variable is generally the traditionally understood biological/reproductive (assigned) sex of the individual in question. So, for instance, in the cases of Bostock and Zarda, assume all aspects of the case are the same, that is, the individuals are romantically/sexually attracted to men and that they were fired due to this attraction. In employing the but-for test, imagine that both Bostock and Zarda are women rather than men. It is clear to Gorsuch and the majority of the court that their firing can be rightly considered discrimination on the basis of sex, or because of sex, since, *but for their sex*, they would not have been fired. In both cases, they were fired because they are men attracted to men; the employers in these cases would have had no problem with women being attracted to men in the relevantly similar way.

This simple test meant to identify cases of unlawful discrimination on the basis of sex can be employed with the Stephens case as well. If Stephens were assigned female at birth, then the request expressing herself as a woman, asking individuals to use feminine pronouns, and requesting that her identity as a woman be respected would not even be needed, let alone cause for termination. It is only due to being assigned male at birth that any of these requests become at all controversial in general or become a specific concern of the employer. Thus, this case, too, fails to pass the "but-for" test for unlawful sex-based discrimination. *But for the fact that she was assigned male at birth, she would not have been fired from the funeral home.* From the decision:

> The statute's message for our cases is equally simple and momentous: An individual's homosexuality or transgender status is not relevant to employment decisions. That's because it is impossible to discriminate against a person for being homosexual or transgender without discriminating against that individual based on sex.[11]

In addition to the employment of the but-for test to justify why these three cases each are a violation of Title VII's prohibition on discrimination because of sex, the court supports its decision further by carefully considering relevant case law in which further nuances of sex discrimination were clarified and stand as precedents to the Bostock cases. However, before explaining these three important precedents, it is important to respond to a possible objection involving the last of the but-for thought experiments employed above.

When considering whether firing a person because they are transgender is an instance of unfair employment discrimination the court employed the use of the simple but-for test for sex-based discrimination. In describing the application of this test above, I posed the question of whether it can be argued that Stephens would have been fired if she were designated female at birth, rather than being designated male at birth as was her history. When applying the but-for test to the cases of Bostock and Zarda, I simply asked the reader to imagine if both individuals were women rather than men. My first choice of language was chosen for simple ease of explanation, but even though there was a hidden assumption that the two plaintiffs are assumed cisgender, the explanation focuses on what is relevant to the case at hand. Both men were fired because they were men, were perceived as men, and were also sexually/ romantically attracted to men. In this case, what they were assigned at birth is irrelevant. For example, it is easy to imagine an individual, say a man who is trans, being fired for being gay, and his employer never realizing, or caring, that he was assigned female at birth. This is not only true because one's assignment at birth is generally not known, and also because it is not a necessary condition for being and expressing oneself as a gay man. In the Stephens case, that fact that she is a woman was not recognized by her employer, but the fact that she is a person who was *assigned male at birth* was seen as sufficient reason for dismissal. Thus, in her case, I direct readers to consider what might have occurred if she was not so assigned. The application of the but-for test for sex-based discrimination in her case tracks to her assignment at birth and not to her gender identity. Thus, a slight modification of the but-for test is in order. Gorsuch does not mention this technical aspect, probably due to not wishing to make obvious that the recognition of trans persons does mean that the but-for test may take a different form in different contexts.

However, some textualists may object that using the *assigned sex at birth* language may run counter to the meaning of the word "sex" as first used in Title VII's language. It is arguable that the meaning of the word "sex" is not exactly the same as the designation of the "assigned sex at birth" construction. Clearly, the second construction is popular with trans affirming persons because it underscores that a sex designation is "assigned" as opposed to something objectively identified. This comparison of the use of the "but-for" test, I believe, reveals a weakness of textualism itself. That is, it cannot be refuted that language has evolved to make linguistic and cultural room for trans and non-binary persons, but since this language was not used by statute authors of the past, then textualists would have to make one of two choices. Either rule that trans and gender non-binary persons are wholly outside the protection of law that relies on designations of biological sex, or that our sex assignment at birth is legitimized for all such legal purposes regardless of our gender identity and lived experiences. Obviously, neither of these results are acceptable.

PRECEDENTS AND LESSONS

While it is clear that Gorsuch, writing for the majority, believes that a simple application of the but-for requirement for sex-based discrimination is primarily what is needed here, he does identify three cases that serve as relevant precedents and further support the majority's conclusion. From each of these cases, Gorsuch identifies a "lesson" that can be then applied to the Bostock set of cases. The first case mentioned is that of *Phillips v. Martin Marietta Corp.*, which was decided in 1971.[12] Here, the employer argued that the policy of refusing to hire women with young children was not prohibited by Title VII, since they had no such policy regarding women who did not have young children. That is, the employer argued that it was not *sex* that they were discriminating against, per se, but *motherhood*. Using the analogy from the beginning of this chapter, the employers contended that discrimination on the basis of motherhood was more like discrimination on the basis of astrological sign than discrimination against the specific categories identified in Title VII. The fact that Martin Marietta Corp. did not have a policy against hiring men with young children proved to be sufficient for the court to regard this policy as a violation of Title VII. It is instructive to note that in this case, the simple but-for test gives the same result as in the Bostock cases. That is, Phillips would not have been refused employment *but-for* her sex, for if she would have been a man with young children she would not have been discriminated against in this way. This case is important to the reasoning behind the Bostock ruling since, while the "but-for" test seems compelling, one could argue that sex discrimination was only part of the explanation for the discrimination, for one had to be both a woman *and* a mother of small children to be refused employment consideration. This is relevant since one might argue that in the cases of Bostock, Zarda, and Stephens, their discrimination was not only or solely based on the sex or sex assignment at birth, but their sexual orientation (in the first two cases) and gender identity (in the case of Stephens). In response to this objection, Gorsuch rightly points out that the law could have been written with a stricter standard, say, having the discrimination based "solely" or even "primarily" because of sex.[13] Because this is not the way the law was written or applied in precedential cases, the but-for test results are conclusive even if discrimination was not on the basis of sex alone.

The second case that was seen as precedent-setting is that of *Los Angeles Dept. of Water and Power v. Manhart*.[14] In this case, the policy at issue was that the employer required women employees make a larger contribution into their pension fund than it did their counterparts who were men. The reasoning behind this policy seemed to have been, at least on the face of it, well intentioned, since, according to the employers, the goal of the policy was the promotion of equity between the men and women employees.[15] The justification, supported by relevant statistics of different life expectancies of men and women, is that since women tend to live for a longer period of time, having women employees contribute more to their own retirement is only fair, goes this argument, since they will be pulling from those retirement funds for longer than will the men of the company. If this policy were not in place, it was argued, the company would be paying more over time into the retirements of their women employees as compared to their retired employees who are men. Not only does the intention of equity promotion seem less objectionable than that of blatant sexism, it is also the case that the company in question had a record of treating women fairly, generally speaking. The court, however, ruled that *Los Angeles Dept. of Water* did, in fact, violate Title VII and its prohibition against discrimination on the basis of sex. By now it may be clear how the "simple test" will give this result, but it is worthwhile to explicate its application.

Recall that applying the "but-for" test of Title VII discrimination because of sex involves a thought experiment in which one imagines how the outcome of the policy would be changed if the sex or sex assignment at birth (whichever is relevant) of one of the affected women is changed. For example, if, say, Elena works at Los Angeles Dept. of Water and is being asked to make proportionally larger contributions to her retirement account than her fellow employees who are men, then what would be the effect if we imagine that Elena is a man rather than a woman? The but-for application is so intuitive that the answer to the question is evident before the question is even posed. Of course, if our fictional Elena was a man and not a woman as per our story, she would not be affected by the policy and would not be required to pay extra into her retirement account. In other words, *but for her sex*, she would not be negatively impacted. The court, in this 1978 case, ruled in favor of Manhart and against the employer.[16]

There are two other noteworthy aspects of this case. First, according to the court, it does not matter that the attitudes of the writers/enforcers of the policy in question were not outwardly sexist or that the organization generally treated its women employees equitably. Just because there was little evidence that the employer held discriminating attitudes towards women as a group, and that the statistics used did, in fact, support the claim of different life expectancies between the two groups, this does not mean that the "simple test" meant to indicate discrimination against an *individual* woman would not still be conclusive. As made clear by Gorsuch, Title VII is to be applied on the individual and not the group level:

> True, women as a class may live longer than men as a class. But "[t]he statute's focus on the individual is unambiguous," and any individual woman might make the larger pension contribution and still die as early as a man. . . . The employer violated Title VII because, when its policy worked exactly as planned, it could not "pass the simple test" asking whether an individual female employee would have been treated the same regardless of her sex. ID., at 711.[17]

As we will see later in this chapter, Alito's dissenting opinion does seem to blur the distinction between a collective and an individual harm, which may be one of the reasons that Gorsuch specifically focuses on this element of the law. In essence, generally treating those of a common and protected identity justly as a group does not mean that it is impossible to treat an individual of that protected identity unjustly and *because* of that identity. In the case of Manhart, the policy on the level of women as a class might seem fair, yet it is unjustly discriminatory for any one *individual* based on the but-for test.

The third and last case that the majority of the court regards as instructive and precedent-setting is that of *Oncale v. Sundowner Offshore Services, Inc.*, 523 US 75 (1998). In this case the plaintiff was a man who claimed to be sexually harassed by his coworkers who were of the same sex. The court, ruling in favor of the plaintiff, recognized that sexual harassment between men was not what was envisioned by the authors of Title VII, but that this by itself was irrelevant to the question of whether the individual plaintiff was discriminated against because of his sex:

> "[A]assuredly," the case didn't involve "the principal evil Congress was concerned with when it enacted Title VII." *Id., at 79*. But, the Court unanimously explained that it is "the provisions of our laws rather than the principal concerns of our legislators by which we are governed." *Ibid*. Because the plaintiff alleged that the harassment would not have taken place but for his sex—that is, the plaintiff would not have suffered similar treatment if he were female—a triable Title VII claim existed.[18]

The relevance of the Oncale ruling to the Bostock decision cannot be overstated, for it demonstrates the principle that the imagined scope of the application of the law by its original authors is not relevant to its future application. The US stands in a class by itself as a country that, from the beginning, espoused the values of universal liberty for its citizens while actively engaging in the worst human rights abuses in history. The program of attempted genocide and immoral group-based harm against Indigenous Americans, the horrific state-sponsored enslavement of those of African descent and the harm of discriminatory and inhumane treatment after 1863, the unjust treatment of those of Asian ancestry, the prohibition of women (white and otherwise) from being able to participate in the democratic process, and all the ills that these original sins spawned, persisted while the great American experiment of Enlightened Liberty was espoused by the privileged and powerful. If we accept that the authors' understood scope of the sentiment that "all men are created equal" was referring only to white, propertied men, and that this narrow scope of application should persist through time, then any of the civil rights advances in the last 245+ years would have been against the spirit of the founding fathers. The originators of Title VII envisioned that cisgender women would be using the statute as protection against sexual discrimination by men in a patriarchal society. They did not predict the use of Title VII by a man who was being sexually harassed by other men. Similarly, they did not anticipate that the statute would be employed by those that are gay or transgender, as in the Bostock decision, which confirms similar legal protection for those that are lesbian, bisexual, queer, transgender, gender non-conforming, or non-binary. In other words, at least according to Gorsuch and the majority, accepting the textualist position does not imply that the future appropriate scope of application of a given statute necessarily resides in the minds of its originators. As will be discussed in the next section, the Alito dissent suggests that the statute's originators' intention for the scope of the application of the law *is* relevant.

As is a point of similarity among all three Bostock cases, the court rulings focused on discrimination against the *individual* plaintiff. In each case, applying the simple but-for test found a violation of Title VII, regardless of whether the relevant group to which the individual belonged was discriminated against *as a collective*. In the first case considered, *Phillips v. Martin Marietta Corp.*, again, women as a class were not discriminated against, but women who happened to also have young children were treated in ways prohibited by Title VII. In *Manhart*, it certainly can be argued that, as a group, statistical measures could be identified to justify the disparate treatment between men and women with regard to their pension contributions, but this did not justify treating individual women differently. In a similar way, in *Oncale*, it is not the case that men, as a group, faced unjust discrimination. In each of these cases, the harm, or at least the harm that is at issue here, only *shows up* on the level of the individual. The but-for test was conclusive in each case, thus illustrating that these kinds of factors are not sufficient to dispel what the majority of the court sees to be the most straightforward and justified conclusion.

In summary, Gorsuch explicitly identifies the three lessons of the three precedent-setting cases. First, and in his words, "it's irrelevant what an employer might call its discriminatory practice, how others might label it, or what else might motivate it."[19] So, while employers might prefer to describe their discrimination to be on the basis of motherhood or perhaps lifespan expectancy, Gorsuch has argued that the application of the meaning of the words of the statute, and aided by the but-for test, is conclusive. Indeed, using our earlier example, even if an employer discriminated against women born under the sign of Scorpio, but not men, such discrimination would violate Title VII. Similarly, if an employer discriminated against men born under the sign of Scorpio, but not women, this policy too would violate the statute. It may be the case that the employer characterizes the discrimination on the basis of Scorpio-ness and not gender since, as Gorsuch points out, one may be likely to describe such actions with a focus on what is subjectively seen as the most important or unique aspects of the event, in this case Scorpio-ness. Still, this does not preclude discrimination that can be rightfully linked to protected categories.[20]

The second lesson is related to the first just articulated. As Gorsuch clearly states, "the plaintiff's sex need not be the sole or primary cause of the employer's adverse action."[21] Instances of the violation of Title VII obviously need to be closely linked to one or more of the protected categories but need not be the *only* or sole characteristic of the individual that is relevant when discussing unjust discrimination. In the cases presented, and arguably any such case that may be brought before the court, a secondary non-protected trait of the employee can be the source of, or identified as the basis of, discrimination. In the cases reviewed, it was being a mother or one with a longer life expectancy that was appealed to. These two lessons are intimately tied together since the employer may wish to characterize the discrimination on the basis of the non-protected trait and prudentially call it by that name. These two lessons are instructive in the Bostock cases since Alito and others argue that the discrimination in the cases of Bostock, Zarda, and Stephens was not because of sex, but was discrimination on the basis of sexual orientation and gender identity, two categories not explicitly mentioned in the language of Title VII.

The third lesson that Gorsuch explicitly identifies is related to the relationship between individual discrimination and a more general treatment of collectives to which the individual may have some relation. Again, this last lesson is associated to the other two and is part of a typical pattern of falsely justifying unjust discrimination. The general pattern is as follows: Individual S is part of collective of individuals for whom Title VII explicitly prohibits employment discrimination. Label this collective, W. S also has traits that put them in a collective called G. Upon firing S, their employer needs to justify the act in their attempt to avoid losing a court challenge. This justification typically involves three related claims. First, the employer might claim that firing S is not an instance of discrimination on the basis of W, but on the basis of G, a non-protected category. *(Lesson one: It does not matter what you call the discrimination.)* Relatedly, since the employers claim that this was discrimination on the basis of G, it is not discrimination on the basis of W and thus not legally prohibited. *(Lesson two: The protected category need not be the only or primary reason for the discrimination.)* Lastly, the employer may argue that it generally treats individuals who are W quite equitably, so the firing of S is not discrimination on the basis of W. *(Lesson three: Discrimination involves how the individual in question is treated, not how a related collective is treated.)* It is the conclusive application of the but-for test, the three primary lessons of precedent cases just discussed, and also the conclusion that the appropriate scope of the application of Title VII is not determined by the predicted scope held by the originators of the statute that make up the bulk of the court's opinion. It should be noted that the conclusiveness of the "but-for" test was not seen irrelevant in any of the cases, despite the fact that the statute's original authors may not have envisioned this particular future application of the law.

ALITO'S DISSENT JOINED BY
THOMAS AND KAVANAUGH

Alito's dissent might be described by some as "searing" or perhaps "scorching," but I think I would describe it as an exercise in grasping at straws in an effort to justify his own worldview. While Gorsuch's rendering of the opinion of the court reads like that of a patient, but quite analytically minded, elementary school teacher painstakingly explaining something to her charges, Alito's dissent is more like that of the old white uncle who is so constantly pissed off at the changing world that no one wants to invite him to Thanksgiving dinner. The cranky uncle is still invited, however, for his, like Alito's, is a lifetime appointment.

Alito describes the court's opinion as a "pirate ship sailing a textualist flag,"[22] and as "preposterous,"[23] "arrogant,"[24] "a "brazen abuse of authority,"[25] "illogical,"[26] and bent upon foisting upon the American people an "exotic understanding of sex discrimination"[27] that would have never crossed the minds of the statute's originators in 1964. Not surprisingly, Alito sees the court's decision as a kind of inappropriate judicial "update" on the original meaning of Title VII and an example of irresponsibly legislating from the bench. In this section, I will explain the main arguments that Alito provides and offer my own analysis of his position. I will stick to a discussion of the main ideas, although it is not without a great deal of self-control since the fallacies of equivocation and straw man seem to assert themselves with great frequency.

As a textualist, Alito believes that the meanings of the terms employed in the text of Title VII are key to determining the relationship between Title VII prohibitions and the Bostock cases. Quoting Scalia, he writes that the duty of the Supreme Court is to interpret these terms to "mean what they conveyed to a reasonable person at the time they were written."[28] Like Gorsuch, Alito believes that the word "sex" involves the typical binary separation of human beings and other animals in two, generally thought to be disjoint and exhaustive, reproductive categories. Recall that Gorsuch understood the term "because of" to be ascertained through the use of the simple "but-for" test to determine causal relationships. It is noteworthy that Alito never discusses this understanding of "because of" nor specifically critiques its use in his dissent. This is noteworthy especially since it is the cornerstone of the court's decision.

Whereas Gorsuch considered the meanings of the terms "sex," "because of," and "discrimination," Alito's dissent focuses on the phrase "on the basis of sex/because of sex" to argue that, since the term "sex" is distinct from the meaning of the term "sexual orientation" or "gender identity," then "discrimination because of sex" must also be distinct from "discrimination on the basis of sexual orientation" or "discrimination on the basis of gender identity."[29] By focusing on the meaning of "discrimination on the basis of (because of) sex," Alito steps over the "but-for" meaning and relies on what he believes to be the 1964 meaning of the notion of "discrimination on the basis of sex." Ignoring the "but-for" test and focusing on what he believes is the true textualist position, Alito invites a subtle, yet important shift in the focus of the analysis. When discussing the meaning of the phrase "discrimination on the basis of sex," to lawmakers in 1964, Alito's analysis slides into considerations of the *imagined scope* of the statute, a slide that is arguably one to be avoided for reasons already discussed. To assert that the authors of Title VII did not envision it being used to prohibit employment discrimination against LGBTQ people is quite obviously true—just as it is obvious to assert that those called our *Founding Fathers* didn't envision that the phrase "all men are created equal" would apply to Black women, Indigenous Americans, and others, and that the civil rights era would, socially, legislatively, and judicially, challenge this country to live up to its so-celebrated ideals.[30] Furthermore, Alito is not persuaded by the majority's arguments regarding the three cases identified as relevant precedents to Bostock. Alito wrongly describes Gorsuch's analysis as wholly irrelevant to the question before the court: "The Court tries to cloud the issue by spending many pages discussing matters that are beside the point."[31]

In essence, Alito wants to change the algebra of grouping individuals with respect to sex, sexual orientation, and gender identity. Instead of noting, as I believe would Gorsuch, that (in a hypothetical case) discrimination against a lesbian is discrimination against a woman for being a *certain kind* of woman, a kind of woman who rejects the gender expectation of heterosexuality, Alito sees this kind of discrimination as one best described as discrimination against a *lesbian*, or perhaps a *homosexual*, which, because the concept of sexual orientation is distinct from that of sex itself, is not prohibited by Title VII. Alito states,

> The Court's argument is not only arrogant, it is wrong. It fails on its own terms. "Sex," "sexual orientation," and "gender identity" are different concepts, as the Court concedes. *Ante*, at 19 ("homosexuality and transgender status are distinct

concepts from sex"). And neither "sexual orientation" nor "gender identity" is tied to either of the two biological sexes. Both men and women may be attracted to members of the opposite sex, members of the same sex, or members of both sexes. And individuals who are born with the genes and organs of either biological sex may identify with a different gender.[32]

Dismissing his use of the preposition "with," in the last sentence (trans persons generally do not claim to identify *with* their gender, but *as* their gender), I think that most agree that the terms "sex," "sexual orientation," and "gender identity" do have distinct meanings. Certainly, if one were to investigate, one would find that being a competent language user requires that these terms not be considered synonyms. Still, one can agree with Alito that the terms "sex," "sexual orientation," and "gender identity" are distinct in meaning, but this premise does not lead to a meaningful conclusion with regard to the case at hand. This is made especially obvious when Alito asserts that "neither 'sexual orientation' nor 'gender identity' *is tied to* either of the two biological sexes."[33] The term "tied to" is quite vague but it seems clear that these two notions are *tied to* sex in that their meaning relies on an interpretation of the commonly understood yet overly binary notion of biological sex that both Alito and Gorsuch accept. Gorsuch revealed this mistake in his hypothetical example of an employer who was explicit in their "homosexuals need not apply" rule. Relevant here is that explaining this rule to one who was unfamiliar with the term "homosexual" would require reference to sex-assigned-at-birth (biological sex). Indeed, the meaning of the term requires such.

Alito, however, seems to have a much more restrictive understanding of the idea of "tied to" sex. He wishes to sever any connection of sexual orientation and gender identity to sex itself with the claim, "Both men and women may be attracted to members of the opposite sex, members of the same sex, or members of both sexes. And individuals who are born with the genes and organs of either biological sex may identify with a different gender."[34] The premise here is undoubtedly true, but unhelpful. It is as if identities such as "lesbian" or "gay" are not descriptors of men and women (cisgender or otherwise), but only certain *types of persons*. That is, it is as if the broad and problematic grouping "homosexual" erases gender identity and the experience of being a man or a woman or a gender non-binary person. Similarly, it is as if being "transgender" is to be within a grouping of individuals who identify as transgender in a way that is totally independent of sex assignment at birth or their gender history. In other words, Alito seems to think that being "homosexual" (his word) or transgender is to persist in a category of persons that are simplistically and erroneously reducible to only this one characteristic. I expect that Kimberlé Crenshaw would not be impressed.[35]

Consider a parallel example that I believe illustrates Alito's error in yet another way. It is arguable that the notion of masculinity is *tied to* the biological sex of maleness and femininity is *tied to* the biological sex of femaleness, but that does not keep individuals of different sexes, sexual orientations, and of differing "genes and organs" from expressing their gender differently. In this case, "tied to" refers to how femininity is socially constructed as natural and normative to those assigned female at birth just as masculinity is thought to be related to being assigned male at birth. Similarly, being attracted to men is *tied to* or *thought natural for* individuals assigned female at birth and being attracted to women is *thought natural* for those assigned male at birth. Individuals of various sexual orientations, gender identities, expressions, or sexual designations at birth can express masculinity and femininity in ways that can get them unjustly fired from their jobs. A woman who displays masculine traits is protected under Title VII because *but for the fact she is a woman*, she would not be fired for displaying masculinity or what some interpret as such. This is similarly the case for a man expressing what is understood as typical femininity. Thus, particular gender expressions can be expressed by anyone (just as can different kinds of sexual orientations); however, one can't infer from this claim alone that such expressions are not relevant to violations of Title VII. Same-sex sexual or romantic attraction can be felt or expressed by anyone, and like gender expression, it is *tied to* assigned sex at birth not in any necessary way but through the social construction of the cisgender heterosexist gender binary.

Gorsuch's application of the "but-for sex" simple test is clear, Zarda and Bostick are men attracted to men, a proclivity that is not at issue if expressed by women; Stephens wished to live as a woman, a request not controversial if one is assigned female at birth. Thus, if all aspects of the context remain the same and only the relevant gender or sex category is changed, none of these three plaintiffs would have been fired. Alito wishes to make this point moot by offering a different kind of grouping that highlights a fallacious and unjustified logic, a discriminatory logic that reasons that non-dominant sexual orientations and gender histories render certain forms of discrimination not just irrelevant but impossible. That is, Alito would have us believe that discrimination on the basis of being a lesbian is not related to the lesbian being a woman and that discrimination due to being a gay man is unrelated to the individual being a man. Compare Alito's conclusion with unjust laws of the not distant past that regarded it legally impossible for a man to rape his wife. It was as if the designation of "wife," akin to the idea of "property," erased the identity of the wife as a woman and, in this dominant culture, rendered her vulnerable to abuse as such. In both cases, it is as if the fact that the individual is *likely* to be abused, raped, or discriminated against is justification for why it is legally *impossible* to protect them from such.

In competition with Gorsuch's but-for thought experiment as explained, Alito offers his own. Assume there are four individuals who are all employed at the same place and who, taken together, illustrate all of the different permutations of sexual attraction possible, if one assumes the gender binary notion of biological sex. Using Alito's example but giving the fictional individuals names for easy reference, let us assume that Gary, a man, is attracted to men; Sarah, a woman, is attracted to men; Leslie, a woman, is attracted to women; and Sam, a man, is attracted to women as well (in other words, Sarah and Sam are straight, Gary is gay, and Leslie is a lesbian). Assume further that Sarah and Sam continue their employment whereas Gary and Leslie are both fired. Alito describes this case like so: "The discharged employees have one thing in common. It is not biological sex, attraction to men, or attraction to women. It is attraction to members of their own sex—in a word, sexual orientation."[36] Alito believes that this example is illustrative of cases of discrimination against those who are gay and lesbian, and that such discrimination is irrelevant to the workers' sex or sex assigned at birth. The fact that the employees' sexual orientation is relevant to the case is indisputable, but the question here is whether this amounts to discrimination *because of sex*. Recall that the review of the precedent-setting case of *Phillips v. Martin Marietta Corp.* gave rise to the general lesson that biological sex (or sex assigned at birth) need not be the *only* or sole cause of the discrimination. We learned that one cannot discriminate against parents of young children who are also women and claim this is not discrimination because of sex. In Alito's hypothetical example, the employer is discriminating against Leslie because she is a lesbian, a person who is sexually attracted to women and is also a woman. The parallelism of the two cases cannot be ignored, nor can the obvious fact that sexual orientation is indeed *tied to* sex. Gorsuch is correct that the scenario just explained simply involves two instances of discrimination on the basis of sex and also sexual orientation, and this description appropriately applies to the employer's treatment of both Leslie and Gary.

There is another more nuanced and problematic assumption inherent in Alito's example. The example involves an employer who discriminates against Gary and Leslie because Gary is gay and Leslie is a lesbian. According to Alito, the employer treats these two fictional individuals the same, and it is certainly possible that the employer is ready to fire anyone who displays what can be considered as same-sex attraction or, more broadly, doesn't conform to heterosexual norms. There are probably many employers who view same-sex sexual orientation this way, especially given that "homosexuals" like "heterosexuals" have been socially constructed as different *kinds* of people through colonial and pseudo-scientific fallacious reasoning.[37] Yet, this fact cannot obscure the fact that gay men and lesbian women have very different experiences and histories within the dominant culture and that within the group of gay men and lesbians there are vastly different experiences that vary due to physical ability, race, ethnicity, economic class, and a myriad of other factors. "Gay men and lesbian women" are hardly a homogeneous group (the same could be said for gay men or lesbians taken as two different groups), and the stereotypical attributes of the group, if at all descriptive, are descriptive only to the culturally dominant white cisgender experience within that group. Furthermore, it is certainly not uncommon for individuals (LGBTQ or otherwise) to have different discriminating attitudes toward gay men and lesbian women, or different attitudes toward individuals who have same-sex attraction but other identities.

Given these complexities, it is certainly imaginable that the employer in Alito's example does not discriminate against homosexuals across the board, but only gay men, or only lesbian women. Consider case one: The employer fires Gary because the employer regards being gay as being woman-like, and thus believes that Gary is not doing what he should to support a certain heterosexual version of manhood, masculinity, or the power structure of heteropatriarchy. The employer does not fire Leslie because he assumes that lesbianism is trivial and childish and that she will soon find a good man who will more than change her "preference." Case two: Assume the employer fires Leslie and not Gary since Leslie needs to take her role as a subservient heterosexual wife and mother for the good of society, whereas Gary's attraction is simply the result of a particularly robust and masculine sex drive.

Now, in considering these two cases, it is not the case that the employer is discriminating against homosexuality across the board. The discrimination is more obviously based on being a gay man (case one) or a lesbian woman (case two). Alito's thought experiment, slightly tweaked, makes it clear that the treatment of Leslie or Gary cannot be seen as unjust or just depending on how gay men and lesbians are treated *as a group*. In case one, Gary is fired because he is a man and a gay man; that is, he is *a certain kind of* man. In case two, Leslie is fired because she is a lesbian who is a woman; that is, she is a *certain kind of* woman. By Alito's reasoning, neither is unlawfully discriminated against if they both are fired, but this conclusion is revealed as weak when considering the cases that involve only Leslie or Gary being fired, for the similarities to the Phillips case (discrimination against women with young children) are much less easy to deny. This points to Alito's confusion, since the characterization of unlawful discrimination against an individual does not depend on how a second individual is treated. In other words, discrimination on the basis of sex should not be absolved if discrimination on the basis of same-sex attraction is also at play.

Due to the fact that whiteness is generally seen as the assumed race of individuals unless stated otherwise, it is probable that both Gary and Leslie were imagined as white persons in the above example. Assume instead that

Leslie is Black and Gary is white. Now, assume the employer has both racist and heterosexist biases; these result in him finding fault in nearly everything that Leslie does. The employer fires Leslie because he simply cannot tolerate any individual who is a lesbian, a woman, and is Black. On the other hand, even though Gary is gay, he finds his gayness to be acceptable, even endearing, a reaction that is most certainly tied to his whiteness. "He reminds me of my old Uncle Lawrence—what a queen! Ha Ha!" Gary's whiteness protects him from discrimination and Leslie's identities make her more of a target of the same.

Legal theorist and a pioneer in critical race theory Kimberlé Crenshaw revolutionized legal theory and social analysis through her work in intersectionality. As she explains, the origination of the notion resulted from a particular case, that of Emma DeGraffenried.[38] The case involved the kind of complexity that I just attempted to illustrate. In this case, DeGraffenried was denied employment because she was a Black woman. Even though the cause of the discrimination seemed both blatant and unjust, she was told she wasn't discriminated against due to her sex since the company had a long-time practice of hiring white women as administrative assistants. She was told that she was not discriminated against because of being Black, either, because the company had a long practice of hiring Black men in industrial or labor jobs in the company. Crenshaw notes that the opinion of the court at the time was that DeGraffenried's treatment cannot be seen as discrimination since doing so would represent a kind of preferential treatment for Black women; they would have "two swings at the bat," whereas those experiencing discrimination on the basis of just one aspect of their identity only got the one swing. Quite obviously, this denied the common occurrence that many individuals are discriminated against for a multiplicity of reasons. This denial is based in the experience of those who do not have the experience of being marginalized in multiple ways and thus have an insufficiently complex lens with which to understand discrimination and bias.

Crenshaw made it clear that "sex discrimination" had been constructed as only applying to white women and "discrimination on the basis of race" had been constructed as only applying to Black men. Discrimination against an individual on the basis of both race and sex, especially before her influential work, didn't fit either of the two constructs and so went unjustly unrecognized. Crenshaw made it clear that discrimination against Black women was not nullified by a lack of discrimination against Black men. Similarly, discrimination against Black women was not nullified by a lack of discrimination against white women. In Crenshaw's example, Emma DeGraffenried was discriminated against because she was a Black woman, a person who was Black *and* a person who was a woman. Using analogous reasoning in the case under discussion, Leslie's discrimination as a lesbian woman should not be nullified because the employer does not discriminate against white Gary. In the case in which Leslie is imagined as a Black lesbian woman, her discrimination should not be regarded as acceptable since white Gary is insulated from discrimination because he is white and because the form of white gayness exhibited by Gary reminds the employer of his beloved Uncle Lawrence. Indeed, this is true even if it is Gary's whiteness alone that serves as such an insulator, Queeny Uncle Lawrence notwithstanding. Thus, Alito's attempt to group all thought-to-be-homosexuals together in one group, and then claim that discrimination on the basis of sexual orientation is not relevant to Title VII, fails.

ALITO'S DISTRESS OF CONSEQUENCES

Before looking more closely at textualism itself, there is one last and important critique of Alito's dissent that is significant. Here, I mean significant in the sense that his reasoning is so worrisome that it can't be ignored, and perhaps is so egregious that it reveals some of his attitudes about not only the ramifications of the court's decision here, but his particular views regarding trans persons in general. Until this point of the dissent, the case of Stephens and the reasoning of her case runs roughly parallel to that of Bostock and Zarda. I admit that my own experience reading the dissent was that, while I recognized ways in which Alito's arguments were in error to various degrees, I was tentatively glad to see that at least there was no obvious and specific anti-transgender sentiment expressed. This changed when I read his Section IV. Perhaps based on the anti-trans rhetoric of the last five years, I was waiting for the shoe to drop and for Alito to argue that Stephens's case was raising a very different issue than those of Zarda and Bostock. I imagined arguments that concluded that discrimination against transgender persons was entirely a different matter than discrimination against non-trans LGB individuals because, perhaps, our identities were somehow fabricated or illegitimate. Perhaps since Alito is denying Title VII protection in all three cases, his incredulity that transgender persons would be protected from employment discrimination did not appear until the end of his dissent.

In the last section of his dissent, Alito dispenses with even an attempt to argue for a conclusion based on the law itself, or anything even remotely related to textualism, but instead argues against the majority conclusion on the basis of predicted consequences:

> What the Court has done today—interpreting discrimination because of "sex" to encompass discrimination because of sexual orientation or gender identity—is virtually certain to have far reaching consequences. Over 100 federal statutes

prohibit discrimination because of sex. . . . The Court's brusque refusal to consider the consequences of its reasoning is irresponsible.[39]

Most of the consequences that Alito describes involve those that he believes follow from the court's conclusion that discrimination on the basis of gender identity is a form of discrimination on the basis of sex. Alito rightly realizes that as a result of this ruling, transgender persons will wish to argue for our rights as relevant to Title VII and in other areas of the law. Predictably, Alito mentions the usual imagined terrors of full and just transgender social inclusion. Of course, he first mentions bathroom use:

> Under the Court's decision, however, transgender persons will be able to argue that they are entitled to use a bathroom or locker room that is reserved for persons of the sex with which they identify, and while the Court does not define what it means to be a transgender person, the term may apply to individuals who are "gender fluid," that is, individuals whose gender identity is mixed or changes over time.[40]

I will not rehash the arguments I made in chapter 3 here, but it is worthy of mentioning that Alito mentions gender fluid people as particularly concerning, which is a position relatively new in this national debate, since generally those with this identity have not often been explicitly named as dangerous or cause for concern. Assuming that our legal system, at least theoretically, supports the position that no individual should be barred from meaningful participation in society, then the colonial and unjustified assumptions of the binary sex-gender system need to be jettisoned. Again, there is no justifiable reason that transgender, gender non-binary, or gender fluid persons should be barred from participation in society in all respects. The fact that Alito regards a kind of invitation to change unjust laws as a *negative* consequence displays his obvious anti-trans bias.

Alito's list of concerns of full trans inclusion include worries that Title XI will be employed to insure inclusion of transgender students in educational settings, that transgender athletes will seek to participate in athletic competition, that transgender college students will challenge archaic residence hall policies, that transgender persons will seek to have appropriate health care and that such health care be not excluded from being covered by relevant health insurance policies, that transgender persons will be able to cite verbal harassment in the form of disrespectful pronoun use as a form of sexual harassment, and the fear that transgender or LGBQ individuals will be able to cite employment discrimination if they are discriminated against in seeking employment as teachers.[41] Alito attempts to tie the above potential legal challenges to threats of "freedom of religion, freedom of speech, and personal privacy and safety."[42] While these are the commonly imagined and exaggerated thought-to-be dangers of our age, what is most relevant here is that it is the inclusion of transgender persons that is identified as the source of the fear. Quite obviously, Alito believes that it is transgender, including gender fluid and gender non-binary, persons who are the problem, and that our nation's laws, which continue to speak of liberty and equal opportunity for all, even after centuries of falling so short of these ideals, should not accept further challenges to insure such equal opportunity.

> This potential is illustrated by pending and recent lower court cases in which transgender individuals have challenged a variety of federal, state, and local laws and policies on constitutional grounds. . . . Although the Court does not want to think about the consequences of its decision, we will not be able to avoid those issues for long. The entire Federal Judiciary will be mired for years in disputes about the reach of the Court's reasoning.[43]

To be clear, it is not just a full court docket of difficult cases that is worrying Alito, but he erroneously believes that recognizing that employment discrimination against transgender persons is prohibited by law will result in the infringements of others' rights:

> Before issuing today's radical decision, the Court should have given some thought to where its decision would lead. As the briefing in these cases has warned, the position that the Court now adopts will threaten freedom of religion, freedom of speech, and personal privacy and safety. No one should think that the Court's decision represents an unalloyed victory for individual liberty.[44]

Alito here suggests that rights and inclusion of transgender persons are not just contested, but that there is a zero-sum game between trans inclusion and liberty for cisgender persons. In this way, he gives a not-so-subtle nod toward those who regard trans inclusion to be personal loss for them as individuals and a collective loss for the country. The rights considered by Alito to be threatened can be argued to be some of the most foundational liberties of the country. Thus, he suggests that trans inclusion is not just unwarranted, but is inconsistent with these fundamental liberties and, as such, a threat to this nation's continuance and collective identity. The fact that such a small percentage of the population is regarded as this dangerous is related to the scapegoating strategies that were discussed in chapters 5 and 6, and also to the fragility of some of the underlying beliefs of the dominant US culture. Here I refer not to the valuing beliefs regarding freedom of speech, religion, or personal privacy, but to the belief that the sex-gender binary is an essential and necessary part of our coercive legal system.

With regard to legal interpretation, there two ways to characterize Alito's reasoning here. First, one could argue that he is breaking ranks with textualism altogether in his argument for avoiding the dire consequences of transgender inclusion. Textualism is not concerned with the *consequences* of judicial decisions but the relationship between these decisions and the *meaning* of the originating statute. Textualism is decidedly backward-looking. It is backward-looking towards textual or original meanings and not forward-looking to positive or negative consequences. On the other hand, if we try to understand Alito's view to be consistent with a most rigid and status-quo-maintaining sort of textualism—a kind of originalism for which it is the statute authors' meaning, intention, scope of application, and imagination to what a future just society might resemble is relevant to the interpretation and future application of the statute—then we have a different conclusion. If it is *this* kind of overly strict textualism that Alito wishes to employ, then nearly any movement away from, or challenge to, the status quo of the past will be regarded as unconstitutional. Given this, perhaps Alito has the following conditional in mind, "If one employs strict textualism, then status-quo-challenging future legal cases will be less likely." So, "If status-quo-challenging future cases are very likely, then one has not employed strict textualism." This kind of reasoning would both benefit those who have historically been privileged and uphold and strengthen those meanings/social constructions that serve to privilege the same. This is surely unacceptable. There is reason to think that even a less obviously status-quo-preserving textualism may be unacceptable, more broadly, in that it holds present and future generations hostage to the ideas, categories, and ways of being that were seen as normative or natural in the past but have lost their relevance to contemporary and future lives.

Regardless of the specifics of Alito's reasoning here, the fact that he explicitly identifies that it would be a *negative* consequence for transgender and gender transgressive persons to legally investigate and fight for our rights is unprecedented in its blatant disregard for the well-being and flourishing of a clearly oppressed subgroup of Americans. The kinds of legal challenges he dreads would mean that the reconsideration of legal sex, fair and inclusive athletic competition, and fair and respectful treatment of gender transgressive persons are all inappropriate and not worth the attention of national and regional courts. Alito decries the fact that the Bostock ruling means that a purely legislative remedy to these kinds of cases has been preempted and "has effectively ended—any chance of a bargained legislative resolution."[45] Perhaps he predicts that no such legislative compromise would ever favor transgender persons and our full inclusion into society. Unfortunately, this kind of belief may be warranted. Even over a decade after the ENDA (Employment Non-Discrimination Act) fiasco of 2007, when the inclusion of protections for transgender persons was dropped so as to have a greater chance of legislative approval, it isn't difficult to imagine that the inclusion of a bargained legislative resolution on LGBTQ employment rights would leave the most vulnerable groups of individuals without protection. Indeed, it is why this issue needed to be handled by the courts; political bargaining, particularly as it affects highly politicized identities, far from guarantees justice.

CONCLUSION

I mentioned in the introduction of this chapter that the Obergefell ruling can, in an important way, serve as the beginning of a new stage in the nation's recognition of LGB equality. It also serves as related, at least temporally if not causally, to a nearly nation-wide backlash and unprecedented targeting of transgender, gender non-binary, and gender non-conforming persons. The Bostock ruling is similarly important, not just as the chosen endpoint of this study, but as a court case that has the *potential* to change people's lives for the better. Of course, I realize that much—now illegal—discrimination on the basis of gender identity will continue just as it did before the Bostock decision. The individuals more likely to be discriminated against are also the same who do not have the funds or the privilege to mount a legal discrimination lawsuit. The Bostock decision may make it much less likely that those of the gender transgressive community that benefit from white privilege are discriminated against, but this group of individuals was less likely to experience this in the first place. Paraphrasing theorist Dean Spade, the law can now tell itself that it prohibits discrimination on the basis of gender identity and sexual orientation and the US can tell other countries that this form of discrimination is legally prohibited. A just society requires more than just laws. On the other hand, if one accepts, at least to some degree, the legal system we have, then this is an incredibly positive outcome.

How the trans-targeting portion of the population will respond to Bostock remains to be seen. I assume many will just ignore this positive assertion of transgender rights in favor of the anti-trans movement that has already gained such momentum. This is especially true since the new wave of anti-transgender proposed legislation seems to target children and girls who wish to play sports. These are much different questions than employment discrimination and so some may simply deny any relevance of this ruling to new anti-transgender tactics and proposals. Of course, a negative reaction to the decision that includes effort to achieve an even greater dominance of conservative justices and an ever more strict textualism may be forthcoming. It is also important to consider the response of certain anti-trans lawmakers to this decision: Might they begin to be concerned that they will soon be seen as being on the wrong side of history, public opinion, and justice? One of the concerns that led me to want to take a close look at the politicization of transgender identity was that I feared that it is easier to politicize a group of individuals than undo the damage after it is done.

Of course the future is unknown and unknowable. What is known is that the politicization of trans identity has been immensely harmful in a way that is inversely proportional to one's social privilege. As often articulated in this work, dismantling anti-transgender oppression requires the dismantlement of other systems of oppression that have been in place before this country's inception. Given the events and demonstrations of the last few years, it is my hope that this is an understanding shared by many, even those that do not experience multiple marginalizing systems.

NOTES

1. At the time of finishing up this manuscript, the coronavirus death toll in the US has grown to over 800,000 souls.
2. *Bostock v. Clayton County Georgia*, Certiorari to the United States Court of Appeals for the Eleventh Circuit, June 15, 2020, 3 https://www.supremecourt.gov/opinions/19pdf/17-1618_hfci.pdf.
3. Judge Kavanaugh's dissent relies on the distinction between a literal and a "common sense" reading of the law. His "literal meaning" of the law involves thinking of meaning as a function of individual words, as opposed to phrases.
4. Bostock, 37.
5. Duncan Kennedy, "Freedom and Constraint in Adjudication: A Critical Phenomenology," *Journal of Legal Education* 36, no. 4 (1986): 518 (also in Kennedy, *Legal Reasoning: Collected Essays*).
6. Title VII of the American Civil Rights Act of 1964, United States Equal Opportunity Commission, https://www.eeoc.gov/statutes/title-vii-civil-rights-act-1964.
7. Bostock, 5.
8. Arguably, though not an argument presented by Gorsuch, a focus on these notions that are connected to but not basic to the meaning of "sex" or, more specifically, "biological sex" seems as though it would be a move toward conception-textualism rather than meaning-textualism, as per the distinction made by Perry. More will be said regarding this kind of argument later in this chapter.
9. As will be made clear, the court argues that discrimination because of *sex* need not be the sole reason for the discrimination but is simply a necessary aspect of what may be a more complex intention.
10. Bostock, 5.
11. Bostock, 9.
12. 400 US 543 (1971).

13. Bostock, 6.
14. 435 US 702 1978.
15. It should be noted that the statistic in question identifies life expectancies of cisgender men and cisgender women only.
16. Given that this court case was argued with the Cisgender Assumption fully in place, I have maintained that unfounded assumption in the above application of the but-for test and the remainder of this section.
17. Bostock, 13.
18. Bostock, 14.
19. Bostock, 14.
20. Bostock, 16.
21. Bostock, 14.
22. Bostock, slightly paraphrased, 3.
23. Bostock, 3.
24. Bostock, 6.
25. Bostock, 3.
26. Bostock, 11.
27. Bostock, 25.
28. Bostock, 3, and A. Scalia and B. Garner, *Reading Law: The Interpretation of Legal Texts* (St. Paul, MN: Thompson West, 2012), 16.
29. I don't analyze Kavanaugh's dissent in detail, but it is similar to Alito's argument here in that it wishes to understand the phrase "discrimination on the basis of sex" by considering the meaning of the phrase all together, rather than breaking it into constituent parts.
30. Relevant to this discussion is John Perry's "Textualism and the Discovery of Rights," in *Philosophical Foundations of Language and the Law* (Oxford: Oxford University Press, 2011).
31. Bostock, Alito dissent, 6.
32. Bostock, Alito dissent, 7–8.
33. Ibid., italics mine.
34. Ibid.
35. Kimberlé Crenshaw, an influential legal theorist to be further discussed later in this chapter, would certainly not support reducing any individual to a single defining characteristic.
36. Bostock, Alito dissent, 17.
37. Jonathan Ned Katz, *The Invention of Heterosexuality* (Chicago: University of Chicago Press, 2007).
38. Kimberlé Crenshaw, "The Urgency of Intersectionality," Ted Talk, TEDWomen, 2016, https://www.ted.com/talks/kimberle_crenshaw_the_urgency_of_intersectionality?language=en#t-12624.
39. Bostock, Alito dissent, 44.
40. Bostock, Alito dissent, 45.
41. Bostock, Alito dissent, 44–54.

42. Bostock, Alito dissent, 45.
43. Bostock, Alito dissent, 53–54.
44. Bostock, Alito dissent, 45.
45. Bostock, Alito dissent, 45.

Epilogue

When I first envisioned this project many years ago, I identified the year of 2020 to be the cut off year of my research into anti-transgender proposed legislation, rates of violence, and hateful rhetoric. Five years seemed a fine amount of time for careful tracking and analysis; the Bostock decision put a kind of natural endpoint to the project and created, so interestingly, a five-year period bounded by two of the most pro-LGBTQ SCOTUS rulings in US history. Obviously, this five-year period turned out to be one in which trans and other gender transgressive persons have been politicized and targeted, in a way not seen before in this nation's history. As mentioned in both chapters 1 and 8, wins in the courtroom do not always produce justice on the streets. This is an understatement.

The momentum of anti-trans proposed legislation did seem to slow down through 2020. This came as a great relief. I would hope that during a global pandemic politicians would find ways of helping their constituents stay alive, rather than unnecessarily targeting trans persons in ways that reduce our ability to participate fully in society and puts us at an increased risk of harm. However, as I write this epilogue in the summer of 2021, it is clear that a new wave of anti-transgender legislation is again being proposed. This second tidal wave of targeting trans persons is mostly focused in two areas:

1. Prohibiting children who are trans from receiving care that has been medically approved and agreed upon through consultation of the medical professional, the child, and the parents or guardians, and
2. Prohibiting children and adults who are trans from participating in sports.

The number of bills and the fervor that accompanies the faulty arguments used by their proponents have received national attention. Even Pete Buttigieg, transportation secretary, mentioned in a recent interview (July

2021) that lawmakers needed to "stop picking on trans kids."[1] Indeed, if only they would heed his advice.

This new wave of anti-transgender backlash means that the global pandemic did not force a dramatic redirection or cessation of these efforts, rather just a brief period of relative inactivity. Given that these two kinds of legislation have only become popularized in 2021, I won't present a detailed analysis of these proposals here. I'd ask my reader though to be careful of the disinformation that exists to sway your opinion. Children do not, in fact, have a "medical sex change." At most some children socially transition so they can feel more like themselves both at home and at school. This is important not just for general well-being but also for their academic success. Some individuals, if they medically qualify, are prescribed hormone blockers, a treatment which is a medically approved and supervised way to avoid the often very difficult-to-accept, and sometimes irreversible, physical changes that puberty brings. I spoke of my own experience of this herein and would have loved to have had access to the treatments that are now thoughtfully prescribed. Any form of transition, including social transition, is not for everyone, by any means, but medical professionals, parents, and the individuals involved should be able to make choices that alleviate suffering and increase flourishing. To attempt to outlaw this medical intervention in the general case is both profoundly insensitive and uninformed.

The second kind of anti-transgender proposals involve barring trans athletes from competition. These kinds of efforts generally target girls and women who are trans, for reasons that I alluded to in chapter 3. These efforts are also wrongheaded and rely on ignorance and misguided mythology of testosterone rather than cogent argumentation and scientific literacy. Dr. Veronica Ivy has already written substantially on this issue, and so I direct my readers to her authoritative work. Of special note is "Including Trans Women Athletes in Competitive Sport: Analyzing the Science, Law, and Principles and Policies of Fairness in Competition," that she authored with Aryn Conrad in 2018.[2] See also "If 'Ifs' and 'Buts' Were Candy and Nuts: The Failure of Arguments against Trans and Intersex Women's Full and Equal Inclusion in Women's Sport," in 2021.[3] As Dr. Ivy so cogently argues, sport is a human right even for those that powerful others wish to dehumanize and ostracize.

Religious freedom laws, that have been proposed and sometimes adopted in the past five years and were a particular favorite of former vice president Pence, are not thoroughly discussed in this volume. Dr. John Corvino, a philosopher who has done so much for LGBTQ philosophy through his cogent arguments for the moral acceptability of queer relationships, wrote, along with two interlocutors, *Debating Religious Liberty and Discrimination*.[4] His analysis is exceedingly insightful and so I direct my readers to his scholarship to learn more about how to recognize the fallacious reasoning on which these proposals rely. The idea that treating transgender, gender non-binary, and gender non-conforming persons disrespectfully because we are an affront to one's religious practice is an argument from "arrogant perception" that lacks both empathy and reason.

I believe that the forces against trans, gender non-binary, and gender non-conforming persons fully participating in our society are neither satisfied nor trounced. I'd like to think that five, ten, fifteen, or even a generational twenty years from now, most will regard the efforts of the present anti-trans offensive to be embarrassingly misguided. Yet, based on the stubborn near intractability of other oppressive systems in this country, I am concerned that the politicization of trans identities will persist. Oppressive systems and politicization tend to obstinately endure. My pessimism on this issue is countered by the evidence that a rejection of strictly binary identities is becoming less common in our youth. More and more young people are identifying as trans, non-binary,[5] and otherwise have more accepting attitudes towards LGBTQ communities in general. This doesn't mean that those of us who are older wait for the younger generations to take the helm, but that we actively promote flourishing together.

NOTES

1. Clara Hill, "Pete Buttigieg Calls Out Politicians for 'Picking On' Transgender Kids," *Independent*, July 7, 2021, https://www.independent.co.uk/news/world/americas/us-politics/pete-buttigieg-lgbtq-rights-defense-b1879949.html.

2. Veronica Ivy and Aryn Conrad, "Including Trans Women Athletes in Competitive Sport: Analyzing the Science, Law, and Principles and Policies of Fairness in Competition," *Philosophical Topics* 46, no. 2 (2018): 103–140, https://www.muse.jhu.edu/article/764815.

3. Veronica Ivy, "If 'Ifs' and 'Buts' Were Candy and Nuts: The Failure of Arguments against Trans and Intersex Women's Full and Equal Inclusion in Women's Sport," *Feminist Philosophy Quarterly* 7, no. 2 (2021), Article 3.

4. John Corvino, Ryan T. Anderson, and Sherif Girgis, *Debating Religious Liberty and Discrimination* (New York: Oxford University Press 2017), 5.

5. Madeleine Carlisle, "Young People Are Taking Control of Their Gender Identity: New Research Examines Diversity of Nonbinary Youth," *Time* magazine, July 12, 2021, https://time.com/6079326/nonbinary-lgbtq-youth/.

Bibliography

Abadi, Mark. "North Carolina Has Lost a Staggering Amount of Money Due to Its Controversial Bathroom Law." *Business Insider*, September 21, 2016, http://www.businessinsider.com/north-carolina-hb2-economic-impact-2016-9.

Abraham, Ralph. "Abraham for Governor," Abraham Campaign, August 22, 2019. Video: https://www.youtube.com/watch?v=0YkAm6NY8oU.

Alder, Madison. "Fact Check, Was the White House Lit in Rainbow Colors on Obama's Last Night in the White House?" *Republic*, https://www.azcentral.com/story/news/politics/fact-check/2017/01/20/fact-check-white-house-lit-rainbow-colors-obamas-last-night-office/96843594/.

Alexander, Harriet. "God Let 9-11 Happen in Anger at Transgender Silliness, Says American Evangelical." *Telegraph*, May 14, 2016, https://www.telegraph.co.uk/news/2016/05/13/god-let-911-happen-in-anger-at-transgender-silliness-says-americ/.

Andersson, Jasmin. "Butch Lesbian Opens Up about 'Increased Harassment' She Faces When She Uses Public Toilets." *iNews*, UK, January 19, 2021, https://inews.co.uk/news/uk/butch-lesbian-public-toilet-women-abuse-government-review-gender-neutral-facilities-833787?fbclid=IwAR3Ne6JYqGGL9FC5jF0-INlZZrDoh8PT7ScFGKxVOMKaHEdAVgTJzbgsIkE.

Anonymous. Interview with Idaho-born Latina woman who is transgender and living out of the state. She wished to stay anonymous. January 29, 2021.

Assunção, Muri. "Ohio Lawmaker Blames Trans People, Open Borders, Gay Marriage, Drag Queen Advocates, for Deadly Mass Shootings." *New York Daily News*, August 5, 2019, https://www.nydailynews.com/news/politics/ny-candice-keller-gop-ohio-blames-gay-marriage-transgender-drag-queen-20190805-rftgwkv-vt5ehpgp3daboujo2ry-story.html.

Appiah, Kwame Anthony. "Racisms." In *Anatomy of Racism*, edited by David Theo Goldberg. Minneapolis, MN: University of Minnesota Press, 1990.

Astor, Maggie. "Violence against Trans People Is on the Rise, Advocates Say." *New York Times*, November 9, 2017, http://assets2.hrc.org/files/assets/resources/A_Time_To_Act_2017_REV3.pdf.

Bibliography

Avery, Ben. "LGBT Rights Fight Reignited Four Years After N.C.'s 'Bathroom Bill' Controversy." *NBC News*, December, 8, 2020, https://www.nbcnews.com/feature/nbc-out/lgbtq-rights-fight-reignited-4-years-after-n-c-s-n1250390.

Barnes, Elizabeth. "Justice, at What Cost?" *History Today* 68, no. 12 (2018).

Bartholomew, James. "The Awful Rise of Virtue Signalling." *Spectator*, April 18, 2015, https://www.spectator.co.uk/2015/04/hating-the-daily-mail-is-a-substitute-for-doing-good/.

Beck, Julia. Interviewed by Tucker Carlson. *Tucker Carlson Tonight*, Fox News, February 12, 2019, https://www.youtube.com/watch?v=aQns3VsYdd4.

Bettcher, Talia Mae. "Evil Deceivers and Make Believers: On Transphobic Violence and the Politics of Illusion." *Hypatia* 22, no. 3 (Summer 2007): 43–65.

Bible, The. Leviticus.

Blumberg, Antonia. "Julián Castro Gives Nod to Trans Community While Sharing His Abortion Views." *HuffPostPolitics*, June 26, 2019, https://www.huffpost.com/entry/julian-castro-democratic-debate-reproductive-justice_n_5d141d98e4b0e455603742aa.

Bollinger, Alex. "31 Anti-Transgender Bills Proposed in 20 States as the GOP Target Transgender Children Nationwide." *LGBTQ Nation*, February 5, 2021, https://www.lgbtqnation.com/2021/02/31-anti-transgender-bills-filed-20-states-gop-targets-schoolchildren-nationwide/.

Bostock v. Clayton County Georgia. Certiorari to the United States Court of Appeals for the Eleventh Circuit, June 15, 2020, 3. https://www.supremecourt.gov/opinions/19pdf/17-1618_hfci.pdf.

Boylan, Jennifer Finney. "Really, You Are Blaming Transgender People for Trump?" *New York Times*, December 2, 2016, https://www.nytimes.com/2016/12/02/opinion/really-youre-blaming-transgender-people-for-trump.html.

Brandwatch, Ditch the Label. "Exposed: The Extent of Transphobia Online," https://www.brandwatch.com/reports/transphobia/.

Browning, Bill. "National Center for Transgender Equality Has Endured Multiple Bomb Threats Over the Past Year." *LGBTQ Nation*, August 29, 2019, Referenced, September 11, 2019, https://www.cnn.com/2017/04/28/us/la-riots-korean-americans/index.html.

Browning, Bill. "Trump Supporter Starts 'Kill Transgenders' Chat at Rally." *LGBTQ Nation*, July 27, 2020, https://www.lgbtqnation.com/2020/07/trump-supporter-starts-kill-transgenders-chant-rally/?fbclid=IwAR1WKbyhnDHyQjSndtYMDOPqjLRfYPgu1N5ClSXx-Z_fWB3qGwp6pL2CTmk#.Xx8wirQHdDU.facebook.

Calhoun, Cheshire. "In Defense of Same-Sex Marriage." In *The Philosophy of Sex: Contemporary Readings*, edited by Alan Soble and Nicholas Power, 206. Lanham, MD: Rowman & Littlefield, 2008.

Card, Claudia. "Recognizing Terrorism." *Journal of Ethics* 11 (2007): 1–29.

Carlisle Madeleine, "Young People Are Taking Control of Their Gender Identity: New Research Examines Diversity of Nonbinary Youth." *Time*, July 12, 2021, https://time.com/6079326/nonbinary-lgbtq-youth/.

Carter, C. Allen. *Kenneth Burke and the Scapegoat Process*. Norman: University of Oklahoma Press, 1996.

Cannon, Loren. "Trans-Marriage and the Unacceptability of Same-Sex Marriage Restrictions." *Social Philosophy Today* 25 (2009): 75–89.
Cheung, King-Kok. "(Mis)Interpretations and (In)Justice: The 1992 Los Angeles 'Riots' and 'Black-Korean' Conflict." *Melus* 30, no. 3 (Fall 2005): 3–40.
Combahee River Collective. "A Black Feminist Statement" (1977). In *This Bridge Called My Back: Writings by Radical Women of Color*, edited by Cherríe Moraga and Gloria Anzaldúa (New York: Persephone Press, 1981).
Corvino, John, Ryan T. Anderson, and Sherif Girgis. *Debating Religious Liberty and Discrimination*. New York: Oxford University Press, 2017.
Crenshaw, Kimberlé. "The Urgency of Intersectionality." Ted Talk, TEDWomen, 2016, https://www.ted.com/talks/kimberle_crenshaw_the_urgency_of_intersectionality?language=en#t-12624.
Cudd, Ann E. "Analyzing Backlash to Progressive Social Movements." In *Theorizing Backlash: Philosophical Reflections on the Resistance to Feminism*, edited by Anita M. Superson and Ann E. Cudd. Lanham, MD: Rowman & Littlefield, 2002.
Curry, Tommy J. "Michael Brown and the Need for a Genre Study of Black Male Death and Dying." *Theory and Event* 17, no. 3, supplement (2014), https://muse.jhu.edu/article/559369.
Diaz, Alexa. "HUD Chief Ben Carson Reportedly Made Dismissive Comments about Transgender People during a California Trip." *LA Times*, September 2019, https://www.latimes.com/politics/story/2019-09-20/housing-secretary-ben-carson-transgender-comments-san-francisco.
Dreier, Fred. "The Complicated Case of Transgender Cyclist, Dr. Rachel McKinnon." *Velo News*, October 18, 2018, https://www.velonews.com/2018/10/news/commentary-the-complicated-case-of-transgender-cyclist-dr-rachel-mckinnon_480285.
D'Oro, Guiseppina. "The Ontological Backlash: Why Did Mainstream Analytic Philosophy Lose Interest in the Philosophy of History?" *Philosophia* 36, no. 4. (December 2008).
DeAlmeida, Luis Duarte. "Legal Sex." In *Oxford Studies in the Philosophy of Law Volume 2*, edited by Leslie Green and Brian Leiter. Oxford: Oxford University Press, 2013.
Dreher, Ron. "Paglia: Transgender and Civilization's Decline." *American Conservative*, March 8, 2017, https://www.theamericanconservative.com/dreher/paglia-transgender-civilizations-decline/.
Du Bois, W. E. B. *The Souls of Black Folks*. Chicago: A. C. McClurg, 1931.
Dworkin, Andrea. *Intercourse*. New York: Free Press, 1987.
Eilperin, Juliet. "Gay Marriage Will Cost Tens of Millions." *Washington Post*, July 1, 2013. http://www.washingtonpost.com/blogs/the-fix/wp/2013/07/01/how-much-will-the-gay-marriage-fight-cost-over-the-next-three-years-tens-of-millions/.
Feinberg, Leslie. *Transgender Warriors: Making History from Joan of Arc to Dennis Rodman*. Boston, MA: Beacon Press, 1996.
Fischer, Bob, ed. *Ethics, Left and Right: The Moral Issues that Divide Us*. New York: Oxford University Press, 2019.
Fredrickson, George M. *Racism: A Short History*. Princeton: Princeton University Press, 2016.

French, Peter. *Collective and Corporate Responsibility.* New York: Columbia University Press, 1984.

Friedman, David M. *A Mind of Its Own: A Cultural History of the Penis.* New York: Free Press, 2001.

Frye, Marilyn. *The Politics of Reality: Essays in Feminist Theory.* Trumansburg, NY: Crossing Press, 1983.

Faludi, Susan. *Backlash: The Undeclared War against American Women.* New York: Crown, 1991.

Gattaca. Official Trailer, Written and Directed by Andrew Niccol, Produced by Danny DeVito, Michael Shambert, Stacey Sher, Gail Lyon, 1997. YouTube, https://www.youtube.com/watch?v=W_KruQhfvW4.

Gilson, Tim. "Transgenderism: The Fastest-Growing Insanity the World Has Ever Seen." *Stream Magazine*, https://stream.org/*transgenderism*-fastest-growing-insanit/.

Girard, René. *I See Satan Fall Like Lightning.* Translated with a foreword by James G. Williams. Maryknoll, NY: Orbis Books, 2001.

Girard, René. *The Scapegoat.* Baltimore, MD: Johns Hopkins University Press, 1986.

Glenn, Gary, president of the Michigan chapter of AFA, 2001. From Southern Poverty Law Center web page :https://www.splcenter.org/fighting-hate/extremist-files/group/american-family-association.

GLSEN School Climate Survey, 2019. https://www.glsen.org/sites/default/files/2020-10/NSCS-2019-Executive-Summary-English_1.pdf.

Green, Emma. "White Evangelicals Believe They Face More Discrimination than Muslims." *Atlantic*, March 10, 2017 (based on PRRI Survey, 2017), https://www.theatlantic.com/politics/archive/2017/03/perceptions-discrimination-muslims-christians/519135/.

Grinberg, Emanuella, and Dani Stewart. "Three Myths That Shape the Transgender Bathroom Debate." CNN, March 7, 2017, https://www.cnn.com/2017/03/07/health/transgender-bathroom-law-facts-myths/index.html.

Gunn Allen, Paula. *The Sacred Hoop: Recovering the Feminine in American Indian Traditions.* Boston, MA: Beacon Press, 1986/1992.

Hale, Jacob. "Are Lesbians Women?" *Hypatia* 11, no. 2 (Spring 1996): 94–121.

Herman, Jody L. "Gendered Restrooms and Minority Stress: The Public Regulation of Gender and Its Impact on Transgender People's Lives." *Journal of Public Management and Social Policy* 19, no. 1 (2013): 65–80, 77.

Hill, Clara. "Pete Buttigieg Calls Out Politicians for 'Picking On' Transgender Kids." *Independent*, July 7, 2021, https://www.independent.co.uk/news/world/americas/us-politics/pete-buttigieg-lgbtq-rights-defense-b1879949.html.

Holmes, Juwan J. "Black Trans Teen Found Dead in Parking Garage Could Add to a Record Year of Anti-Trans Violence." *LGBTQ Nation*, February 2, 2021, https://www.lgbtqnation.com/2021/02/black-trans-teen-found-dead-parking-garage-add-record-year-anti-trans-violence/?fbclid=IwAR0jveorFVxpzEdHQkuN79bk1NqPliBCvSRhLllTt1n-gWL63X1FML-dKPc.

Holmes, Juwan J. "Trans People Have Become Pawns in the Kentucky Governor Race." *LGBTQ Nation*, September 16, 2019, https://www.lgbtqnation.com/2019/09/rightwing-pac-scare-mongering-trans-rights-kentucky-governors-election/

?fbclid=IwAR0H8qbHtfs-5oyPQPHk2kgZ1PGuj5qwe-j84m_AQY6UiOu_P9qwRC9s11g.

Honneth, Axel. "Integrity and Disrespect: Principles of a Conception of Morality Based on the Theory of Recognition." *Political Theory* 20, no. 2 (1992): 190.

Human Rights Watch. "In Harm's Way: State Reponses to Sex Workers, Drug Users, and HIV in New Orleans" (2013). https://www.hrw.org/sites/default/files/reports/usnola1213_ForUpload_3.pdf.

Hunte, Ben. "Transgender People Treated 'Inhumanly' Online." BBC News, October 25, 2019, https://www.bbc.com/news/technology-50166900?SThisFB&fbclid=IwAR0qpV2Ifs5iNWwq3qiaG8XGFxhJZXUcfvFWmwDbZaeJi4QRV30OlbN23PI.

Hunter, Nan D. "Expressive Identity: Recuperating Dissent for Equality." *Georgetown Law Faculty Publications and Other Works* 118 (2000). https://scholarship.law.georgetown.edu/facpub/118.

Ifill, Gwen. "Widespread Backlash to Donald Trump's Muslim Ban." PBS News, December 11, 2015, https://www.pbs.org/weta/washingtonweek/episode/widespread-backlash-donald-trumps-proposed-muslim-ban.

Ivy, Veronica. "If 'Ifs' and 'Buts' Were Candy and Nuts: The Failure of Arguments against Trans and Intersex Women's Full and Equal Inclusion in Women's Sport." *Feminist Philosophy Quarterly* 7, no. 2 (2021), Article 3.

Ivy, Veronica, and Aryn Conrad. "Including Trans Women Athletes in Competitive Sport: Analyzing the Science, Law, and Principles and Policies of Fairness in Competition." *Philosophical Topics* 46, no. 2 (2018):103–140, https://www.muse.jhu.edu/article/764815.

Jackson, Alyssa. "The High Cost of Being Transgender." CNN, July 31, 2015, https://www.cnn.com/2015/07/31/health/transgender-costs-irpt/index.html.

Jeffreys, Sheila. *Gender Hurts: A Feminist Analysis of the Politics of Transgenderism*. New York: Routledge, 2014.

Johnston, Elizabeth. "Activist Mommy." June 14, 2017, https://www.youtube.com/watch?v=L0MGOVKxvW0.

Juang, Richard M. "Transgendering the Politics of Recognition." In *Transgender Rights*, edited by Paisley Currah, Richard M. Juang, and Shannon Price Minter. Minneapolis: University of Minnesota Press, 2006.

Jurcaba, Yo, "New York Repeals 'Walking While Trans' Law after Years of Activism." NBC News, February 2021, https://www.nbcnews.com/feature/nbc-out/new-york-repeals-walking-while-trans-law-after-years-activism-n1256736.

Kander, John, composer, Fred Ebb, lyrics. Theme song for the Martin Scorsese film *New York, New York*.

Katz, Jonathan Ned. *The Invention of Heterosexuality*. Chicago: University of Chicago Press, 2007.

Kennedy, Duncan. "Freedom and Constraint in Adjudication: A Critical Phenomenology." *Journal of Legal Education* 36, no. 4 (1986): 518.

Kennedy, Pagan. *The First Man-Made Man*. New York: Bloomsbury, distributed to the trade by Holtzbrinck, 2007.

Kertscher, Tom. "Conservative Group That Claims Joe Biden Backs Sex-Changes for Kids, Is False." PolitiFact, The Poynter Institute, October 27, 2020. https://

www.politifact.com/factchecks/2020/oct/27/american-principles-project/conservative-groups-claim-joe-biden-backs-sex-chan/.

Koyama, Emi. "Whose Feminism Is It Anyway? The Unspoken Racism in the Trans Inclusion Debate." In *The Transgender Studies Reader*, edited by Susan Stryker and Stephen Whittle. New York: Routledge, 2006.

Kunzelman, Michael, and Astrid Galvan. "Trump's Words Linked to More Hate Crime? Some Experts Think So." Associated Press, August 7, 2019, https://apnews.com/article/7d0949974b1648a2bb592cab1f85aa16.

Lah, Kyung. "The L.A. Riots Were a Rude Awakening for Korean Americans." CNN, April 29, 2017, accessed September 11, 2019, https://www.cnn.com/2017/04/28/us/la-riots-korean-americans/index.html.

Lamargue, Kevin. "Trump Says Transgender Policy Is Meant to 'Protect the Country.'" NBC News, October 23, 2018, https://www.nbcnews.com/feature/nbc-out/trump-says-transgender-policy-seeks-protect-country-n923266.

Lang, Nico. "Anti Trans Facebook Ads Target Georgia Voters Ahead of Critical Run Off Election." *Them*, January 5, 2021. https://www.them.us/story/anti-trans-facebook-ads-target-georgia-runoff-election-voters?fbclid=IwAR1ru5stQDRFqh7jf6I7Bq4pnz6PDQbJmGU-dyE1oPGD7VuebRC5zQUDgHM.

Legislature of the State of Idaho in the House of Representatives, House Bill 509. https://legislature.idaho.gov/wpcontent/uploads/sessioninfo/2020/legislation/H0509.pdf.

Littleton v. Prange. 9 S.W.3d 223 (1999).

Loller, Travis. "Transgender Plaintiffs Sue Tennessee, to Change Birth Certificate Gender." NBC News, https://www.nbcnews.com/feature/nbc-out/transgender-plaintiffs-sue-tennessee-change-birth-certificate-gender-n997996.

López, Ian Haney. *Dog Whistle Politics: How Coded Racial Appeals Have Reinvented Racism and Wrecked the Middle Class.* Oxford: Oxford University Press, 2013.

López, Ian Haney. "Dog Whistle Politics." Duke University Sanford School of Public Policy. Video, March 8 2017, https://www.youtube.com/watch?v=00FNvIC5N7g.

Lugones, María. "Heterosexualism and the Colonial/Modern Gender System." *Hypatia* 22, no. 2 (Winter 2007): 186–209.

Mannix, Andy. "CeCe McDonald Murder Trial, Behind the Scenes of the Transgender Woman's Case." *CityPages*, May 9, 2012, https://web.archive.org/web/20140114115204/http://www.citypages.com/2012-05-09/news/cece-mcdonald-murder-trial/2/.

May, Larry. "Mobs and Collective Responsibility." *Social Philosophy Today: Freedom, Equality, and Social Change* 2 (1989): 300–311.

Mayer, Jeremy D. "Nixon Rides the Backlash to Victory: Racial Politics in the 1968 Presidential Campaign." *Historian* 62, no. 2 (Winter 2002): 351–356.

Mellema, Gregory. "Scapegoats." *Criminal Justice Ethics* 19, no. 1 (Winter/Spring 2000).

Murphy, Meghan, Saba Malik, and Kara Dansky. Speech, "Fighting the New Misogyny." February 2020, https://www.eventbrite.com/e/fighting-the-new-misogyny-a-feminist-critique-of-gender-identity-tickets-85012638089.

Nathanson, Paul, and Katherine K. Young. *Spreading Misandry: The Teaching of Contempt for Men in Popular Culture*. Montreal: McGill-Queen's University Press, 2001.

Nathanson, Paul. Interview by Laura Ingraham, "Transhumanism and the Assault on Traditional Gender and Masculinity." *The Laura Ingraham Podcast*, https://podcastone.com/episode/Transhumanism-and-the-assault-on-traditional-gender-and-masculinity-.

O'Scannlain, Diarmuid F. "We Are All Textualists Now: The Legacy of Justice Antonin Scalia." *St. John's Law Review* 91, no. 2 (Summer 2017): 303–311, https://scholarship.law.stjohns.edu/cgi/viewcontent.cgi?article=6793&context=lawreview.

Obama, Barack. July 14, 2015, https://www.whitehouse.gov/thepressoffice/2015/07/14/remarks-president-naacp-conference.

Obergefell et al. v. Hodges. Director, Ohio Department of Health et al., June 26, 2015, http://www.supremecourt.gov/opinions/14pdf/14-556_3204.pdf.

Oyewùmí, Oyéronké. *The Invention of Women: Making an African Sense of Western Gender Discourses*. Minneapolis: University of Minnesota Press, 1997.

Pasulka, Nicole. "The Case of CeCe McDonald: Murder—or Self-Defense against a Hate Crime?" *Mother Jones*, May 22, 2012, https://www.motherjones.com/politics/2012/05/cece-mcdonald-transgender-hate-crime-murder/.

Perry, John. "Textualism and the Discovery of Rights." In *Philosophical Foundations of Language in the Law*, edited by Andrei Marmor and Scott Soames, 105–129. Oxford: Oxford University Press, 2011.

Philostratus, Flavius. *The Life of Apollonius of Tyana, the Epistles of Apollonius and the Treatise of Eusebius*. Trans. F. C. Conybeare, Loeb Classical Library, 2 vols. Cambridge, MA: Harvard University Press, 1912. 1: 363–367.

Raymond, Janice. *The Transsexual Empire: The Making of the She-Male*. New York: Teachers College Press, 1979.

Rawls, John. *A Theory of Justice*. Cambridge, MA: Harvard University Press, 1971.

Ridler, Keith. "Correction, Transgender Birth Certificates, Idaho Story." Associated Press, October 25, 2019, https://apnews.com/article/dc535a4b404c447c96b7328c54a08e72.

Robinson, Brandon Andrew. "The Lavender Scare in Homonormative Times: Policing, Hyper-Incarceration, and LGBTQ Homelessness." *Gender & Society* 34, no. 2 (2020).

Rubin, Gayle S. "Thinking Sex: Notes for a Radical Theory of the Politics of Sexuality." 1984, http://www.feminish.com/wp-content/uploads/2012/08/Rubin1984.pdf.

Sánchez, Carlos Alberto. "On Documents and Subjectivity: The Formation and Deformation of the Immigrant Identity." *Radical Philosophy Review* 14, no. 2 (2011): 197–205.

Sartre, Jean-Paul. Excerpt from *Being and Nothingness*. In *Being Ethical: Classic and New Voices on Contemporary Issues*, edited by Shari Collins, Bertha Alvarez Manninen, Jacqueline M. Gately, and Eric Comerford. Peterborough, ON: Broadview Press, 2017.

Schmider, Alex. "2016 Was the Deadliest Year on Record for Transgender People." November 9, 2016, https://www.glaad.org/blog/2016-was-deadliest-year-record-transgender-people.

Schwartz, Hunter. "Obama's Latest 'Evolution' on Gay Marriage; He Lied about Opposing It, Axelrod Says." *Washington Post*, February 10, 2015.

Shiva, Vandana. Interviewed in *The Call of the Mountain: Deep Ecology and Arnie Naess*, Director Jan van Boeckel, Producer, Karin van der Molen/Pat van Boeckel, 1997. Paraphrase.

Shrier, Abigail. *Irreversible Damage: The Transgender Craze Seducing Our Daughters*. Washington, DC: Regency, 2020.

Shultz, Marisa. "Trump Jr. Derides Transgender Cyclist Who Won Championship." *New York Post*, October 21, 2019.

Snapp, Shannon D., Jennifer M. Hoenig, Amanda Fields, and Stephen T. Russell. "Messy, Butch, and Queer: LGBTQ Youth and the School-to-Prison Pipeline." *Journal of Adolescent Research* 30, no. 1 (2014): 57–82.

Snorton, C. Riley. *Black on Both Sides: A Racial History of Trans Identity*. Minneapolis: University of Minnesota Press, 2017.

Snyder, Timothy. *On Tyranny: Twenty Lessons from the Twentieth Century*. New York: Tim Duggan Books, 2017.

Spade, Dean. *Normal Life: Administrative Violence, Critical Trans Politics, and the Limits of the Law*. Brooklyn, NY: South End Press, 2011.

Spade, Dean, and Craig Willse. "Marriage Will Never Set Us Free." Organizing Upgrade: Engaging Left Organizers in Strategic Dialogue, September 6, 2013, http://www.organizingupgrade.com/index.php/modules-menu/beyond-capitalism/item/1002-marriage-will-never-set-us-free.

Steinmetz, Katy. "The Transgender Tipping Point." *Time*, May 28, 2014.

Stryker, Susan. *Transgender History: The Roots of Today's Revolution*, 2nd ed. New York: Seal Press, 2017.

Sverdlik, Steven. "Collective Responsibility." *Philosophical Studies: An International Journal for Philosophy in the Analytic Tradition* 51, no. 1 (January 1987): 61–76.

Tilleman, Morgan. "Transforming the Provocation Defense." *Journal of Criminal Law and Criminology* 100, no. 4 (2010).

Turban, Jack L., Dana King, Jeremi M. Carswell, and Alex S. Keuroghlian. "Pubertal Suppression for Transgender Youth and Risk of Suicidal Ideation." *Pediatrics* 145, no. 2 (February 2020).

Tani, Maxwell. "Joe Biden Just Gave a Rousing Gay Rights Address That Sounded a Lot Like a Campaign Speech." *Business Insider*, July 9, 2015, http://www.businessinsider.com/joe-biden-just-gave-a-rousing-gay-rights-address-that-sounded-a-lot-like-a-campaign-speech-2015-7#ixzz3hdGSgfXV.

Vint, Sherry. "The New Backlash: Popular Culture's 'Marriage' with Feminism, or Love Is All You Need." *Journal of Popular Film and Television* 34, no. 4 (Winter 2007).

Venkatraman, Sakshi, and Brooke Sopelsa. "'Transgender Black Marxists' Seek to Overthrow the U.S., Trump Backer Bachmann Says." NBC News, September 9,

2020, https://www.nbcnews.com/feature/nbc-out/transgender-black-marxists-seek-overthrow-u-s-trump-backer-michele-n1239683.

Ware, Wesley. "Rounding Up the Homosexuals: The Impact of Juvenile Court on Queer and Trans/Gender-Non-Conforming Youth." In *Captive Genders: Trans Embodiment and the Prison Industrial Complex*, edited by Eric A. Stanley and Nat Smith. Edinburgh: AK Press, 2011.

Weber, Paul J. "Texas House Speaker Didn't Want Suicide Over 'Bathroom Bill.'" ABC News, July 3, 2017, http://abcnews.go.com/Politics/wireStory/texas-house-speaker-suicide-bathroom-bill-48419478.

Wesley, Saylesh. "Twin Spirited Woman: Sts'iyóye smestíyexw slhá:li." *Transgender Studies Quarterly* 1, no. 3 (August 2014).

Whaley, Monte. "Smile Called Provoking Act in Transgender Case." *Denver Post*, May 7, 2016 (updated from September 18, 2008), https://www.denverpost.com/2008/09/18/smile-called-provoking-act-in-transgender-case/.

Whitford, Emma. "When Walking as Trans Is a Crime: The NYPD Says It Is Taking a More Sensitive Approach to Sex Work, but Not Everyone Benefits." *NY Magazine, The Cut*, January 31, 2018, https://www.thecut.com/2018/01/when-walking-while-trans-is-a-crime.html.

Wildmon, Don. American Family Association website, 1999, from Southern Poverty Law Center, https://www.splcenter.org/fighting-hate/extremist-files/group/american-family-association.

Wood, John R. "Reservations in Doubt: The Backlash against Affirmative Action in Gujarat, India." *Public Affairs* 60 (Fall 1987): 408–430.

Wurth, Margaret H., Rebecca Schleifer, Megan McLemore, Katherine W. Todrys, and Joseph J. Amon. "Condoms as Evidence of Prostitution in the United States and the Criminalization of Sex Work." *Journal of the International AIDS Society* 16, no. 1 (2013), DOI:10.7448/IAS.16.1.18626. https://www.ncbi.nlm.nih.gov/pmc/articles/PMC3664300/.

Yancy, George. *Backlash: What Happens When We Talk Honestly about Racism in America*. Lanham, MD: Rowman & Littlefield, 2018.

Index

Abraham, Ralph, 155–56
Alito, Samuel, 5, 18, 174; "but-for" thought experiment, 188–92; dissenting opinion on Bostock case, 171, 176, 177, 181, 183, 184; distress of consequences, 192–96; language, attempts to understand, 19–20, 172, 184, 198n29; as a textualist, 185–86; "tied to," use of term, 187, 189
Allen, Paula Gunn, 26–27
American Bar Association Resolution 113A (2013), 103
American Family Association, 85–86
"Analyzing Backlash to Progressive Social Movements" (Cudd), 93–94
Andersson, Jasmine, 66
Andrade, Allen, 100, 142
anthropological philosophy, 133
anticipatory obedience, 124
anti-transgender bathroom bills (ATBBs). *See* bathroom bills
Apollonius of Tyana, 134–35, 136, 141, 144, 145, 151
Appiah, Anthony, 153
Araujo, Gwen, 100, 101
"Are Lesbians Women?" (Hale), 26
Arthur, John, 17
assimilationism, 11, 141

athletic competition, 43, 77, 156, 193, 195, 201

Bachmann, Michele, 122–23
backlash, 1, 53, 95, 102, 201; describing and defining, 81–82; as a collective response, 82–83; directional considerations, 82, 84–85; dog-whistling as an aspect of, 152, 159; gender non-conformance, backlash against, 3; to marriage equality legislation, 10, 30–31, 57, 169; as opportunistic, 88–89; scapegoating tactics, use of, 107–8; scope, considerations of, 82, 103–4; violence as a form of, 97–98; the vulnerable, as targeting, 86–87; Yancy, writings on, 90–93
Baldwin, James, 90
Barnes, Elizabeth, 87, 101–2
Barrett, Amy Coney, 20
Bartholomew, James, 162
bathroom bills, 46, 57, 70, 74, 76; anti-transgender bathroom bills, 63–69; cisgender fear of non-binary persons in restrooms, 10; Michigan Womyn's Festival, trans-exclusion policy of, 71; as morally inappropriate, 4, 76; NC HB 2, 42, 52–53, 55, 57, 61, 96,

121, 161; as socially ostracizing, 37, 61, 67, 68, 69, 75; TN HB 1111, 54, 56
Beck, Julia, 122
Beede, Amos, 39
Being and Nothingness (Sartre), 50
Beshear, Andy, 123, 155
Bettcher, Talia Mae, 56, 65, 101, 163
Bevin, Matt, 123, 155
Biden, Joe, 28, 57, 62
Bill of Rights, 12, 15, 32n12
Black, Bonaire (Bonny), 38
Black Lives Matter movement, 154
Black on Both Sides (Snorton), 143–44, 158
Booker, Cory, 163
Bostock, Gerald Lynn; Bostock decision covering case of, 169, 172; "but-for-sex" test, applying to situation of, 188; sexual orientation, firing due to, 170–71, 176, 177–78, 180, 184
Bostock v. Clayton (2020), 2, 5, 18, 28, 36, 192, 195; Gorsuch writings on, 171, 179–80; Obergefell, paving the way for, 19, 29; potential to change people's lives, 196; relevant precedents to, 182, 186; textualist application, 33n36, 173; three different cases, combining, 169–70, 172; Title VII prohibitions and, 1, 7, 51, 177–78, 183, 184, 185
Boylan, Jennifer Finney, 126
Boys Don't Cry (film), 89
Brown, Michael, 55, 144
Burke, Edwin, 132
Bush, George W., 39
"Butch Lesbian Opens Up About Increased Harassment" (Andersson), 66
Buttigieg, Pete, 201–202

Calhoun, Cheshire, 15–16, 17, 23
Campaign for American Principles (CAP), 123
Card, Claudia, 39

Carson, Ben, 123
Carter, C. Allen, 132
carve-out bills, 37, 43–44, 85
Castro, Julián, 163–64
Central Park Five, 111
Charlottesville rally, 96–97, 152–53
Chen, Mel Y., 143
Christian Parent's Guide to Discussing Homosexuality with Teens (Gilson), 86
Civil Rights Act, 84
Clinton, Hillary, 126, 154
Collective and Corporate Responsibility (French), 96
"Collective Responsibility" (Sverdlik), 95
colonization, 20, 81, 113, 142, 189; Africa, legacy of European colonial rule in, 27; decolonization of gender identities, 7, 28; gender diversity, as marginalizing, 35, 158, 193; marriage in European/colonial culture, 7, 12, 14, 26
Combahee River Collective, 73
Compton Cafeteria Riots, 86
Conrad, Aryn, 202
Corvino, John, 202
COVID-19 pandemic, 17, 90, 170
Cox, Laverne, 58
Craig, Charlie, 85
Crenshaw, Kimberlé, 187, 191, 198n35
"crime of passion" defense, 98–99
cross-dressing, prohibitions against, 35, 113
Cruz, Ted, 85
The Crying Game (film), 75, 99
Cubilette-Poblanco, Layleen, 39

Dale, Candy, 51
Davis, Kim, 84–85
"Dear White America" (Yancy), 90–91
Debating Religious Liberty and Discrimination (Corvino et al.), 202
DeBoer, April, 17
DeGraffenried, Emma, 191

De Koe, Ijpe, 17
DeVine, Phillip, 89, 132
Diagnostic and Statistical Manual of Mental Disorders (DSM), 14, 99, 139
Dillon, Michael, 158
Ditch the Label (organization), 146
Dog Whistle Politics (López), 152
dog-whistling, 31, 87, 109, 158, 163; as a backlash response, 77, 104, 107, 108; the base, turning out via, 30; heeling of constituencies and, 159–60; as an intentional performance, 166–67; López as characterizing, 110, 152–54; racism and biases as accompanying, 1–2; transphobic dog-whistling, 154–57; virtue signaling as an aspect of, 4–5, 151, 160–62, 164, 165
domestic abuse, 40
double bind of trans folk, 65, 101–2, 163
Dreier, Fred, 92–93
Du, Soon Ja, 87–88
Du Bois, W. E. B., 91
Due Process Clause, 12–13, 173, 188
Dworkin, Andrea, 76

Eliade, Mircea, 142
The Empire Strikes Back (Stone), 122
Employment Non-Discrimination Act (2007), 195–96
Equal Protection Clause, 12–13, 51
Equal Rights Amendment, 20–21
Ethics, Left and Right (Fischer, ed.), 4

Feinberg, Leslie, 23, 158
Fifth Amendment, 12
Fischer, Bob, 4
Flavius Philostratus, 134
Floyd, George, 55, 170
FORGE (advocacy group), 40
Fourteenth Amendment, 12–13, 18, 19–20
Fredrickson, George, 41, 88, 89

"Freedom and Constraint in Adjudication" (Kennedy), 174
French, Peter, 96
Friedman, David M., 75
Frye, Marilyn, 50, 65

Gattaca (film), 54
Gender Hurts (Jeffreys), 72
Gilson, Tom, 86
Girard, René, 4, 140; characteristics of scapegoating, naming, 135–37, 138–39, 167; mimetic desire of, 144–48; on the monstrous as a rejection of differentiation, 141–44; scapegoating approach of, 108, 127, 133
GLSEN (nonprofit organization), 62
Gore, Kayla, 46
Gorsuch, Neil, 5, 171, 174; "because of," understanding of term, 176–77, 180, 185–86; "but-for-sex" test, applying, 177, 178–79, 180, 185, 188–89; precedent-setting cases, three lessons of, 183–84; Title VII, applying to the individual, 181–82
Griswold v. Connecticut (1965), 15
Guierrez, Viccky, 39

Hake, Sean Ryan, 39
Hale, Jacob, 26
Harlins, Latasha, 88
Hate Crimes Prevention Act, 99
health care access, 36, 37, 41, 43, 44–46
Henderson, Russel, 99
Herring, Kiwi, 39
Hesse, Herman, 139
"Heterosexualism and the Colonial Modern Gender System" (Lugones), 26
Hitler, Adolf, 107, 124, 147
Honneth, Axel, 67, 68
House bills: AR HB 1628, 44; AR HB 1894, 46; AZ HB 1027, 49; AZ HB 1070, 48; AZ HB 2293, 44; AZ HB 2294, 44; CO HB 922, 160; CO HB 1206, 160; ID HB 509, 51–52; IN

HB 1361, 46; MN HB 1183, 44; NC HB 2, 42, 52–53, 55, 57, 61, 96, 121, 161; NC HB 142, 55; OK HB 2426, 43–44; SD HB 1076, 46; TN HB 1111, 54, 56; VA HB 1667, 44; VA HB 2011, 44
Huckabee, Mike, 85
Hulme, Jay, 146
Hunte, Ben, 146
Hunter, Nan, 101

identity documents, correcting of, 37, 43, 46–52, 59n20
Ifill, Gwen, 94
"Including Trans Women Athletes in Competitive Sport" (Ivy/Conrad), 202
"In Defense of Same-Sex Marriage" (Calhoun), 15
Individualistic Account, concept of, 144
Ingraham, Laura, 123
invisibilizing, practice of, 37, 51, 107, 122
Irreversible Damage (Shrier), 72
I See Satan Fall Like Lightning (Girard), 134
Ivy, Veronica, 92–93, 117–18, 202

January 6th insurrection, 37, 124
Jeffreys, Sheila, 72, 122
Jenner, Caitlyn, 121
Johnston, Elizabeth, 121
Jorgenson, Christine, 35, 157
Juang, Richard M., 68
"Justice, at What Cost?" (Barnes), 87

Kavanaugh, Brett, 171–72, 177, 185, 197n3, 198n29
Keller, Candice, 86
Kempf, Edward, 99
Kennedy, Anthony, 11–12, 13, 17, 18, 21, 22, 28
Kennedy, Duncan, 174
Kennedy, Pagan, 158
King, Rodney, 87

Knudslie, Christa Leigh Steele, 39
Kostrura, Thomas, 17
Koyama, Emi, 72–74
Ku Klux Klan, 84

Lambert, Anna Mae, 89
Lambert, Lisa, 89
Laude, Jennifer, 100
Lawrence v. Texas (2003), 13, 14
Lee, Bill, 53
lesbian seagulls, 140
liberty, 9, 12, 182; Alito on trans inclusion and liberty as a zero-sum game, 194; ATTBs and trade-off of liberty for security, 68–69; Kennedy on the burden of liberty regarding same-sex couples, 18; Scalia on the liberty to govern oneself, 19; Thomas on liberty from governmental intervention, 21, 22–23
Littleton, Jonathon, 28
Littleton Van de Putte, Christie Lee, 28, 49
Loeffler, Kelly, 62
López, Ian Haney, 110, 152, 158, 159, 166; dog-whistling, on internalized bias in, 156–57; racism, understanding of term, 160; Republican Party, on Southern Strategy of, 153–54
Los Angeles Dept. of Water and Power v. Manhart (1978), 180–82, 183
Lotter, John, 89, 132
Lotz, Ann Graham, 121
Loving v. Virginia (1967), 13, 21–22
Lugones, María, 26, 27, 50–51, 70

Maher, Bill, 126
"man in a dress" caricature, 35
"Mapping and Contextualizing Black, Queer, and Trans Resistance in North Carolina" (presentation), 38
marriage equality movement, 3, 9, 10, 24, 42; Kim Davis, resistance against, 84–85; prioritization of

movement, 2, 11, 16, 23–25, 169; transgender experiences of backlash from, 30, 31, 37, 57, 64
Masterpiece Cakeshop case, 85
May, Larry, 96–97
McCrory, Pat, 53
McDonald, CeCe, 97, 117
McKinney, Aaron, 99
Medina, Johanna (Joa), 39
Mehlman, Ken, 154
Meili, Trisha, 111
Mellema, Gregory, 108, 109–11, 125, 131
"Messy, Butch, and Queer" (Snapp et al.), 115
Michigan Music Festival, 71–76
mimetic desire, 144–46, 148
A Mind of Its Own (Raymond), 75
Mullins, David, 85
Murphy, Meghan, 122

Nathanson, Paul, 123, 137, 141
National Center for Transgender Equality (NCTE), 42–43, 104
Newsom, Gavin, 8
Nissen, Tom, 89, 132
Nixon, Richard, 82, 153
nonideal theory, 29

Obama, Barack, 8, 9, 83, 99, 121, 124, 156
Obergefell, James, 17
Obergefell v. Hodges (2015), 2, 13, 22, 43, 104, 173; Bostock decision as a reaction to, 29, 170; legacy of ruling, possibilities for, 30–31; LGBTQ rights, as a win for, 7, 29–30, 169, 196; new and privileged class resulting from, 11, 25; Obama, looking favorably on, 8, 9; responses of those threatened by, 58, 77, 86; as the tip of an iceberg, 28, 85; transgender persons not considered in, 10, 36; violence in the wake of, 37, 40–41, 90

Oncale v. Sundowner Offshore Services (1998), 182, 183
"On Documents and Subjectivity" (Sánchez), 48
On Tyranny (Snyder), 124
O'Rourke, Beto, 163
Out of the Ordinary (Dillon), 158
Oyewùmí, Oyéronké, 26–27

Paglia, Camile, 122
Paul, Alice, 20–21
Pemberton, Scott, 100
Pence, Mike, 202
penis, social issues regarding, 45, 102, 119; in feminist writings, 76; "no penis policy" of Michfest, 72–75; social construction of, 77
Permeability to Culture Account, 144
Phallostethus cuulong fish, 140
Phillips, Jack, 85, 180
Phillips v. Martin Marietta Corp. (1971), 179–80, 183, 189, 190
pile-up, concept of, 83
Poe v. Ullman (1961), 13

racism, 4, 49, 144; anti-Black racism, 113, 125, 191; anti-trans animus and, 2, 73, 89, 93, 132; dog-whistling as linked with, 153–54, 156, 159–60; in Exonerated Five case, 111–12; marginalization through, 1, 35; racially motivated backlash, 82, 83, 84, 90–92, 103; as scavengeristic, 41, 88; structural racism, 125, 157–58, 160; as a tool, 54, 90; violence as linked with, 38, 64–65
Racism: A Short History (Fredrickson), 41
rallies, hateful language at, 37, 124, 152–53
Rawls, John, 68
Raymond, Janice, 75, 76, 122, 136
"Really, You Are Blaming Transgender People for Trump?" (Boylan), 126
"Recognizing Terrorism" (Card), 39

religious freedom bills, 44, 45, 57, 138, 202
"rest in power" response, 38
Reyes, Matias, 111
Richards, Renée, 157
Roberts, John, 18, 19–20, 173
Roe v. Wade (1973), 13, 155
"Rounding up the Homosexuals" (Ware), 114
Rowse, Jayne, 17
Rubin, Gayle S., 25

same-sex marriage, 12, 20, 28, 36, 141; anti-transgender backlash in wake of, 84–85, 93; carve-out bills in response to, 37, 43; Due Process Clause, influence on ruling, 18–19; HB 1111, allowing discrimination against those in, 56; LGBTQ community, as priority of, 2, 23–25, 169; momentum for, 7–11, 29; Obergefell decision ceasing prohibition of, 1, 3, 173; political importance of championing, 15; ruling as not sufficiently competent, 16–17, 30
Sánchez, Carlos Alberto, 48–50
Sartre, Jean-Paul, 50
Scalia, Antonin, 18, 19–20, 171, 172, 183, 185
The Scapegoat (Girard), 136
scapegoating, 4, 61, 68, 87, 157, 165, 194; as a backlash response, 77, 104, 107–8, 125, 152; blameworthiness and, 109–11, 131–32, 151; characteristics of, 135–37, 138–39; Girardian account of, 127, 133, 139–41, 142, 144–48, 167; in "Miracle of Appolonius of Tyana," 134–35, 136; as an ongoing concern, 1, 121; political weaponizing of, 31, 62, 124, 148, 169; S-B scapegoating types, 109, 111–13, 117–18, 119, 126; of trans/gender non-conforming persons, 113–20
"Scapegoats" (Mellema), 108

Schmitz, Dean, 97
Schultz, Scout, 39
Scott, Allison, 55
Scott, Jason, 46
Scottsboro Boys trial (1931), 112
Senate bills: AZ SB 1511, 46; CO SB 361, 160; SC SB 4949, 54; TX SB 17, 96
Sewally, Peter/Mary Jones, 143–44
sex discrimination, 1, 174, 180, 191; Alito on "exotic understanding" of, 185; Bostock rulings on, 2, 7, 178; relevant variable as assigned sex of the individual, 177
sexual predators, 69, 70, 76, 101, 112, 136, 154, 161
sex workers, 100, 117, 118–19
Shepard, Matthew, 99
Smith, Susan, 112
Snapp, Shannon D., 115, 116–17
Snorton, C. Riley, 89, 132, 143, 158
Snyder, Timothy, 124
social media, 38, 42, 92, 146, 147–48, 162, 166
Southern Poverty Law Center (SPLC), 86, 121
Spade, Dean, 23, 24, 25, 196
Spreading Misandry (Nathanson), 123
"Spreadsheet Project," 57
Stephens, Aimee, 174, 178, 188, 192; Bostock decision, as represented in, 169, 172; firing at workplace, 170–71, 176, 179; gender identity, discriminated on the basis of, 180, 184
Stonborough, Ms., 66
Stone, Sandy, 122
Straus, Joe, 57
Stryker, Susan, 158
Sverdlik, Steven, 95

Teena, Brandon, 89
testosterone, 45, 75, 77, 202
textualism, 179, 183, 186, 192; Alito on the textualist court, 185; overview,

172–75; Scalia as championing, 18, 171; "sex," defining, 176–77; strict application of, 20, 195, 196
A Theory of Justice (Rawls), 29
Thomas, Clarence, 18, 19, 21–23, 177
Thompson, Shante, 39
Till, Emmett, 112
Tilleman, Morgan, 100, 101, 102
Tisdel, Lana, 89
Title IV of Higher Education Act (1965), 31
Title VII of American Civil Rights Act (1964), 175, 180, 193; in Bostock decision, 169, 171, 172, 192; "but-for-sex" rule, applying under, 177, 178, 181, 183, 188; gender discrimination, deeming unconstitutional, 1, 7, 51; imagined scope of the statute, 182, 184–85, 186; Los Angeles Dept. of Water as violating, 180–81; *Oncale v. Sundowner* case and, 173–74; "sex," meaning of word as first used in bill's language, 19, 179
Trans-Exclusionary Radical Feminists (TERFs), 92, 122, 126
Transgender Day of Remembrance, 37–38, 41–42, 164
"Trans-Marriage and the Unacceptability of Same-Sex Marriage Restrictions" (Cannon), 9, 26
trans panic defense, 98–100, 102–3, 149n11
The Transsexual Empire (Raymond), 72, 122
Trans Thinking/Thinking Trans (conference), 38
Trump, Donald, 9, 17, 57, 151, 155, 170; anti-trans climate of Trump years, 148; gender issues, saying little on, 123–24; hate crime increase during administration, 40; immigrants, false narrative on, 75, 136, 142; political polarization under presidency of, 138; protector of the country, portraying as, 156; transgender people, blaming for Trump's win, 126
Trump, Donald, Jr., 37, 117–18
Turner v. Safley (1987), 22
"Twin-Spirited Woman" (Wesley), 27
Two-Spirit people, 27, 56

Vint, Sherry, 82
violence, 11, 73, 75, 87, 137; in 2015–2020 timeframe, 3, 10, 25, 37–40; anti-Blackness and anti-trans violence, 89; bathroom bills and, 4, 64–69, 76; cisgender women, feared violence against, 125, 126, 136, 161; as directed backlash, 97–98, 104, 107; gay panic/trans panic defense and, 99–103; the marginalized, violence against, 1, 7, 40; in "Miracle of Apollonius," 135; trans-directed violence, 31, 37–42, 48, 62; white skin as a reminder of violence, 74
virtue signaling, 152, 162; failed bill proposals, utilizing for, 160; as flip side of dog-whistling, 151, 161; manufactured fears, alleviating via, 4–5; objections to the idea of, 164–68; pro-trans virtue signaling, 163–64
Vogel, Lisa, 71, 74

Ware, Wesley, 114, 115
Warren, Earl, 173
Warren, Elizabeth, 164
Warren, Karen, 2
Washington Week (television program), 94
Wesley, Saylesh, 27
White House rainbow, 8, 9
white supremacy, 8, 40, 70, 86–87, 89–90
Whitford, Emma, 118–19
"Whose Feminism Is It Anyway?" (Koyama), 72

Wilchins, Riki, 72
wrong place/wrong time cases, 66, 88–89, 132

Yancy, George, 90–93
Youchum, Quartney Davia Dawsonn, 39

Zablocki v. Redhail (1978), 22
Zapata, Angie, 100, 101, 142
Zarda, Donald, 188, 192; Bostock decision as covering case of, 172; sexual orientation, fired due to, 170, 176, 180, 184; Title VII legislation and, 169, 171, 177–78

About the Author

Loren Cannon graduated with his doctoral degree from Arizona State University in 2006. Since graduation, he has taught at Humboldt State University, where he manages a teaching load of five classes per semester as a full-time lecturer. Dr. Cannon's teaching schedule includes many different classes, but his specialties are environmental ethics, philosophy of law, trans theory, and various courses in ethics. Known for his dedication in the classroom, Dr. Cannon was selected to receive the Distinguished Award for Teaching Excellence in 2017 from his peers and developed and teaches the first and only trans theory (credited) course at his university. Dr. Cannon's philosophical work on *Trans Marriage* (2009) and his essay against bathroom bills (2019) have both been anthologized in applied ethics textbooks, and his work has been published in such journals as *Public Affairs Quarterly*, *Journal for Social Philosophy*, *Hypatia*, and *Journal for Philosophy in the Contemporary World*, as well as more autobiographical pieces as book chapters. When not working, Dr. Cannon enjoys various outside activities in the beauty of the north coast of California and spending time with his wife and dog-children.

www.ingramcontent.com/pod-product-compliance
Lightning Source LLC
Chambersburg PA
CBHW020117010526
44115CB00008B/862